19.95

MY FAVORITE

HERB

MY FAVORITE

HERB

How North America's Great Chefs
Savor the Flavor of Herbs

BY LAUREL KESER

Callawind
Publications Inc.

MONTREAL

My Favorite Herb: How North America's Great Chefs Savor the Flavor of Herbs

CATALOGUING IN PUBLICATION DATA
Keser, Laurel, 1948–
    My favorite herb : how North America's great chefs savor
the flavor of herbs

Includes bibliographical references and index.
ISBN 1-896511-12-0

    1. Cookery (Herbs)   I. Title.

TX819.H4K48 1999   641.6'57   C99-900319-4

Cover design by Shari Blaukopf. Book design by Marcy Claman. Copy editing by Sarah Weber. Indexing by Christine Jacobs.

10 9 8 7 6 5 4 3 2 1

Printed in Canada.
All product/brand names are trademarks or registered trademarks of their respective trademark holders.

Callawind Publications Inc.
    3383 Sources Boulevard, Suite 205, Dollard-des-Ormeaux, Quebec, Canada H9B 1Z8
    2083 Hempstead Turnpike, Suite 355, East Meadow, New York, USA 11554-1730
    E-mail: info@callawind.com   http://www.callawind.com
Distributed in North America by Firefly Books Ltd.
    3680 Victoria Park Avenue, Willowdale, Ontario, Canada M2H 3K1

This book is dedicated to:

my mother, Elaine Lewis, who started me out young in the kitchen

❧❧

my sons, Raymond and Brian Carr, who cheerfully (usually) devoured my kitchen creations

❧❧

my husband, Larry, who still does and without whose love, support, and dishwashing
services the seeds of this book would never have germinated much less blossomed

table of contents

acknowledgments

*h*ATS OFF, OR SHOULD I SAY TOQUES OFF, to all the great chefs whose creative culinary talents are showcased on these pages. And special thanks to their assistants and public relations professionals who paved my way to interviews and recipe collecting.

Special thanks also to:

→ Marcy Claman for her enthusiasm for this project and her vision to see its worth

→ Sarah Weber, whose keen eye and sense of order were essential ingredients

→ Bill Neely of Indian Rock Produce for his produce prowess and foraging abilities

→ Vince Cozza of Cozza's Butcher Shop for his meaty words of wisdom

→ Fred Cristiano and his staff at Laurel Seafood for their fish tales

→ Rose Milza, Family and Consumer Sciences Educator (Rutgers Cooperative Extension of Camden County), who always has all the answers

Many thanks also to these knowledgeable and helpful folks:

→ Lorraine Kiefer of Triple Oaks Nursery & Herb Garden

→ Steve Horowitz of Herb Thyme Farms

→ Conrad Richter of Richters Herbs

→ Judy Miles of Miles Estate Herb & Berry Farm

→ Robin Siktberg, horticulturist, of The Herb Society of America

→ Holly Ferkol, librarian, of The Herb Society of America

introduction

*h*OME COOKS ARE LEARNING what professional chefs have known for some time now: Fresh herbs add dazzle to any dish. Ask chefs which herb is best and you'll find that some are partial to parsley and others say sage is the rage. Still others remember rosemary and many pay tribute to thyme.

On the pages of this book you'll learn about 51 North American chefs and their favorite herbs. In addition, you'll find more than 125 of their recipes, all tested and scaled to family-sized proportions.

Selecting chefs to include in this book was truly an awesome task. There are many excellent herb-loving chefs across North America, and there was just so much room on these pages. Primarily, I searched for chefs who show a passion for herbs. As I questioned chefs across North America about their favorite herb, some were hard-pressed to pick one. "I can only have one?" asked some. "I love them all," asserted others.

Still other chefs have favorite herbs for different seasons. Some favor a certain herb with certain dishes. Some use dried herbs for certain things, but, overall, most prefer to use fresh herbs. For some chefs that means growing their own. You'll meet one city chef with a rooftop herb garden. You'll be introduced to several chefs who maintain extensive on-site herb gardens, as well as to some who have home herb gardens. You'll encounter other chefs who search out local farmers to grow their herbs to order and one who has live plants delivered each day. And, you'll learn how these chefs use their favorite herbs.

I hope you enjoy reading about these chefs and their herbs as much as I enjoyed talking with them and learning from them.

When you've finished reading, try your hand at creating their dishes in your kitchen. And when you're in their neighborhood, stop by, say hello, and sample their specialties.

herbs 101

getting to know herbs

*O*NE OF THE THINGS I LIKE about herbs is the rules. Essentially, there are no rules. Sure, traditionally basil is married to tomatoes, but if you like basil with turnips, there are no herb police to clamp on the handcuffs.

The lack of rules leaves you free to experiment and gives you an excuse to be a child again. Remember your first fingerpainting experience? First you stuck your finger gingerly in the paint. You looked at it, felt it, and squished it between your fingers and then onto the paper. Later you may have explored what happened when you mixed colors. You might even have ventured a taste.

Employ the same technique to learn about herbs. Pluck a leaf from its stem. Rub the leaf between your fingers to release the essential oils and aroma. Wash, shake, and air-dry a sprig, or dry it with a towel. Inspect the herb — its color, shape, and the texture of its leaf. Some herbs are very similar in appearance; when confronted with unlabeled bunches of herbs at the market, the uninitiated may mistake cilantro for parsley or marjoram for oregano. Don't neglect the stem. You'll find that while most herbs have round stems, some, such as those in the mint family, have a square stem.

Next taste the herb. Nibble on the leaf. (An exception is the bay leaf. Taste it if you wish, but the leaf itself is hard to digest. Usually bay leaf is used just to impart its flavor, and is removed from the dish before serving.) What does it taste like? Is it sweet or tart, strong or mellow? Does it remind you of something else? Many herbs mimic other flavors. Taste the stem if it's not too woody; often the stem is as flavorful as the leaf, or even more so. You might even want to try a blossom. Don't be put off by strong-tasting herbs at this point. Many mellow out nicely when combined with other ingredients. Just get to know them for now.

Explore one herb at a time until you have a good feel for its possibilities and a sense of which herbs you like. Then try cooking with herbs. Use an herb chart or the examples in this book to guide you while you gain experience and confidence. Initially, add only small amounts of each herb until you learn its special properties. Once they are familiar to you, let your taste buds and your creativity be your guide.

why fresh herbs?

*f*RESH HERBS CONTAIN AN ESSENTIAL OIL that evaporates during the drying process. It's that oil that provides most of the flavor. Fresh herbs also give a splash of color to our plates that dried herbs just can't.

"Fresh herbs have a completely different taste; there's a flatness to dried herbs," says Jerry Traunfeld, chef at The Herbfarm Restaurant, which has extensive herb gardens.

Dieters find that salads containing fresh herbs require less dressing. Herbs also help those on salt-free diets tolerate their saltless foods. In addition, many herbs — parsley and stinging nettles, for instance — are chock-full of vitamins and minerals.

Throughout this book, fresh herbs (washed and thoroughly towel dried) are used unless a recipe specifies using dried herbs.

preserving herbs

*i*N A PERFECT WORLD, we'd all have fresh herbs right outside the kitchen door all the time. Since, alas, there's no such thing as a perfect world, here are some ways to keep your favorite fresh herbs with you when the season wanes.

chervil

Herb Butters

One easy way to preserve almost any herb is in butter. Just toss a handful of herbs (washed and towel dried) into your food processor. Chop, add about ½ pound (1 cup) of butter, and process until the herbs are well distributed. You could start with Michael Thomson's recipe for cilantro chile butter (page 56).

Use single herbs such as parsley, chervil, basil, or chives, or use any combination you like. You can also add other spices or flavorings. Try garlic with basil or oregano. Add one of the lemon herbs with pepper or dill to grilled fish. Sometimes I like to add a few drops of honey.

Store herb butter in freezer-safe custard cups with lids or in small plastic containers like those from soft margarine, or form it into a log, wrap it in plastic wrap, and place it in the freezer for up to one year. Use slices from the herb butter log as you need them, and put the rest back in the freezer. You can also use rubber butter molds to form the butter into shapes; release the butter shapes, and freeze them on a cookie sheet. When the butter is frozen, store the individual pieces in a plastic bag in the freezer until needed.

Herb Pestos

Pesto is basically a purée of fresh herbs with cheese (usually Parmesan), nuts (usually pine nuts, but just about any nut can be substituted), and a bit of liquid. Traditionally the liquid is olive oil, but some people substitute chicken stock for a lighter version. Several pesto recipes are included in this book: lemon basil pesto (page 26), cilantro habanero pepito pesto (page 60), and mint pesto (page 123).

Similar to butters, pestos are an excellent way to use fresh herbs. Don't limit yourself to the ever popular basil pesto; any herb or combination of herbs can be used.

Pesto freezes well. I like to freeze it in ice cube trays so I can pop out a cube or a few depending on how much pesto I need. You're not limited to using pesto just for pasta, either. Use a cube to flavor steamed or sautéed vegetables. Toss some into soups, stews, and sauces. Top grilled fish, chicken, or meat with a defrosted cube of pesto. Brush some onto grilled or toasted bread. Stir some into dips, spreads, sour cream, or cream cheese.

If you run out of ice cube trays, just pop out the cubes and store them in a plastic bag.

Herb Vinegars

chives

Another easy way to have the flavor of herbs year round is to make herb vinegars. There are several methods for making herb vinegar. Personally, I'm of the "kiss" philosophy — keep it simple, sweetie. Although purists might disagree, I find no difference in herb vinegars prepared the simple way and those prepared with heat. While some books recommend heating the vinegar, the only time I heat it is if I'm in a hurry to have some herb vinegar, maybe for a gift, or when using herbs like chive blossom or purple basil. Hot vinegar pulls more of the color from these herbs and turns white vinegar purple or red respectively, thus adding visual interest as well as flavor. Using the cold pack method, it takes longer for the flavors to infuse into the vinegar.

Most often I simply place a handful of clean herbs in a sterilized bottle or jar, add the vinegar, close the container tightly, and store it in a cool, dry place for at least a month. Many herbs, parsley, for example, retain their color better if they're blanched before putting them into the container.

Lorraine Kiefer, herb lecturer and co-owner of Triple Oaks Nursery & Herb Garden, teaches students to clean herbs in inexpensive vinegar rather than washing them in water. Place distilled vinegar (no sense wasting costly wine vinegar) in a large bowl, and gently swish the herb sprigs in the vinegar. Any debris will sink to the bottom of the bowl and you won't have diluted your flavored vinegar.

You can use a number of different vinegars to make herb vinegar. Wine vinegars are more expensive but have a good flavor. Cider vinegar, malt vinegar, champagne vinegar, sherry vinegar, white wine vinegar, and red wine vinegar are all suitable. You're limited only by the ingredients available and your imagination. Start with single herb vinegars, using your favorite herbs. Basil is popular, tarragon is the queen of herb vinegars, and rosemary is worth remembering. Move on to combinations such as basil and oregano or tarragon and rosemary, or one of my favorites — parsley, sage, rosemary, and thyme (it has a poetic ring, doesn't it?). The most important thing is that the herbs be fresh. They're most flavorful if harvested just before the blossoms open.

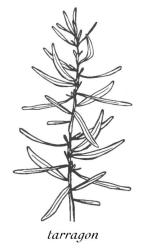

tarragon

Don't forget other seasonings as well. Drop in a few peppercorns; add some green onions or a strip of red or green pepper; include a strip of lemon peel, a cinnamon stick, or a hot chile pepper. Edible flowers, too, make attractive and flavorful vinegars. Try chive, nasturtium, or calendula blossoms.

Now that you've made your vinegar, remember to use it. Substitute herb vinegars for plain vinegar in any recipe, from salad dressings and vinaigrettes to marinades and desserts. When you use flavored vinegars, you need less salt and fat to flavor your foods. In general, for salad dressing, combine three parts oil to one part vinegar. The stronger the vinegar flavor, the less oil you may need to use.

In herb vinegars, the flavor of the herb is infused into the vinegar. You can also infuse herb flavors into simple syrup (page 221), cream, water, broth, and oil, in fact, into just about any liquid.

Herb Oils

You will find several recipes in this book for flavored oils. From a safety standpoint, herb oils, however, are a bit trickier than herb vinegars. The acidity in vinegar acts as a preservative. Oils, on the other hand, have no such safety net, and introducing other ingredients increases the risk of spoilage. Therefore, it's generally recommended that flavored oils be made in small quantities, refrigerated, and used quickly. This is especially important when adding garlic to herb oils, as botulism is a real threat here.

Follow the example of the recipes in this book (chive-infused oil, page 48; habanero-infused oil, page 90; wild sorrel and stinging nettle oil, page 187) to make oils with your favorite herbs. You can strain out the herbs after a period of steeping or leave them in. I find oils with the herbs strained out last longer but don't look as colorful. I've kept some oils for a month in the refrigerator.

Use herb oil anytime a recipe calls for oil — for sautéing, frying, and marinating, and for dressings or simply as a garnish on the plate.

herbs 101

Drying Herbs

Drying herbs concentrates their essential oils. Therefore, one-third less dried herbs than fresh herbs gives a similar result. You can use this formula anytime you want to substitute fresh herbs for dried herbs in a recipe, or vice versa.

Try drying any herb you like. You'll find some more acceptable than others. Generally speaking, soft leaves such as basil don't dry well. Harder leaves such as rosemary and sage tend to dry better. When using dried herbs, rehydrate them by steeping them in liquid for a few minutes before using. If you're using them to flavor steamed vegetables, for example, steep them in the steaming liquid before adding the vegetables. Rehydrating isn't necessary when making long-cooking dishes like soup.

There are also several ways to dry herbs. The most primitive method — used for centuries — is simply to hang them to air-dry. Tie herb sprigs into bunches using a rubber band around the stems, and hang the bunches, upside down, in a cool, dark, dry place where they will not collect dust. Rubber bands are recommended because they will tighten as the stems dry and shrink.

One problem with this method is that in today's homes, it's difficult to find a cool, dark, dry place to hang herbs undisturbed for the several weeks it can take them to dry. In addition, it's nearly impossible to maintain a dust-free area, and the thought of accumulated dust on my herbs — well we just won't go there.

Some people tie the herbs in a paper bag to keep the herbs clean while drying. The bag, which should have a few small holes for air circulation, will also catch any dried leaves that fall off the stem.

Go instead to the oven or dehydrator. To dry herbs in the oven, you need a very low temperature (no more than 120°F) and 24 to 48 hours. The oven method works best if you have a gas oven with a pilot light. The heat from the pilot light is often low enough to keep from overheating the herbs.

I prefer to dry herbs in a dehydrator. Dehydrators, available in kitchenware and department stores, have several racks to hold the herbs and usually include a heat source and a fan to circulate the air. These handy appliances dry herbs in hours rather than weeks.

With most dehydrators, you can dry a lot of herbs at a time, and the low temperature helps retain their flavor and color. The drying time is anywhere from minutes to a couple of hours for most herbs.

It's easiest to dry most herbs on their stems, and then strip the leaves off after drying. Store dried herbs in airtight containers out of direct light, and use them within a few months.

Freezing Herbs

Many herbs can be frozen, and there are many ways to do this. Some people like to freeze whole sprigs of annual herbs such as dill. Other herbs, such as basil, can be chopped and stored in small containers or ice cube trays. Most herbs can be tightly packed into the trays by themselves. If you prefer, you can add a small amount of water, broth, or oil, depending on how you ultimately want to use the herbs. Toss a cube into a sauce, soup, stew, or vegetable pot near the end of the cooking time. Some herbs retain their color better if blanched first, but doing so usually results in a loss of flavor.

herb blends

*t*HERE ARE A NUMBER OF HERB BLENDS that are traditionally used to season various foods. Most often, a basic set of herbs forms the base of each blend. Individual cooks then add to or vary the blend, depending on their taste and the availability of herbs. It's easy to make your own herb blends. The most common are described below.

Bouquet garni is a classic herb blend used to flavor soups, stews, broths, and stocks. It always includes parsley, thyme, and bay. Sometimes chives, marjoram, or basil is added along with carrots, celery, leeks, or onions. Whole sprigs of herbs can be tied together with kitchen twine or the leaves placed in an herb ball or muslin bag. Leaving one end of the twine long and tying it to the pot handle makes the bouquet garni easy to remove at serving time. Some people sandwich the herbs between celery or leek stalks and tie them together. Bouquet garni is also available in dried form, although some say the dried versions lack flavor.

Herbes de Provence is another classic herb blend from southern France. It usually includes marjoram, thyme, summer savory, basil, rosemary, sage, and lavender. This blend is used mostly for meats and poultry, or often for seasoning sauces and flavoring vegetables.

Fines herbes, still another classic French blend, is made of finely chopped herbs. It's usually made with parsley, chervil, chives, and tarragon, but marjoram, thyme, or rosemary may be included. Other herbs such as salad burnet, savory, and watercress are sometimes added. This blend is best added during the last few minutes of cooking, since chopped, fresh herbs lose flavor during prolonged cooking.

anise hyssop

Agastache foeniculum

HERE'S AN HERB THAT'S SURPRISING and delicious. It's one of several herbs that are underused in North American kitchens yet revered by European cooks. Beekeepers introduced anise hyssop to Europe. Nectar from the flowers makes a fragrant honey. You can brew the leaves and flowers for a special tea or put some blossoms into fruit salads. Add anise hyssop to baked goods and to desserts such as ice creams and sorbets. Chopped leaves complement pork and add interest to rice. Try some with chicken, fish, or beef. Toss some chopped leaves and a couple of blossoms into your green salad, as well. As with many culinary herbs, the flavor is diminished when heated, so when using anise hyssop in cooked foods, add it just before serving or at the end of the cooking time.

Anise hyssop is among the ancient herbs mentioned in the Bible, although its use at that time was mainly medicinal. In medieval times, it was believed to ward off evil eyes. In Elizabethan times, anise hyssop became more widely used in the kitchen for teas, soups, and stews.

A member of the mint family, anise hyssop has heart-shaped leaves and produces lavender-blue flowers that are both decorative and flavorful. Although I have read that anise hyssop is not suitable for container gardening, if you have a sunny window, you can bring a plant in for the winter. Mine not only flourished over the past winter when others succumbed to indoor conditions, but it also presented me with lovely blooms.

When you taste anise hyssop, you will detect a combination of flavors including mint, root beer and, of course, anise. You could make a fair substitute by mixing some mint with a bit of chervil, tarragon, or fennel tops. Anise hyssop makes a good partner for lemon grass, scented geranium, or pineapple sage.

frank mcclelland

*f*RANK McCLELLAND, WHO DECLARES HIMSELF to be "first and foremost a cook and secondly a gardener," first encountered anise hyssop more than 12 years ago. While working at the Country Inn at Princeton in western Massachusetts, he developed an herb garden in which to grow some of the herbs that were not available to him otherwise at the time. He had read about anise hyssop and decided to try it. "I really loved its scent and I quickly incorporated it into my kitchen. It has a wonderfully sweet, anise-scented foliage and beautiful purple blossoms." Today, he buys organic produce from a local grower and maintains an herb garden that also helps supply L'Espalier.

Anise hyssop, he says, has a wide range of uses in the kitchen, from marinating meats and fish to scenting broths. "The leaves bring a lovely, soft licorice flavor while the flowers have a strong nectar that also adds visual appeal to dishes." Anise hyssop can even be used in pastries with fruit. In addition to using anise hyssop in the recipes given here, McClelland uses it in a Maine crab salad and with marinated spring lamb.

When he was only 23, McClelland had already been chef at the Harvest in Cambridge and at L'Espalier. He moved to an executive chef position at the Country Inn at Princeton, returning to L'Espalier as executive sous-chef in 1986.

McClelland and his wife, Catherine, fulfilled a lifelong dream when they bought L'Espalier in 1988. He combines his two vocations — cooking and gardening. McClelland once grew 50 varieties of fresh herbs as well as rare fruits and vegetables in a rooftop garden at L'Espalier. He now grows most of his herbs in a larger garden at his home.

In the kitchen at L'Espalier, he carefully creates concentrated flavors by infusing vegetables with herbs and other seasonings. His garden includes anise hyssop, of course, along with lovage, tarragon, rosemary, several varieties of thyme, flat-leaf parsley, basil, and lemon verbena. He also has a separate mint garden where he grows several varieties of mint.

L'Espalier features French American cuisine using regional New England ingredients served in three elegant dining rooms, each with its own fireplace. L'Espalier is located in an 1886 townhouse in the heart of fashionable Back Bay, one block from the Hynes Convention Center, Prudential Center, and Copley Place.

L'Espalier is one of only four Boston restaurants to earn the *Mobil Travel Guide* Four-Star Award. The restaurant was ranked number one for food in Boston by the *Zagat Survey*, and *Nation's Restaurant News* inducted L'Espalier into its Fine Dining Hall of Fame. It was also named one of the nation's best restaurants by *Condé Nast Traveler* and received a Best of Boston Award from *Boston* magazine. *Yankee* magazine travel guide selected L'Espalier as an Editor's Pick. *Gourmet* readers ranked L'Espalier as the Top Table in Boston. McClelland was a 1998 nominee for the American Express Best Chef: Northeast James Beard Award.

*executive
chef/owner*
⍆⍆⍆
L'Espalier
Boston, Massachusetts

Striped Bass, Potato-Cucumber Purée, and Littleneck Clams with Fumet and Anise Hyssop

Striped Bass:
6 (8-ounce) striped bass fillets
Olive oil
Zest of 1 lemon
Zest of 1 orange
Salt and pepper

Potato-Cucumber Purée:
2 pounds Idaho potatoes, peeled and chopped
1 large cucumber, peeled, seeded, and diced
1 cup heavy cream
¼ pound unsalted butter (½ cup) plus
   2 tablespoons, at room temperature
Ground nutmeg
Salt and pepper

Littleneck Clams:
Vegetable oil
Cornmeal
Salt and pepper
18 littleneck clams, cleaned and shucked
Milk

Fumet:
1½ teaspoons olive oil
2 cloves garlic, minced
1 shallot, minced
1 tablespoon chopped tarragon
½ teaspoon coriander seed
½ cup amontillado sherry
2 cups white wine
2 cups fish stock (page 217)
Juice of 2 cucumbers*
Salt and pepper

*If you do not have a juicer, purée the cucumbers in a food processor, and strain.

1 pound mixed greens
½ cup cooked peas
½ cup anise hyssop leaves, cut into julienne
4 tomatoes, peeled, seeded, and cut into julienne
1 small cucumber, seeded and cut into julienne

➤ To prepare the fish, brush the fillets on all sides with olive oil, and arrange them on a 17 by 13 by 1-inch pan lined with parchment paper. Sprinkle the lemon and orange zest over the fillets, and refrigerate for 60 minutes.

➤ To prepare the purée, place the potato in a medium saucepan, cover with water, and bring to a boil. Cook the potato until tender. Drain. Push the potato through a ricer or medium sieve. Add the cucumber, cream, and butter, and mix thoroughly. Season with nutmeg, salt, and pepper, and keep warm.

➤ One of my favorite aspects of inventing a new dish is to include the element of surprise — an unexpected taste or sensation that isn't noticed immediately. In this dish, the anise hyssop highlights the cucumber in the garnish. Including cucumber in the potato purée creates a unity of flavors in this dish.

❀ To prepare the clams, heat a small amount of vegetable oil in a deep fryer or large sauce-pan to 350°F. (If you are using a saucepan without a temperature control, you can use a candy or fat thermometer to check the temperature of the oil.) Place the cornmeal in a shallow dish with some salt and pepper. Dip the clams in milk, dredge them in the cornmeal mixture, and shake off any excess. Fry the clams until golden brown, place them on a pan lined with paper towels, and keep warm.

❀ To prepare the fumet, heat the olive oil in a medium saucepan over medium-high heat. Add the garlic and shallot, and sauté until translucent. Add the tarragon and coriander seed, and stir to incorporate. Add the sherry, and cook for about 1 minute. Add the wine, and, over medium heat, reduce the liquid by half, about 30 minutes. Incorporate the fish stock, and reduce the liquid by half, about 20 minutes. Add the cucumber juice, and bring to a boil. Reduce the heat, and simmer until hot, skimming off any foam. Remove from the heat. Strain the fumet, season it with salt and pepper, and keep warm.

❀ To cook the fish, preheat the oven to 425°F. Heat a large ovenproof sauté pan over medium-high heat. Season the fillets with salt and pepper, and place them in the pan skin side up. Add more olive oil if needed. Sauté the fillets until golden brown, turn, and finish by roasting them in the oven to the desired doneness.

❀ To serve, spoon some of the potato-cucumber purée onto a plate, put some mixed greens on top, and place a fillet on the greens. Arrange some fried clams, peas, anise hyssop leaves, and julienned tomato and cucumber over and around the fish. Spoon some fumet around the plate.

Yield: 6 servings

Chilled Melon Soup with Anise Hyssop

2 very ripe cantaloupes
2 cups champagne
2 tablespoons sugar

Salt
2 tablespoons anise hyssop leaves (about 12 leaves)

❀ Place a serving bowl in the refrigerator to chill. Peel and seed 1 cantaloupe, and cut it into chunks. Place the chunks in a blender with the champagne and sugar. Blend for 1 minute, and strain. Cut the other melon in half, and remove the seeds. With a spoon, shave out the ripe meat in thin ribbons, and place them in the chilled bowl. Ladle the soup over the shaved melon. Add salt to taste. Cut the anise hyssop leaves crosswise into thin slices, sprinkle them over the soup, and serve.

Yield: 6 servings

❀ This is one of my favorite summer preparations. I love the combination of the sweet melon, the acidity of the champagne, and the mintiness of the anise hyssop.
❀ Although this soup makes a lovely first course, it may also be served as a refreshing finale.

Summer Berry Shortcakes with Anise Hyssop–Banyuls Sauce

Summer Berry Shortcakes:
4 cups all-purpose flour
7 tablespoons sugar
3 tablespoons baking powder
2 teaspoons salt
⅔ cup chopped anise hyssop leaves

Zest of 1 orange
4 tablespoons soft butter
2 cups heavy cream
2 tablespoons butter, melted

Anise Hyssop–Banyuls Sauce:
6 cups mixed berries (approximately)
1 tablespoon sugar
1 cup Banyuls*

½ cup simple syrup (page 221)
¼ cup finely minced anise hyssop leaves

Port is an acceptable substitute for Banyuls.

1½ cups heavy cream, whipped

✦ To prepare the shortcakes, preheat the oven to 350°F. Sift together the flour, sugar, baking powder, and salt. Mix in the anise hyssop and orange zest. Mix in the soft butter and the cream to make a soft dough. Roll the dough on a lightly floured surface to a thickness of 1 inch. Cut the dough into 12 (2-inch) rounds, and brush them with the melted butter. Bake the shortcakes until golden brown, about 15 to 20 minutes. Let them cool slightly on a wire rack.

✦ To prepare the sauce, place 1 cup of the berries and the sugar in a blender or food processor. Purée, and strain through a fine strainer. Add the purée to the remaining berries with the wine, the simple syrup, and the anise hyssop. Bring to a simmer, and simmer for 4 minutes. Remove the sauce from the heat, and let cool to room temperature.

✦ To serve, split the shortcakes and place 4 halves in each of 6 large soup bowls. Spoon some sauce over the shortcakes, and top with whipped cream.

Yield: 6 servings

✦ Banyuls is a dessert wine from Provence. It is not always easy to find and can be a bit of an extravagance. Its rich, cherry-like flavors accentuate the intensity of the best summer berries and the subtle spice of the anise hyssop.

✦ Enjoy a cup of herb tea with this summer dessert.

basil

Ocimum

bASIL IS ONE OF THE MOST COMMON and most obtainable herbs. It's readily available at supermarkets and produce stands and is easily grown in a kitchen or windowsill garden. This pungent herb is also a member of the mint family and boasts a royal background. It's known as "the herb of kings" because the Greek name for it, *basileus,* means "king" and its strong aroma is said to be "fit for a king." The French refer to it as the *herbe royale,* and Italians consider it a sign of love. Basil is used extensively in Mediterranean, Thai, and Italian cuisines and is native to India, Africa, Iran, and Asia. It's an ingredient in the classic herb blend, herbes de Provence.

There are hundreds of varieties of basil; the most common is sweet, or garden, basil. Its large, shiny, deep-green leaves emit a sweet, rich, spicy aroma, and its flavor is a combination of clove and mint. Basil is often paired with tomatoes.

Holy basil is considered a sacred herb in India. The sweeter Genovese variety is the basil most often used in Italy to make pesto.

Basil is considered a copycat herb because a number of basil varieties mimic other flavors. Lemon basil, popular in Indonesia, adds a citrusy flavor. Cinnamon basil has an intense cinnamon-basil flavor, which is especially good with rice, fish, poultry, and marinades, and in teas and flavored vinegars. Anise basil adds the essence of licorice and enhances fish, poached fruits, baked apples, and melon salads.

Thai basil combines the clove-mint flavor with a hint of coriander and pepper. This variety appears, of course, in Thai dishes such as chutneys, marinades, and jellies.

Basil also adds zip to pasta, meat, soup, egg dishes, and seafood and goes well with garlic, onions, and olives. Basil contains potassium and small amounts of calcium.

joe simone

executive chef

Tosca
Hingham, Massachusetts

*J*OE SIMONE DRAWS ON HIS ITALIAN HERITAGE and on Italian tradition and uses basil on a daily basis. "Basil is a very fundamental herb in my kitchen. I like the fresh, clean flavor of basil, and I like that it complements many, many things."

Contrary to popular belief, basil is not just for tomato sauce. Simone heats a bit of butter in some olive oil and adds basil and cream to make a sauce for his lobster ravioli. If you have extra basil leaves, tear them into pieces and toss them into a salad, suggests Simone. "Herbs and lettuce are fabulous together."

According to Simone, basil is a lot like mint in its flavor profile and, therefore, is easy to pair with other flavors. He suggests adding julienned basil leaves to grapefruit segments. He also offers a very simple, quick tomato sauce: Warm several cloves of garlic in olive oil. When the garlic sizzles, toss in a handful of basil and a can of whole tomatoes with juice. Simmer for about 20 minutes, put the mixture through a sieve, and you have a quick pasta sauce. Simone, an aficionado of Italian and Mediterranean cuisine, travels extensively throughout Italy and Europe, studying and sampling regional dishes to add to his repertoire. His roots, however, are firmly planted in New England and are evident in the dishes he prepares from the region's bounty.

In Tosca's open kitchen, Simone takes center stage, orchestrating such dishes as wood-roasted New Bedford scallops with fennel and Provençal tomatoes, late summer corn and porcini pizza with spiced arugula, and lobster and scallop ravioli in lemon basil cream. He also uses basil in his signature dish, grilled leg of lamb with basil and warm potato salad, for which the recipe is given opposite.

Simone spent many seasons fine-tuning his culinary skills at Al Forno in Providence and the Wauwinet Inn on Nantucket. He also spent six years at Papa Razzi as the concept chef, overseeing operations at 14 restaurants serving more than 40,000 guests a week.

Simone was honored for culinary excellence by the Italian Associazione Cuochi Vincenza, an award the association has presented to only one other restaurant in the United States. He is an active member of the Chefs Collaborative 2000, as well as the Oldways Preservation and Exchange Trust, an organization dedicated to preserving traditions in food, cooking, and agriculture.

Tosca, the flagship restaurant of Eat Well, Inc., is located on historic Hingham Harbor in the 1910 Granary Marketplace building. The restaurant's theatrical setting includes rustic brick, imported tiles, and mahogany.

Grilled Leg of Lamb with Basil and Warm Potato Salad

1 large bunch basil
½ cup extra virgin olive oil
2 tablespoons Dijon mustard
2 tablespoons balsamic vinegar
1 boneless leg of lamb (about 4 pounds), butterflied

Kosher salt and freshly ground pepper
2 pounds potatoes (about 8 medium), preferably
    Yukon gold, cut into 1-inch pieces
2 tablespoons grated Parmigiano-Reggiano cheese

✦ Remove the basil leaves from their stems, and wash the leaves carefully in cold water. Place them on paper towels to dry.

✦ Whisk ¼ cup of the olive oil with the mustard and the balsamic vinegar. Chop 20 basil leaves coarsely, and stir them into the marinade. Set aside the remaining basil leaves.

✦ Season the lamb with salt and pepper. Rub the marinade all over the lamb. Cover the lamb loosely with plastic wrap, and let it stand at room temperature for 2 hours or overnight in the refrigerator. Allow the refrigerated lamb to reach room temperature before grilling it.

✦ Preheat the grill or the oven broiler. Meanwhile, place the potatoes in a saucepan, cover with cold water, and bring to a simmer. Cook for about 15 minutes until the potato is tender but not falling apart. While the potatoes are cooking, finely chop the remaining basil leaves on a cutting board with a pinch of salt. Continue chopping until the basil and salt nearly form a paste.

✦ When the grill is ready, use a rubber spatula to scrape the marinade off the lamb. Reserve the marinade. Grill the lamb for 8 to 10 minutes per side for medium rare, basting it with the reserved marinade during the last 2 minutes of cooking. Remove the lamb, and allow it to stand while you finish the potato salad.

✦ Drain the potatoes, and put them back in the saucepan with the basil. Toss the potatoes with the basil, and add the remaining ¼ cup of olive oil and the cheese. Mix well, and do not worry if the potatoes begin to break down. Taste, and adjust the salt and pepper. Slice the lamb against the grain, and serve with the warm potato salad.

Yield: 4 to 6 servings

Note: Be careful not to overcook the lamb. If overcooked, it can have a gamey taste that many people don't like. Remember that the lamb will continue to cook during the time it is left standing.

✦ **Marinating the lamb in basil and balsamic vinegar adds a tender, sweet note to this popular spring dish.**
✦ **Serve simply prepared seasonal vegetables with this dish.**

Tuscan Tomato and Bread Soup with Fresh Basil

1 medium red onion, cut into ¼-inch pieces (about ½ cup)
2 tablespoons extra virgin olive oil
¼ cup coarsely chopped basil leaves
1 (28-ounce) can plum tomatoes, packed in juice

¼ cup shaved Parmigiano-Reggiano cheese*
*Use a vegetable peeler to shave the cheese.

2 cups chicken stock (page 219) or vegetable stock (page 218)
Kosher salt and freshly ground black pepper
1½ cups small pieces hearty style, day-old bread

Olive oil

❧ Put the onion and oil in a stockpot, and set it over medium heat. Cook, stirring often, until the onion wilts and becomes translucent, about 10 minutes. Add the basil, and cook until the mixture becomes fragrant, about 2 minutes. Add the tomatoes with their juice, and bring to a simmer. Mash the tomatoes with a fork to break them up coarsely. Add the chicken stock, season with salt and pepper, and bring to a boil. Immediately reduce the heat, and simmer for 15 minutes. Add the bread, and simmer for 5 minutes. Check the seasoning.

❧ To serve, ladle the soup into warm soup bowls. Sprinkle the cheese on top of the soup, and drizzle on a small amount of olive oil.

Yield: 4 servings

Orange and Basil Granita

4 average-sized sprigs basil
3 cups spring water

1 cup freshly squeezed orange juice (about 3 oranges)
1 cup sugar

❧ Wash the basil and remove the leaves. Reserve the stems. Carefully dry the leaves with paper towels, and cut the leaves into very thin ribbons. (This is easy to do if you stack 3 or 4 leaves on top of each other and then roll them up.)

❧ In a nonreactive saucepan, bring the spring water and basil stems to a simmer. Add the orange juice and sugar, and simmer for 3 minutes. Strain the mixture into a large glass bowl. Add the ribbons of basil, stir, and transfer the basil mixture to a large Pyrex baking dish. The dish should be large enough so that the liquid is no more than ½-inch deep. Place the dish in the freezer overnight.

❧ To serve, grate the granita with a fork to form crystals, and serve them in a chilled bowl or goblet.

Yield: 4 to 6 servings

aNN COOPER LIKES OPAL BASIL, a variety with dark purple leaves and a slightly anise flavor, and uses a fair amount of it to create herbal treats such as opal basil and Gewürztraminer sorbet and garden pesto. But it's the citrusy lemon basil variety that really lights her fire.

*certified
executive chef*
⊱⊰
**The Putney Inn
Putney, Vermont**

"It has a nice fresh flavor — a bright flavor," she says. "It makes really nice pestos, is good on pastas, and even in sorbets."

Despite the short growing season in Vermont, The Putney Inn maintains a garden where Cooper harvests lemon basil and other herbs for use in the meals served at the inn. She says lemon basil's "semi-citric flavor" goes well with fish, in dressings and marinades, and on grilled vegetables. She advises handling lemon basil gently. "You don't want to bruise it," she says. Get it from the garden or the store, and put it right in the refrigerator. It'll keep about three or four days.

Although Cooper has won a number of honors, she isn't one to rest on her laurels. This energetic chef serves as a consultant to a number of culinary operations including the Vermont Butter & Cheese Company, several Vermont restaurants, and her alma mater, the Culinary Institute of America.

She has been chef for Holland Cruises, Radisson Hotels, and the Telluride Ski Company. In addition, she has served as chef for the Telluride Film Festival for the past several years, preparing 12,000 meals during the four-day festival. She also wrote the book *A Woman's Place Is in the Kitchen* (Van Nostrand Reinhold, 1997), in which she examines women chefs — their history, current status, and future opportunities. She is a member of Women Chefs and Restaurateurs and of the International Association of Culinary Professionals. Cooper's adventures aren't just culinary. She celebrated her 40th birthday by trekking up Mount Kilimanjaro in Africa.

Cooper, one of the first 50 women to be certified as an executive chef by the American Culinary Federation (ACF), was named 1995 Chef of the Year by the ACF of the Central Vermont region. Cooper's awards include the ACF Custom Gold Award for Culinary Excellence. In addition, she was the Northeast Regional Winner in the Uncle Ben's Rice Cookoff, grand prize winner in the Hershey's Chocolate Desserts Contest, and she earned a General Foods Nutrition Scholarship.

Located just off Interstate 91, The Putney Inn is a favorite of locals, travelers, and conference groups. Early American furnishings under rough-hewn exposed beams reflect the property's history, which dates back to the 1700s. The menu emphasizes regional New England cuisine prepared with fresh, local ingredients carefully selected by Cooper.

Lemon Basil Pesto

4 to 6 cloves garlic
1 cup lemon basil leaves
1 tablespoon balsamic vinegar
1 tablespoon lemon juice
¾ cup Parmesan cheese

½ teaspoon cracked black pepper
⅓ cup walnuts
¼ cup white wine
1½ cups olive oil

❋ Combine the garlic, lemon basil, vinegar, lemon juice, cheese, pepper, walnuts, and wine in a blender. Slowly add the oil while the blender is running.

Yield: about 1¾ cups

❋ This recipe really lets the citrus flavor of the lemon basil shine.
❋ Serve lemon basil pesto over vegetables, fish, or pasta, or use it to make balsamic pesto vinaigrette (below).

Balsamic Pesto Vinaigrette

1 tablespoon whole grain Dijon mustard
½ cup lemon basil pesto (above)
1 cup balsamic vinegar
1 cup olive oil

1 cup salad oil
⅓ cup champagne vinegar
⅛ cup sugar
1 teaspoon salt

❋ Place the mustard and pesto in a mixer, and on low speed slowly blend in the balsamic vinegar, olive oil, salad oil, and champagne vinegar. Add the sugar and salt, and mix well.

Yield: about 3 cups

❋ Besides being a perfect dressing for a green salad, this versatile vinaigrette makes a great marinade for fish or chicken.
❋ Spoon balsamic pesto vinaigrette over cooked asparagus to add zip to this spring vegetable.

Lemon Basil Bouillabaisse

1¼ medium carrots, diced
1¼ stalks celery, diced
1 medium onion, diced
2 cups diced tomatoes (about 3 medium)
2 cups diced green onions (about 1 bunch)
1 cup diced oven-dried tomatoes
¼ cup minced garlic
Olive oil
1 cup lemon basil

¼ cup white wine
4 cups tomato sauce
2 cups clam broth
1 cup white wine
2 tablespoons lemon juice
1½ teaspoons seafood seasoning (such as Old Bay)
Saffron
White pepper

❧ In a 3½-quart stockpot (or larger), sauté the carrot, celery, onion, tomato, green onion, oven-dried tomato, and garlic in a small amount of olive oil on medium heat until tender. In a blender, purée the basil with the wine. Add the basil mixture, tomato sauce, clam broth, white wine, lemon juice, seafood seasoning, and a pinch of saffron and pepper to the vegetable mixture. Simmer for about 20 minutes.

Yield: 4 to 6 servings

Note: To oven-dry the tomatoes, place washed, dried, quartered tomatoes on a baking sheet, and bake at 200°F until they are dry but not brittle, about 2½ to 3 hours. You will need about 2 pounds of tomatoes for this recipe. Any leftovers can be stored in the refrigerator for a few days. Use them to flavor soups, stews, or sauces.

❧ Bouillabaisse is a seafood stew that originated in the Provence region of France.

❧ Sauté fish and shellfish of your choice, and add to the bouillabaisse. I sometimes ladle some bouillabaisse into a soup bowl and place a charbroiled salmon fillet brushed with lemon basil pesto on top (see the color photo on the front cover illustrating this presentation).

daryle ryo nagata

executive chef

Herons Restaurant & Lounge
Vancouver, British Columbia

*g*UESTS OF THE WATERFRONT CENTRE HOTEL, which houses Herons Restaurant, often spot chef Nagata gathering fresh herbs from his 2,100-square-foot terrace herb garden.

Nagata enjoys answering questions about the garden and encourages guests to taste the herbs. In fact, he enjoys sharing his herbs and culinary expertise so much he's developed a Down to Earth dinner and seminar series in which guests participate in a seminar followed by a six-course, herbal-inspired dinner.

Among the herbs growing in his garden are lavender, stevia, chives, rosemary, Greek oregano, chamomile, lovage, sorrel, thyme, mint, basil, lemon verbena, tarragon, and sage.

Although Nagata likes a lot of different herbs, "basil is probably one of the most versatile herbs we use here. We use it in everything from herbal truffles to pastas and seafood."

He appreciates the many varieties of basil. "Different basils have different flavors or tones to them. They can have peppery tones or a bit of licorice flavor. Purple basil has more of an almost mintish clove flavor. They're all pretty good."

He uses basil for bruschettas and crostinis, to finish sauces, or to toss with pasta. He'll sometimes wrap lemon or purple basil leaves around uniformly cut pieces of cantaloupe and slice them to make refreshing canapés. "The combination of basil and cantaloupe is just pretty exciting; basil goes really well with fruit."

Nagata's favorite basil variety is lemon. "I like the fruitiness it adds. The citrusy tones go very well in pasta, and it works well with other citrusy flavors like sun-dried cranberries and lemon or orange rind."

He likes to make a tomato basil elixir that he serves as a clear soup in an espresso cup with a pesto cheese straw. "When you smell it and taste it, there's this incredible flavor of tomato there, and it just knocks your socks off."

During the Asia Pacific Economic Co-operation conference in 1997, Nagata cooked breakfast for United States President Bill Clinton. Nagata earned a gold medal in the Ottawa and Hull Culinary Salon in 1988. Before coming to Herons, Nagata worked at the Hyatt Regency in Vancouver, the Sheraton Centre in Toronto, the Château Laurier hotel in Ottawa, and Restaurant La Nouvelle Reserve in Quebec. He has also worked in a number of kitchens in Switzerland and England.

Nagata graduated from the Northern Alberta Institute of Technology and is a member of Canadian Chefs du Cuisine and the British Columbia Chef's Association, and was a co-director of Cuisine Canada (British Columbia Chapter), an association of culinary professionals that promotes the growth and study of Canadian food culture.

Lemon Basil and Cranberry Crusted Tournedo of Beef Tenderloin with Balsamic Jus

1½ cups beef stock (page 217)
4 (3-inch) rounds cut from sliced bread
4 (4-ounce) beef tenderloins
Salt and pepper
4 slices bacon
3 tablespoons olive oil

⅓ cup coarsely crushed dried cranberries
⅓ cup finely chopped lemon basil
¼ cup fresh bread crumbs
½ cup balsamic vinegar
2 tablespoons finely diced shallots or onions

✢ Over medium heat, reduce the beef stock to one-third of its original volume. Set aside.

✢ Preheat the oven to 350°F. Place the bread rounds on a baking sheet, and set aside.

✢ Season the beef tenderloins on all sides with salt and pepper. Wrap 1 bacon slice around each tenderloin. Use a toothpick to fasten the bacon to each tenderloin. Preheat a large frying pan over medium heat, and add 2 tablespoons of the oil. Sear the bacon-wrapped tenderloins on all sides, and remove them from the pan. Place them on a baking sheet, and set aside.

✢ Reserve 1 tablespoon of the cranberries and 1 tablespoon of the basil for the croutons. Combine the remaining cranberries and basil with the bread crumbs. Pack even amounts of the bread crumb mixture on top of each tenderloin.

✢ To prepare the balsamic jus, pour the balsamic vinegar into a saucepan and add the shallots. Over medium heat, reduce the vinegar mixture to one-quarter of the original volume. Add the reserved beef stock, and continue simmering until this mixture is reduced to one-quarter of its original volume. Season with salt and pepper.

✢ Meanwhile mix the reserved cranberries and basil with the remaining tablespoon of oil, and brush the oil mixture lightly over the bread rounds. Place the tenderloins on one shelf in the oven, and bake until the desired doneness, 7 to 10 minutes for medium rare. Place the bread rounds on the other shelf, and bake them until golden brown, about 5 to 7 minutes.

✢ To serve, place a crouton on each plate, top with a tenderloin, and drizzle the balsamic jus over the tenderloin.

Yield: 4 servings

Note: Tournedo is a French term referring to a beef tenderloin steak usually about 1 inch to 2 inches thick and frequently wrapped with bacon.

Variations: Instead of bacon, you could use pancetta, an Italian bacon. Other berries such as dried blueberries can be substituted for the cranberries in this recipe.

➤ Here I've taken a classic French recipe and given it a West Coast kind of flair by adding a crust made with cranberries, which are indigenous to this area.

➤ In the winter, I might serve this dish with a variety of sautéed winter squashes. During the summer, we often make a nest of sautéed snow pea shoots for this dish. Other options include serving the tournedos on vegetable and potato latkes, on a rice patty, or on a nest of pasta. Seasonal vegetables and potatoes also go well with this dish.

bay

Laurus nobilis

*i*N ITS FRESH FORM, BAY IS A FAR CRY from the dull, musty, dried version. While bay keeps its flavor better than some other herbs when dried, a fresh bay leaf is much more impressive than a dried one. The scent and flavor of fresh bay are stronger, and its color is a deep, shiny green. Bay is referred to as a noble herb because it was much revered by the ancient Greeks who used it to crown their sports heroes, poets, and scholars.

In the kitchen, bay is used in just about anything. You'll find it in many cuisines, including Greek, Turkish, Italian, Portuguese, Spanish, and Italian. Bay joins parsley and sweet marjoram as one of the liaison herbs, so called because they help marry contrasting flavors. Bay is an ingredient in bouquet garni, which is used to flavor soups, stews, and stocks. Crack bay leaves before adding them to the pot to release their oils and, thus, their flavor. Bay is also added to stuffings, curries, spaghetti sauce, tomato juice cocktails, chowders, chicken soup, game, and fish. It's infused in milk to flavor custards and rice pudding. For a flavorful shish kebab, try inserting leaves on the skewer next to meat chunks.

Bay has a hard-to-describe flavor. Some say it tastes of balsam and honey. Others detect a hint of mint and cloves with peppery overtones. It's one of just a few herbs that hold their flavor during long cooking. In colder climates, it can be hard to find fresh bay, although recently I've begun seeing little packets of bay in one of our large supermarkets. Fresh bay is readily available in places with milder climates such as Louisiana, and you can grow bay in a pot in a sunny window. Fresh bay leaves will keep a few days in a plastic bag in the refrigerator.

You should always remove bay leaves from a dish before serving it because they may stick in the throat of diners and are not compatible with our digestive systems. One tradition, though, says that if you do find a bay leaf in your soup, you can expect to receive good luck. The good luck may be simply that you didn't choke on the bay leaf!

Bay contains calcium, iron, vitamin A, and vitamin C, but, since for safety reasons we generally discard the leaf before serving, you can't count on bay for any significant contribution of nutrients.

jamie shannon

*b*AY IS A FAVORITE HERB OF JAMIE SHANNON, executive chef at Commander's Palace in New Orleans. "Bay leaf is incredible," says the 14-year veteran of one of New Orlean's top restaurants and a graduate of the Culinary Institute of America. "It's hardly ever used by itself as a primary herb, so it's a different flavor for a lot of people. It's so distinctive." Shannon describes bay's characteristics as "velvety and earthy."

Says Shannon, "when you discover the true flavor of bay, it's so unique and so good and it goes with so many things that it will just blow you away." He discovered fresh bay's value by "playing around with bay from my tree, doing different infusions and trying different combinations."

When he wants to make rice, he plucks a couple of leaves off his backyard bay tree and adds them along with rice, salt, and a bit of butter to a pot of water to make "the best rice in the world." He uses bay in all his stews and stocks and in some cold appetizers. One excellent way to use bay, he says, is to extract the oil from fresh bay leaves with a juicer. Add some olive oil, and use the mixture for salad dressings and for cooking fish. If you don't have a juicer, he says, you can infuse the oil instead. Heat about 1 cup of olive oil to 105°F (no higher) with about 8 fresh bay leaves, 10 or 12 if dried. Process the oil and bay leaves in a food processor, and strain. If you have an oven with a pilot light, you can also let the oil and bay steep for several hours in the oven. Bottle the bay-flavored oil, and refrigerate. He cautions that infused oils must always be refrigerated to prevent the oil from spoiling. It's best to make just the amount of infused oil you can use within two to three weeks.

Shannon, a southern New Jersey native, worked in several Atlantic City casino restaurants before making his way to Commander's Palace as saucier under Emeril Lagasse in 1984. When Lagasse left in 1990 to open the renowned Emeril's in the Warehouse District, Shannon stepped up to take the reins as executive chef.

Nestled in the Garden District of New Orleans, a streetcar ride from the French Quarter, Commander's Palace boasts a history dating back to the 1800s. Today, diners can tour the open kitchen on their way to one of several dining rooms or, weather permitting, the outdoor patio. They can also choose to join Jamie in the kitchen at the chef's table. Commander's Jazz Brunch plays to a full house each weekend.

Food & Wine magazine readers rated Commander's Palace the number one restaurant in the U.S., and, in 1996, Commander's Palace received the James Beard Foundation's Outstanding Restaurant Award. In 1998, Shannon was nominated for the American Express Best Chef: Southeast James Beard Award. In addition, the *Zagat Survey* rated it the most popular restaurant in New Orleans, *Southern Living* magazine readers rated it the number one restaurant in the city, and *New Orleans Magazine* named Shannon chef of the year.

executive chef

Commander's Palace
New Orleans, Louisiana

Shrimp Creole

Shrimp Stock:

4 pounds large shrimp, heads on*
Oil
2 bay leaves
1 carrot, diced

½ medium onion, diced (about ¼ cup)
2 cups diced celery
1 tablespoon black peppercorns
3 cups cold water

*If shrimp are not available with the heads on in your area, use the shells only to make the stock. You could buy a few extra shrimp to put in the stockpot in place of the heads.

Creole Sauce:

8 vine-ripened tomatoes
Ice bath
2 medium onions, cut into small dice
2 roasted green peppers (page 220), cut into small dice
½ bunch celery, cut into small dice
2 tablespoons crushed garlic
2 bay leaves
1 tablespoon black pepper

2 cups reserved shrimp stock
3 tablespoons light corn syrup
1 tablespoon coarse salt
1 tablespoon Worcestershire sauce
Hot sauce
1 tablespoon chopped garlic
Oil

8 portions cooked rice, preferably Louisiana popcorn rice,* or rice seasoned with bay (see opposite)

6 green onions, cut on the bias

*This aromatic rice has a scent like popcorn and is available in gourmet shops across the country.

➢ To prepare the stock, peel the shrimp, and remove the heads. Set the shrimp aside. Put some oil, the shells, and the heads in a large saucepan, and place it over medium heat. Add the bay leaves, carrot, onion, celery, and peppercorns. Cook for about 10 minutes until the vegetables are soft. Add the water, bring to a simmer, and continue cooking for 60 minutes.

➢ Strain, and reserve the liquid.

➢ To prepare the sauce, bring 2 gallons of water to a boil. Remove the core from the tomatoes, and score the bottom of the tomatoes with an X. Place the tomatoes in the boiling water for 30 seconds. Remove the tomatoes, and place them in an ice bath. Peel off the tomato skins, and cool the tomatoes. Once cool, cut them in half lengthwise, remove the seeds, and cut the tomatoes into ½-inch dice. Set aside.

➢ Meanwhile, cook the Louisiana popcorn rice according to the package directions, or make rice seasoned with bay.

➢ **This is a classic New Orleans dish and a favorite menu item at Commander's.**
➢ **A loaf of crusty bread completes this robust, Creole meal.**

❀ Place the onion, roasted pepper, celery, and crushed garlic in a large saucepan. Sauté for 5 minutes. Add the reserved tomato, the bay leaves, and the pepper. Sauté for 5 minutes. Add the reserved shrimp stock, corn syrup, salt, and Worcestershire sauce, and simmer over low heat for 45 minutes. Add hot sauce to taste, and adjust the salt and pepper if necessary.

❀ In a sauté pan, sauté the chopped garlic in a little oil until golden brown. Add the reserved shrimp, and sauté for 30 seconds. Add the Creole sauce, and simmer for 2 minutes or until the shrimp are cooked. Remove the bay leaves.

❀ To serve, place an equal number of shrimp in each of 8 large bowls, and cover with an equal amount of sauce. Place a scoop of rice in the center of the shrimp, and sprinkle green onions on top.

Yield: 8 servings

Rice Seasoned with Bay

1 cup long-grain rice (not converted)
2 cups water
3 bay leaves

1 teaspoon butter
Salt and pepper

❀ In a small pot, rinse the rice under cold running water until the water becomes clear. Rinsing removes excess starch from rice and keeps it from becoming sticky or gummy.

❀ Place the rice, water, bay, butter, and some salt and pepper in a medium saucepan, and bring to a boil. Cook until the water level reaches the top of the rice. Do not stir. Turn the heat down to low, and cover the saucepan tightly. Simmer for 7 to 10 minutes. Let stand for 5 minutes covered, then fluff the rice with a fork. Remove the bay leaves. Season with salt and pepper to taste.

Yield: 4 servings

❀ Long-grain rice is preferred because the grains hold their texture and flavor and are less likely to become gummy. The bay adds an incredible flavor to rice.

❀ Make this flavorful rice whenever a meal calls for rice, or serve it with gumbo or as an accompaniment to meat or poultry.

BAYLEAF

Seafood Gumbo with Okra

❧ Take a culinary trip to Louisiana with this classic dish. I always double this hearty gumbo recipe and freeze half. I use dry herbs here because they work better in this slow-simmering dish.

❧ A chiffonade of green onions makes a nice garnish. Serve this gumbo over fluffy white rice such as rice seasoned with bay (page 33).

¾ cup vegetable oil
¾ cup all-purpose flour, sifted
4 large or 5 small onions, diced (about 2 cups)
1 medium bunch celery, diced (about 1 cup)
4 green or red peppers, diced (about 2 cups)
4 bay leaves
2 tablespoons minced garlic
1 teaspoon cayenne or 5 fresh cayenne chiles, diced
Dried basil
Dried oregano

Dried thyme
Salt and pepper
2 quarts seafood stock or cold water
6 gumbo (hard-shell) crabs (tops off, halved, lungs removed, claws cracked)
1 pound andouille sausage,* sliced into ¼-inch pieces
1 pound okra, sliced
1 pound medium shrimp, peeled
1 quart oysters (about 24), shucked, in their own liquid
Hot sauce

Other smoked pork sausage can be substituted; make sure it's smoked and firm.

❧ To make a roux, place the oil in a heavy-bottomed soup pot over high heat, and heat it to the smoking point, about 5 minutes. Slowly add the flour, stirring constantly until the mixture is the color of chocolate, about 3 to 5 minutes. Scraping the sides and bottom of the pot while constantly stirring is the key to making a good roux. Be careful not to burn it, because if you do, it will be unusable and you will need to start over.

❧ Once the roux is ready, add the onion. Cook for 1 minute, and add the celery. Cook for 30 seconds, and add the pepper while scraping the bottom of the pot. The aroma from this mixture will be wonderful; it should not smell burnt. Add the bay leaves, garlic, cayenne, and a pinch each of basil, oregano, thyme, salt, and pepper. Add the stock, stirring constantly. Add the crabs, sausage, and okra, and bring the mixture to a boil. Reduce the heat, and simmer for about 60 minutes, frequently skimming any oil or foam off the surface. After simmering and skimming, the crab meat will look like white strings. Add the shrimp, and cook for 10 minutes. Add the oysters and their liquid, and bring to a boil. Adjust the salt and pepper, and add hot sauce to taste. Remove the bay leaves.

Yield: 12 servings

Note: The best way to approach this recipe is to do all the chopping and cutting ahead of time and lay out all ingredients grouped together in the order used. This is known in French as *mise en place* (everything in its place) and is a useful technique in all cooking but especially so in a recipe like this with a number of ingredients and timed steps.

Timesaver Tips: Have your fishmonger prepare the crabs and shuck the oysters for you. Be sure to ask for some of the oyster liquid as well. You may also buy shrimp already peeled. In some supermarkets, you can buy vegetables already peeled and cut.

Chamaemelum nobile (Roman)
Matricaria recutita (German)

YES, YOU REMEMBER CHAMOMILE. It was the tiny, daisy-like blossoms of this herb that Peter Rabbit's mom brewed into a tea to calm him following his traumatic escape from Mr. McGregor.

Although there are two common types of chamomile, Roman and German, it is the Roman variety that's most often used for culinary purposes. And while it's credited with having soothing qualities and generally is prepared as a tea, chamomile can certainly stand up to the heat in any kitchen. The buds are used most often for culinary purposes, but the leaves are often included in potpourri. In Spain chamomile is used in wines and liquors. Some people infuse it in milk or water that is then used to flavor custards and puddings. Others find chamomile adds a delightful apple scent to a green salad.

Chamomile means "ground apple" in Greek, and in the language of flowers, it stands for "energy in adversity." Once you've had a patch of chamomile in your garden, both of these meanings make perfect sense. Chamomile is sometimes used as ground cover in English gardens because it flourishes even when trampled on. The plants emit a strong apple fragrance when walked on.

Roman chamomile

German chamomile

anthony ambrose

chef/co-owner

Ambrosia on Huntington
Boston, Massachusetts

a COMBINATION OF AMERICAN TRAINING and European travels has sharpened the culinary wits of this innovative chef. He relies heavily on herb infusions in his cooking, and makes use of chamomile as a foundation herb to add a surprising element to a number of dishes, including lobster crêpes, chive and caviar vinaigrette, and salmon tartare (see opposite).

"It's such a magical little flower and herb," says Ambrose. "It takes on some unique characteristics. It can be dominant or submissive, depending on the other flavors."

Ambrose uses fresh chamomile buds from the restaurant garden when in season and likes to experiment by adding other herbs and coming up with a whole new flavor.

He's passionate about Asian seasonings and has been described as a "master of fusion cuisine." He describes his food as "Asian-influenced provincial French."

Ambrose was named one of the industry's Rising Stars of 1995 by *Restaurant Hospitality* magazine. At age 20, he learned the rudiments of French cuisine at the Marlborough Inn in Montclair, New Jersey. Ambrose later moved to the Bay Tower Room in Boston where, under the tutelage of Jasper White of Restaurant Jasper, he began developing his own culinary style. "I not only want to satisfy a diner's appetite and curiosity, but challenge their palates and emotions," says Ambrose.

In 1987, he became the first American chef de cuisine for Julien, the dining room at the Hotel Le Meridian. After a stint as the executive chef of Seasons restaurant at the Bostonian Hotel, he left to open Ambrosia on Huntington with his wife and co-owner Dorene.

Ambrose recently launched a line of herb-infused sorbets called Chef Anthony Ambrose's Chamomile Sorbets. He developed the line after serving chamomile ice cubes to his wife while she was in labor with their son. One of the most popular flavors is a signature item, cocoa chamomile sorbet.

Opened in 1994, Ambrosia was named one of the top 25 new restaurants in the country by *Esquire* magazine, the best new restaurant in Boston by *Boston* magazine's annual readers' poll, and one of the most popular new restaurants by *Zagat Survey* in 1996. *Gourmet* readers rated Ambrosia among the 20 Top Tables in Boston.

Situated in Boston's Back Bay within walking distance of Symphony Hall, Newbury Street, and Boston's finest hotels, Ambrosia on Huntington features a grand staircase connecting the mezzanine level, where diners can view the glass-enclosed kitchen, to the first floor. The wait staff make theatrical trips down the stairs ceremoniously toting their trays of sculpted food into the first-floor, glass-enclosed dining room.

Ambrose has a commercial fishing and tuna license, and often he can be found on the docks bringing in fresh fish for the restaurant and buying lobsters right from the lobster boats that have just arrived in port.

Salmon Tartare with a Sauterne and Chamomile Vinaigrette

Sauterne and Chamomile Vinaigrette:
½ cup sauterne
2 tablespoons olive oil
3 teaspoons lemon juice
1½ teaspoons chamomile buds

1 teaspoon honey
1 teaspoon salt
1 teaspoon snipped chives

Salmon Tartare:
12 ounces fresh salmon (from the belly)

4 thin, 8-inch slices English cucumber

Salad Mix:
2 tablespoons chopped chervil
⅛ cup frisée (young chicory)

⅛ cup dulse (a sea lettuce)
4 teaspoons fresh chamomile leaves and buds

✤ To prepare the vinaigrette, combine the wine, oil, lemon juice, chamomile, honey, salt, and chives. Refrigerate for at least 2 hours.

✤ To prepare the tartare, dice the salmon, and roll it inside the cucumber strips. Set aside.

✤ To prepare the salad, mix together the chervil, frisée, dulse, and chamomile leaves and buds.

✤ To serve, place the cucumber-rolled salmon in the middle of a plate. Top with some vinaigrette and salad mix.

Yield: 4 servings

Note: Dulse is available in Asian markets. It's sometimes available dried and can be reconstituted for this dish.

> ✤ I was drinking chamomile tea with lemon and eating salmon tartare when I realized how well the flavors complemented each other. I later created a vinaigrette that would enhance the chamomile and other herbs.
>
> ✤ This is a fun and very sophisticated salmon preparation for a summer salad or appetizer.

Pan Roasted Lobster with Lillet and Chamomile Garlic Sauce

2 (2-pound) live lobsters (preferably
deep-water lobsters)
3 tablespoons olive oil
Cayenne
Sea salt
1½ teaspoons chopped chamomile buds
1 teaspoon coconut milk

1 teaspoon honey
½ kaffir lime leaf,* slivered
½ teaspoon mashed roasted garlic (page 222)
¼ teaspoon fennel seed
1 tablespoon orange juice
2 tablespoons unsalted butter
2 tablespoons Lillet wine

*Substitute lemon grass or lime peel if necessary.

✦ Remove the claws from the live lobsters at the body. Steam the claws for 9 minutes, remove the meat, and set it aside. Discard the shells, or reserve them for use in another recipe.

✦ Cut the bodies (with the tail still attached) lengthwise. From the body cavity remove the tomalley (the liver), and discard it or save it for another use. Place the split lobsters, split side down, on paper towels.

✦ In a large skillet, heat 2 tablespoons of the oil on high heat. Season the cavities and tails with a little cayenne and sea salt. Place the lobsters, split side down, in the skillet. Reduce the heat to medium, and cook for 4 minutes. Add the remaining olive oil and the chamomile, coconut milk, honey, lime leaf, garlic, fennel seed, and orange juice. Increase the heat, and bring the mixture to a boil. Remove the lobster from the skillet, and add the reserved claw meat. Bring the mixture to a boil once again, add the butter, and reduce the sauce by one-third. Remove the skillet from the heat.

✦ Arrange the lobster bodies, cavity side up, on a plate. Fill the cavity with the claw meat. Add the wine to the sauce in the skillet, and pass the sauce through a fine mesh strainer onto the lobster. Serve immediately.

Yield: 2 servings

Note: The shells can be used for dill-scented Maine lobster cappuccino with oyster and dill ravioli (page 68).

✦ When I was cooking in Brittany, we used to drink Lillet with crushed chamomile buds as an apéritif. I was looking for something delicate that I could combine the chamomile with and discovered lobster is perfect. I prefer deep-water lobster for its richer, juicier flavor. I also recommend selecting a female lobster because it is juicier still.

✦ Serve pan roasted lobster with cardamom-scented steamed sticky rice, soy sauce, and quick-sautéed sugar snap peas.

Anthriscus cerefolium

LACY CHERVIL LEAVES CAN BE A DELICATE ADDITION to any dish, whether as a garnish or as an ingredient. Much loved in France, chervil is virtually unknown in North American kitchens. Like parsley, its North American counterpart, chervil is a member of the carrot family. This is one herb you may have to grow yourself, although I've seen it turn up now and then in gourmet shops or farmers' markets. Sometimes called gourmet parsley, chervil makes an attractive and tasty houseplant. Harvest leaves from the stems on the outside of the plant so it will continue to send out new shoots in the center.

Those fragile, feathery leaves yield a subtle pepper and anise flavor. They're best used uncooked or added to cooked dishes at the very end of the cooking since the flavor doesn't hold up well when cooked. Freeze chopped chervil leaves in ice cube trays, and use the cubes to season soups or hot vegetables. Make chervil vinegar for vinaigrettes; toss chervil leaves into salads, or stir them into soups such as sorrel or spinach soup. Chervil enhances new potatoes, peas, asparagus, carrots, fish, oysters, and poultry. It makes a great flavored butter to serve with fish, seafood, and eggs. Basically, anywhere parsley goes, chervil can too.

Both the leaves and stems of chervil can be used. In French cookbooks, the term *pluches de cerfeuil* means "blanched sprigs of chervil," which are often used in soup. Chervil complements other seasonings such as tarragon, shallots, pepper, marjoram, and lemon. Partnered with chives, parsley, and tarragon, it becomes fines herbes, which the French use to flavor omelets, sautés, and cheese sauces.

A reasonable substitute for chervil can be made by combining flat-leaf parsley with a smidgen of tarragon. Because chervil symbolizes resurrection and new life, it's customary to serve chervil soup on Holy Thursday. Chervil gets its name from the Latin *chaerephyllum,* meaning "a joy-giving leaf," and so is a symbol of cheerfulness.

jody adams

chef/co-owner

Rialto
Cambridge, Massachusetts

*t*HIS ANTHROPOLOGIST TURNED CHEF PROCLAIMS, "I like herbs a lot. There's an herb in just about every dish on the menu." Adams is known for her respect for tradition, seasons, and fresh produce, including, of course, herbs.

"I always look forward to spring when I can get them locally," says Adams, who especially likes to work with New England ingredients. She describes her food as "intensely flavored, honest, and straightforward." Her menu changes with the seasons.

Chervil is one of the herbs she most likes to work with. "I love the flavor with spring and summer vegetables and with fish. It has that tiny bit of anise flavor that's also very fresh and green tasting." For Adams, chervil's delicate flavor works well with parsley, chives, and tarragon.

Besides the flavor, she likes chervil because "it's just so damn pretty. I use it in everything. Right now we have seared halibut in parsley, tarragon, and chervil sauce on the menu." Adams also uses chervil with fava beans and with peas and pearl onions cooked in a light broth. In her cold lobster salad with macerated kumquats, the lobster is tossed with lemon juice and chopped chervil. Her potato salad showcases chervil as well. In that, she says, the flavor of the chervil is allowed to stand on its own. As a garnish, says Adams, the lacy leaves of chervil can't be beat.

While studying anthropology at Brown University, Adams took a part-time job with food writer and teacher Nancy Verde Barr and found she was much happier in the kitchen than in anthropology class. She apprenticed with Barr and moved on to work under chef Lydia Shire at Seasons restaurant. A sous-chef position at Hamersley's Bistro followed, and then a move to Michela's. In 1994, Adams entered a partnership with Michela Larson, Christopher Myers, and Karen Haskell. They opened Rialto to rave reviews, garnering a coveted four-star rating from *The Boston Globe*.

Adams found it "thrilling and really exciting" to be named a 1997 James Beard Award winner. "It's lovely and a confidence booster to be recognized by your peers in that way."

As well as being named best chef by *Boston* magazine, she has been recognized by *Bon Appétit, Esquire, Food & Wine, Condé Nast Traveler,* and *The Boston Globe. Gourmet* magazine cited Rialto as one of the top 20 restaurants in Boston, and Rialto made *Travel & Leisure* magazine's World's Top Restaurants list.

Rialto is located in the Charles Hotel overlooking Harvard Square. Floor to ceiling windows give diners a view of historic Cambridge. Golden walls and walnut, maple, and mahogany woodwork combine with paintings by local artists to create a warm atmosphere.

Veal Stew with Lots of Chervil

2 tablespoons butter

6 small red potatoes (about ½ pound), cut in half

4 medium turnips (about ½ pound), cut into quarters

2 large carrots (about ½ pound), cut into
   1-inch by 2-inch sticks

1 teaspoon salt plus additional salt

¼ teaspoon freshly ground pepper plus
   additional pepper

2 bay leaves

½ teaspoon chopped thyme leaves

1 tablespoon minced garlic

¼ cup minced shallots

2 pounds cleaned veal shoulder, cut into
   1½-inch cubes

½ cup white wine

1½ cups heavy cream

2 tablespoons chopped chervil

1 teaspoon lemon juice (juice of about ½ lemon)

❖ Melt the butter in a large casserole. Add the potato, turnip, and carrot. Season with 1 teaspoon salt, ¼ teaspoon pepper, the bay, and the thyme. Cook for 30 minutes. Add the garlic and shallots, and cook for 5 minutes.

❖ Season the veal with additional salt and pepper, and add to the casserole. Cook over medium heat, stirring constantly, until the surface of the veal is no longer pink, about 5 minutes. Add the wine and cook, stirring occasionally, for 10 to 15 minutes. The meat should have some pink in the center and some spring when pressed with a finger. Remove the meat and any of the vegetables that are cooked through from the pan and reduce the juices to a glaze, about 10 minutes. Add the cream, and reduce by one-third. Return the meat and vegetables to the pan. Add the chervil and lemon juice, and stir. Remove the bay leaves before serving.

Yield: 4 servings

❖ **This is my version of a rich, old-fashioned style veal blanquette. The veal is cooked briefly to keep it moist and tender. The cream creates a silky sauce, and the clean, fresh flavor of chervil enlivens the rich stew.**
❖ **Serve this veal stew as a main course following a green salad. Chervil parmesan biscuits (page 42) would make a good accompaniment.**

Chervil Parmesan Biscuits

2½ cups all-purpose flour
1 tablespoon baking powder
1 teaspoon salt
6 tablespoons unsalted butter, chilled and cut
   into 6 pieces

2 tablespoons finely snipped chives
2 tablespoons freshly grated Parmesan cheese
½ cup finely chopped chervil
1 cup buttermilk
1 to 2 tablespoons extra virgin olive oil

✦ In a bowl, combine the flour with the baking powder and salt. Add the butter, and mix with your fingertips until the butter is in pea-sized pieces. Add the chives, cheese, and chervil, and mix well. Stir in the buttermilk.

✦ Preheat the oven to 400°F. On a floured surface, knead the dough for 30 seconds. Pat the dough evenly into a ¾-inch-thick patty. Let the dough stand for 10 minutes. Using a 2-inch round cutter, cut the dough into biscuits. Gather the scraps and repeat. Arrange the biscuits on a parchment-lined baking sheet, and brush them with the oil. Bake for 25 minutes.

Yield: 24 biscuits

Note: You can make your own buttermilk by placing 1 tablespoon vinegar or lemon juice in a measuring cup and adding enough milk to make 1 cup. Powdered buttermilk, which you mix with water following the package directions, is available also.

bruce auden

*t*O BRUCE AUDEN, CHERVIL IS AN HERB he took for granted while growing up in England. His mother grew it in her garden, and it was readily available in the marketplace. He never thought of chervil as unusual because it's very popular in England and is an ingredient in many English cookbooks. Auden thinks chervil is not used nearly enough in North America.

Auden likes chervil's subtle flavor, and, to ensure he has an ample supply, he grows it in the gardens around Restaurant BIGA. It's not overpowering like some of the stronger herbs such as rosemary, sage, and thyme, he says. Auden likes "picking up tiny sprigs of chervil and standing them up on the plate. It makes a nice presentation." He also grows sage, thyme, Mexican mint marigold, chives, garlic chives, lemon balm, several mints, rosemary, and the spice cardamom. It's after chervil, though, that the family cat was named.

Auden began developing his culinary skills at country clubs and restaurants in the Chicago area. Later he moved to Dallas to open "exposure," which quickly became a favorite with diners as well as the Dallas press. At Charley's 517 in Houston, he gained national attention with his exciting dishes and dramatic presentations. He has been credited with putting San Antonio on the culinary map with his work at Polo's Restaurant in the Fairmount Hotel. During his reign in Polo's kitchen, the restaurant was listed as one of the Best New Restaurants by *Esquire* magazine. He was voted one of the Best New Chefs by *Food & Wine* magazine and was listed in the *Who's Who of Food & Wine* by *The Dallas Morning News.*

Auden has appeared on various food shows, including a segment of the *Regis & Kathie Lee Show,* and has been guest chef on Cunard's Mediterranean cruise ship, the *Sea Goddess.*

Restaurant BIGA is located in a 100-year-old mansion in the Tobin Hill section of San Antonio, Texas. Dine by the fireplace in the cozy Picture Room or choose the Sun Room and look out onto the restaurant's herb garden where you might spot chervil (the herb) as well as Chervil (the cat).

For the curious among you, "biga" is an Italian slang word for the dough starter used to make the rustic country breads served at Restaurant BIGA. Auden's wife Debra, an artisan baker, is Auden's partner and also runs Bakersfield's Bakery, Cafe and School, an adjunct to Restaurant BIGA located about two miles from it.

chef/co-owner

Restaurant BIGA
San Antonio, Texas

Chervil-Hazelnut Crusted Sea Bass with Saffron Lime Sauce

Chervil-Hazelnut Crusted Sea Bass:
1 (3-pound) sea bass or other firm-fleshed white fish
   such as tilapia
¼ cup all-purpose flour
Salt and pepper
¼ cup half-and-half
½ cup chopped hazelnuts
3 tablespoons chopped chervil

Roast Garlic Mashed Potato:
6 servings mashed potato
4 cloves roasted garlic (page 222), mashed
2 tablespoons chopped chervil

Saffron Lime Sauce:
2 shallots, chopped
2 cups dry white wine
Juice of 1 lime
Saffron
¼ cup heavy cream
½ pound unsalted butter (1 cup)
1 teaspoon chopped chervil

Sautéed Spinach:
2 cloves garlic, chopped
1 tablespoon butter
1 tablespoon olive oil
1 pound spinach, washed, stemmed, and dried

24 pomegranate seeds
1 ruby red grapefruit, sectioned
Chervil sprigs

✦ To prepare the fish, divide it into 6 equal portions of about 7½ ounces each. Lightly season the flour with some salt and pepper. Dredge one side of the fish pieces first in the flour mixture and then in the half-and-half. Combine the hazelnuts and chervil on a plate, and press the moistened surface of the fish into the hazelnut mixture. Refrigerate the fish while you prepare the mashed potato and the sauce.

✦ To prepare the mashed potato, make mashed potato as you normally would, and blend in the garlic and chervil. Keep warm until ready to serve.

✦ To prepare the sauce, place the shallots in a small saucepan with the wine, the lime juice, and a pinch of saffron. Reduce the liquid over high heat until almost none remains, about 20 minutes. Add the cream, and bring to a simmer. Off the stove or over very low heat, whisk in the butter until it is fully incorporated, and stir in the chervil. Keep the sauce warm until ready to serve.

✦ To bake the fish, preheat the oven to 400°F. Spray a baking sheet with nonstick cooking spray, and place the fish on the baking sheet. Put it on the center rack of the oven, and bake 15 to 17 minutes. The hazelnuts should be lightly toasted, and the fish will feel firm to the touch. Keep the fish warm while you prepare the sauce and spinach, but not longer than 10 minutes or the fish will dry out.

✦ To prepare the spinach, place the garlic, butter, and oil in a heavy skillet over medium heat. Allow the garlic to brown lightly. Add the spinach. Cook over medium heat until wilted.

✦ To serve, place some mashed potato on a plate and top with some spinach. Add a portion of fish and some saffron lime sauce. Garnish with pomegranate seeds, grapefruit sections, and a chervil sprig.

Yield: 6 servings

✦ Because this is a mild dish, a robust bread such as a sun-dried tomato bread with a nice peppery Tuscany olive oil would be great. You could add some diced vegetables depending on the season. I like tiny squashes or baby beets.

chives

Allium

*i*N LATE SPRING, CHIVE PLANTS PRODUCE delicate lavender blossoms that add color not just to the garden but to salads as well. That's right, snip off those blossoms and toss them into the greens for a flowery touch that's sure to impress.

To get these flowers, you'll probably have to grow them yourself. The shelf life of chives is quite short, and, while I've seen chives in the supermarket's produce department lately, I haven't seen any with blossoms.

The easiest way to cut chives is with scissors. Snip a couple of the grasslike leaves and use as a garnish for your vegetables, potatoes, or meat anytime you want to add a mild onion flavor. Chives are, in fact, the tiniest member of the onion family. Basically, where onions go, chives can too. They're especially good in omelets and with potatoes. Toss some into soups, and whip some into dips and cheese spreads. Add some to bread dough and to fish. For a pretty presentation, tie whole blanched chives around asparagus, small pieces of carrot, or julienned zucchini.

Chives are one of the ingredients in that classic French seasoning fines herbes, a combination of chervil, chives, parsley, and tarragon. A flat-leafed variety known as garlic chives *(Allium tuberosum)* adds a hint of garlic flavor and can stand in for green onions, chives, or garlic. Although chives are available in dried form, the flavor and color of fresh chives are far superior. Frozen chives are the next best thing. Simply snip chives and store them in small plastic containers in the freezer; it's easy to just scrape out a little with a spoon as needed. Keep a pot of chives on a sunny windowsill for winter use.

Nutritionally, chives contain calcium, phosphorous, and sulfur (considered a natural antibiotic), as well as iron and vitamins A and C. When cooking with chives, add them to a dish during the last few minutes of cooking to preserve their flavor and nutritional value.

mark gaier

chef/co-owner
❧—❧

Arrows
Ogunquit, Maine

WHILE FORAGING IN THE ARROWS GARDENS to harvest herbs and vegetables for the day's menu, Gaier gathers a healthy supply of chives, one of his favorite herbs.

"Chives have such a clean, fresh, aromatic flavor that goes with a lot of things. It doesn't overpower dishes like some of the stronger herbs can," explains Gaier. One of his favorite things to make is chive oil. He uses it to marinate chicken. He likes chive oil with halibut, tuna, salmon, and turkey cutlets and has been known to drizzle it over salads and to ladle some over grilled steak.

Gaier's culinary philosophy is to "start with quality, fresh ingredients and keep things simple." The delicate flavor of chives helps him do that. He also likes chives because they're so readily available. "Everywhere I've lived, I've had chives growing. They're easy to grow." He uses the green, grasslike leaves of chives and the flowers as well. He likes to pick them apart and scatter the tiny petals on a plate as a garnish. "It adds a really neat splash of color to the plate," he explains.

Gaier worked closely with Michael Allen, the chef at Chez la Mère Madeleine (Madeleine Kamman's former restaurant). Gaier was also executive chef of New England's Whistling Oyster restaurant before leaving the Northeast to expand his culinary horizons at Jeremiah Tower's Stars Restaurant in San Francisco. Returning to the Northeast, he and partner Clark Frasier opened Arrows in 1988. Gaier was recognized as a "great regional chef" of the Northeast by the James Beard Foundation.

Arrows is located one hour north of Boston in a colonial, clapboard farmhouse built in 1765. The dining room features the original plank floors, post and beam construction, and large glass walls overlooking dense woods, manicured lawns, and a two-and-a-half acre garden where staff grow vegetables, herbs, edible flowers, and berries.

Chive-Infused Oil

20 chives
1 small bunch parsley

1 cup olive oil
¼ cup extra virgin olive oil

❧ Place the chives, parsley, and oils in a blender, and process until the herbs are fully integrated, about 3 to 4 minutes. Store the chive oil in the refrigerator. Bring it to room temperature and shake well before using.

Yield: about 1¼ cups

Variations: Add a small amount of red or white vinegar to the chive oil, and use the mixture to marinate fish or chicken.

❧ Chives turn oil a beautiful green. Chive oil is especially nice with white fish and can also be used to sauté vegetables or to fry potatoes.

Chive Mashed Potatoes

3 pounds Yukon gold or other large white potatoes (about 12 medium), peeled and cut into 1½-inch cubes
2 tablespoons coarse salt

4 tablespoons softened Plugrá butter
1 cup heavy cream
¼ cup finely snipped chives

❧ Cover the potato with cold water. Add the salt, and cook until the potato is very soft. Drain the potato, and immediately transfer to a mixer with a whip attachment. Whip the potato, gradually adding the butter a tablespoon at a time, the cream, and finally the chives. Season with salt to taste.

Yield: 6 servings

Note: Plugrá is the brand name of a high-quality European butter with a high fat content, a product available in some supermarkets and specialty stores. If Plugrá butter is unavailable, substitute any high-quality butter. Mashed potato may be kept warm in a covered stainless steel pan for 60 minutes or so.

❧ I grew up in the Midwest, and my mother's wonderful, light mashed potatoes were often a part of our dinners. At Arrows, the addition of sweet European butter, heavy cream, and fresh chives brings home cooking to a new level of indulgence.

❧ These rich mashed potatoes are a great accompaniment to roasted meats.

Chive Biscuits

2 cups all-purpose flour
1 tablespoon baking powder
½ teaspoon salt

¼ pound butter (½ cup)
2 tablespoons snipped chives
⅔ to ¾ cup heavy cream

→ In a large bowl, combine the flour, baking powder, and salt. With a pastry blender or fork, cut the butter into the flour mixture until it has the consistency of very small peas. Mix in the chives. Add the cream, and stir with a fork just until the ingredients come together and form a soft dough.

→ Preheat the oven to 425°F. On a lightly floured surface, knead the dough gently 10 to 12 times. Let the dough stand for 10 minutes. Press the dough out to a ½-inch thickness, and cut into rounds with a 2-inch floured cutter. Place the rounds on an ungreased cookie sheet about 1 inch apart. Bake them for 8 to 10 minutes or until golden brown.

Yield: 12 to 15 biscuits

→ Biscuits are one of my favorite quick breads. These biscuits are so light and flaky and buttery that they go well with anything. They're great on their own, too.

→ These biscuits make a great shortcake. At Arrows we make a lobster shortcake that's very popular. We split the biscuit and top it with warm lobster in butter with roasted pearl onions.

anne desjardins

chef/owner

L'Eau à la Bouche
Sainte-Adèle, Quebec

*W*HEN YOUNG ANNE DESJARDINS visited her grandmother's garden in early spring, she was thrilled to find little bunches of chives pushing up through the ground. "Chives are the first herb of the season," she says, "and they're so appealing not only for the taste but for decoration as well."

Today chives have an important role in the kitchen at L'Eau à la Bouche. Not only are they a remembrance from her childhood, but they also add a subtle onion taste to many of her dishes. Desjardins sprinkles chives over pan roasted potatoes, and infuses olive oil with chives for sautés and salad dressings. She likes to use the purplish chive flowers in salads and to garnish plates. The flowers, she says, "taste agreeable, but stronger than the leaves."

She likes the delicate flavor that chives impart to many foods. "They don't have the character of strong-tasting herbs like cilantro. Cilantro can overwhelm a dish, but chives don't get in the way of the taste of the dish. They just add a little bit of something." She often chooses chives because "not everyone loves basil or tarragon, but I've never heard of anyone who didn't like the taste of chives."

The garden at L'Eau à la Bouche provides much of the fresh, seasonal produce, including herbs, that Desjardins finds essential in her kitchen. The rest she purchases from local purveyors. In addition to chives she grows edible flowers such as calendula, viola, nasturtium, and day lilies.

She was not destined to be a chef, Desjardins says. In fact, both she and her husband, Pierre Audette, earned degrees in geography. "I just cooked for my pleasure and the pleasure of friends."

Then, 18 years ago, she returned to the Laurentians, her childhood vacation site, and with her husband decided to open "a simple bistro." That simple bistro has evolved into a top-rated fine dining establishment that now includes a 25-room inn the pair added in 1987. *Gourmet* magazine readers named L'Eau à la Bouche tops in the Montreal area for food, service, and wine selection. In 1996 Desjardins was invited to cook at the James Beard House in New York. She was also the first female recipient of the Prix Roger Champoux, the most prestigious honor for a Quebec chef, and she has cooked in honor of Julia Child and Paul Bocuse. L'Eau à la Bouche has earned the Distinguished Restaurants of North America Award for the past several years.

Desjardins studied at the Fondation Auguste Escoffier in Cannes, L'Institut du tourisme et de l'hôtellerie in Montreal, and L'École hôtelière des Laurentides in Sainte-Adèle. Her work has been featured on the television show *Country Inns of North America* and in *Canadian Food, Country Inns, Traveler, Chatelaine, The Montreal Gazette, The Globe and Mail, The New York Times*, and *Gourmet* magazine.

Oyster Mushrooms and Chèvre with Chives

16 very large oyster mushrooms
6 tablespoons extra virgin olive oil
Salt
Juice and zest of 1 lemon
14 ounces fresh chèvre

1 large bunch chives, finely snipped, plus chive flowers
1 large ripe tomato, diced
12 ounces young lettuce such as Boston, lamb, tatsoy, or mizuna
1 tablespoon balsamic vinegar

✤ In a nonstick pan, sauté the oyster mushrooms in 1 tablespoon of the olive oil. Add a little salt, and place the mushrooms in a colander or strainer over a pan to drain. Chop the lemon zest. Mix the cheese with the lemon juice and zest, and add half of the chives. Add salt to taste.

✤ Place one-quarter of the mushrooms in a 9-inch square baking dish. Spread one-quarter of the cheese mixture on the mushrooms, and top with one-fifth of the tomato. Repeat three more times to make four layers.

✤ Preheat the oven to 400°F. Place the baking dish in the oven until the mushroom mixture is hot, about 10 minutes. Meanwhile, sauté the lettuce in a nonstick pan in 1 tablespoon of the olive oil. Add salt to taste. Place the remaining olive oil, tomato, chives, and the balsamic vinegar and some salt in a small saucepan over medium heat. Bring to a boil.

✤ To serve, arrange the lettuce on 4 warmed plates. Place some of the mushroom mixture on top of the lettuce. Pour the hot dressing over the top, and sprinkle on the chive flowers.

Yield: 4 servings

Variations: If oyster mushrooms are not available, you can substitute portobello mushrooms, but you must take care in cleaning the black underside or your dish will turn out rather dark. You could also substitute green onions for the chives, but the onion taste will be stronger.

Shopping Tips: Buy large oyster mushrooms for easier sautéing. They're sometimes called oyster caps or tree mushrooms.

Timesaver Tips: You could assemble this dish early in the day, refrigerate it until about 15 minutes before serving time, and then bake. The baking time may increase slightly depending on how long the dish was refrigerated.

➤ This dish is very tasty and light. I like to work with mushrooms — they mix very well with chèvre and the chives add a subtle onion flavor.
➤ This dish is delicious as a summer first course or as a nice accompaniment for lamb or pork.

Suprêmes of Free-Range Chicken with Baby Carrots and Chive-Scented Lemon Cream

4 tablespoons olive oil
Juice and zest of 2 lemons
1 large bunch chives, preferably some with their
   flowers, snipped
Hot sauce
Salt

4 boned and skinless suprêmes of grain-fed,
   free-range chicken*
32 baby carrots (young garden carrots), peeled
1 cup chicken stock, homemade (page 219) or canned
½ cup heavy cream

Suprêmes of chicken are chicken breasts usually with wings attached.

✤ Mix together 3 tablespoons of the olive oil, the juice and zest of 1 lemon, half the chives, and a little hot sauce and salt. Marinate the chicken in the chive mixture for about 2 hours.

✤ Drain the chicken, and pat dry with paper towels. Heat the remaining oil in a heavy-bottomed skillet over medium heat. Add the chicken, and sear on each side for 3 minutes. Reduce the heat, and add the carrots, the chicken stock, the cream, and the remaining lemon juice and zest. Season with hot sauce and salt. Simmer for 15 minutes, allowing the liquids to thicken and reduce by about half. Check the seasonings, and add most of the remaining chives, reserving some chives and their flowers for the garnish.

✤ To serve, arrange the chicken and carrots on hot plates, and pour the cream sauce over. Sprinkle with the reserved chives and flowers.

Yield: 4 servings

Variation: You could substitute asparagus for the baby carrots.

✤ This dish is quite easy to execute and very tasty. It makes a delicious early spring dinner.
✤ The carrots and chicken can be served alone for a light dinner, or with wild rice, potatoes, or noodles.

coriander

Coriandrum sativum

a LOT OF PEOPLE CONFUSE CORIANDER with cilantro. Here's the scoop. Coriander refers to the seed while cilantro refers to the leaf of the coriander plant.

Since we're talking about fresh herbs in this book, cilantro is taking center stage here. Use cilantro leaves, also known as Mexican parsley or fresh coriander, to add zip to salsas, curries, pickles, and salads. It's a popular ingredient in Mexican, Southeast Asian, Middle Eastern, and Greek cuisines and is used in nearly every cuisine. This strong, earthy herb can be used in stews, sauces, salads, vegetables, and stir-fry dishes. It flavors chutneys, relishes, and yogurt, as well as fish and chicken, and makes pleasant partners of strong flavorings such as lemon grass, lime, and chiles.

Unlike some herbs of which only the leaves are used, the entire coriander plant — seeds, leaves, and roots — is used. The seeds are often used in pickling.

Cilantro root has a more intense flavor than the leaves and is a common ingredient in Thai curries. North Americans most often use the leaves, which are a source of vitamin A and potassium.

Cilantro is a love it or hate it herb. Some people describe it as a blend of parsley and lemon; some say lemon peel and sage. Others say this member of the carrot family tastes like soap.

Although it has been popular in the United States and Canada for just a few years, cilantro has a long history. Cilantro has been used in China since 200 B.C. It was first grown in southern Europe, but fell out of fashion during Elizabethan times. The Romans brought it to Britain, and the ancient Jews included it at Passover feasts.

vietnamese coriander

Polygonum adoratum

aS IF THE WHOLE CORIANDER/CILANTRO thing isn't baffling enough, you'll now be introduced to Vietnamese coriander. Sometimes called Vietnamese mint, Vietnamese coriander is neither coriander nor mint but is actually a member of the buckwheat family and has a flavor very much like that of cilantro. Vietnamese coriander is becoming a favorite cilantro substitute for many gardeners because, unlike cilantro, it doesn't bolt in hot weather and require several successive seedings.

There isn't much known about Vietnamese coriander says Conrad Richter, owner of Richters Herbs in Ontario, who offers the plant in his catalog. He says Vietnamese coriander is widely used by Vietnamese cooks who use fresh herbs more than many other Asian cooks.

According to chef Mai Pham, whom you'll meet later in the lemon grass section, "the highly aromatic leaves are usually eaten raw, in salads and with noodles, and as a garnish for soups." She describes the flavor as "spicy, sharp, and flavorful."

Known as *rau ram* in Vietnam, Richter says Vietnamese cooks don't regard Vietnamese coriander as cilantro at all, and they use it to garnish meat, poultry, and duck eggs. To the North American palate, he says, it seems more like cilantro and makes a very serviceable substitute. "Purists will tell you it's not even the same thing, and there's some truth to that. The flavor is different, but I would argue that many people would not know the difference."

He says the flavor is "similar to cilantro with a more soapy, but not unpleasant, characteristic." Some people have reported detecting a slight lemon flavor as well.

Vietnamese coriander is another of those herbs you may have to grow yourself. It is easy to grow, says Richter, and makes a nice hanging basket.

You can use Vietnamese coriander in much the same way as cilantro to add flavor to fish, chicken, meats, and salads. It goes well with other Asian flavorings such as lemon grass, chiles, green onions, Thai basil, and kaffir lime leaves.

Besides a distinctive taste, Vietnamese coriander also has a distinctive appearance. The plant has small green lancelike leaves on a stem that bears reddish brown horizontal stripes.

michael thomson

*C*OWPOKES AND CITY SLICKERS ALIKE chow down at Michaels where they know they can expect unexpected flavors — a ranch martini garnished with cilantro and a jalapeño shrimp, or ancho chiles in a chocolate mousse, or lamb chops topped with ranch goat cheese and raspberry chipotle sauce. And, if you're a cigar smoker, well, belly on up to the Ancho Chile Bar (a separate room), hitch onto a cow skull tapestry bar stool, and puff away.

The bar stools, working stone fireplace, Andy Warhol American Indian prints, and rustic wood give Michaels an out-on-the-ranch atmosphere. "I wanted it to feel like a getaway from town," says Thomson, who dreamed of opening his own restaurant since he was 16. At 13 he was already working in a neighbor's restaurant in Florida. He said it took him 16 years to achieve his dream. "During that time, I got all the experience I could." He worked in hotels, in chain restaurants, and in fine dining restaurants and was corporate and consulting chef to the Burlington Northern Railroad.

Two of Thomson's favorite ingredients are dried chile peppers and cilantro. He likes cilantro's "vibrant, spicy, peppery flavor." It has even more vibrancy, he says, when mixed with an acid base such as lime juice or vinegar. He likes its versatility and that it "changes the character of food not the flavor." He says "it mellows out when cooked and gives depth to what you're cooking."

When shopping for cilantro, Thomson recommends buying it with the roots. It will last longer, and you can use the roots for stocks and to flavor butter sauces or pestos. While cilantro is often characterized as an ingredient of southwestern cuisine, Thomson's concept blends "the textures and spices of Mexico with the cuisines of the American Southwest." He calls it "contemporary ranch cuisine. Our cuisine is envisioned as a lifestyle, not simply a region of our great country." In keeping with that character, steaks and game are menu staples.

chef/proprietor

Michaels Restaurant and Ancho Chile Bar Fort Worth, Texas

Cilantro Chile Butter

½ cup chopped cilantro
1½ tablespoons finely chopped habanero chile
(about 3 or 4)
1 tablespoon fresh lime juice
1 tablespoon freshly ground pepper

1 tablespoon lime zest
1 teaspoon ancho chile powder*
1 teaspoon granulated garlic
1 pound cold unsalted butter, chopped (2 cups)

You may find ancho chile powder in Mexican markets. If not, purée about half a rehydrated ancho chile in a food processor.

✤ Place the cilantro, habanero chile, lime juice, pepper, lime zest, chile powder, and garlic in a food processor and purée. Add the butter, and pulse just until the butter is combined with the other ingredients.

✤ Using a pastry bag, pipe small rosettes onto a cookie sheet, or roll the butter into a 1½-inch-diameter log onto parchment paper. Refrigerate or freeze until needed. The logs are easily sliced into discs.

Yield: 1 pound seasoned butter

✤ This is a compound butter, not a butter sauce. Store it in an airtight container in the refrigerator for about two weeks or in the freezer for about two months.
✤ Serve on grilled meats such as steak and on fish, poultry, or cooked vegetables. Try it on corn on the cob, or use it in place of plain butter in your favorite bread recipe.

Chipotle Cactus Relish

3 chipotle chiles in adobo sauce
1 cup thinly sliced white onion
¼ cup corn oil
4 cups nopales (fresh or canned), cut into julienne
2 cups minced cilantro

2 tablespoons adobo sauce
½ cup fresh lime juice
1 tablespoon salt
1 tablespoon freshly ground black pepper

✤ Halve the chiles, carefully remove the seeds, and cut the chiles into very fine strips.

✤ In a skillet over medium heat, sauté the onion in the oil until lightly browned. Add the chipotles and nopales. Sauté for several minutes to blend the flavors. Place the cilantro, adobo sauce, and lime juice in a mixing bowl. Add the cooked onion, chiles, and nopales, and mix well. Add the salt and pepper, and mix well. Refrigerate the relish until needed, up to 1 week.

Yield: about 4 cups

✤ This flavorful southwestern relish is full of heat. It's best served at room temperature.
✤ This relish works well as a condiment for any grilled meat or poultry. I personally like this relish with grilled fish and with eggs. You can serve it as a salad and as a garnish for black bean soup.

Cilantro Orzo

1 gallon water

2 tablespoons corn oil

2 tablespoons salt

1 pound orzo pasta

4 tablespoons minced garlic

2 cups chicken stock (page 219)

2 cups chopped cilantro

1 cup chopped white onion (about 2 medium)

1 tablespoon chicken-flavored seasoning (bouillon cubes or paste)

1 tablespoon fresh lime juice

1 tablespoon freshly ground black pepper

½ pound whole unsalted butter, chopped (1 cup)

❧ Place the water, oil, and salt in a large pot, and bring to a boil. Add the orzo, and cook until it is al dente (about 3 minutes). Drain the orzo, and allow it to dry for several minutes. Purée the garlic, chicken stock, cilantro, onion, chicken-flavored seasoning, lime juice, and pepper in a blender or food processor. Place the purée in a pot, add the butter, and bring to a boil. Add the orzo, and simmer for several minutes to fully flavor the orzo. Keep warm until serving time.

Yield: 8 servings

Note: The liquid should be fully absorbed into the pasta before serving it.

Timesaver Tip: Peeled and minced garlic is now available in jars at supermarkets.

❧ **Orzo is a tiny pasta that resembles rice. The cilantro and lime juice add a southwestern zip that wakes up this sleepy pasta.**

❧ **This is a great side dish for grilled meats, fish, and poultry, or for vegetables.**

janos wilder

chef/co-owner

Janos
Tucson, Arizona

"**W**HY DO I LIKE CILANTRO? Let me count the ways," quips Janos Wilder in his poetic fashion. "Cilantro is really almost an icon of southwestern cooking; it grows prolifically here, and it's extremely versatile."

He says cilantro is used in cuisines around the globe — in Thai cuisine, for instance, and even more often in Chinese cuisine. In fact, it was in Chinese food that Wilder first discovered cilantro. As a five-year-old, he says, he was immediately attracted to it. He was raised in northern California, and one of his favorite dishes there was a Chinese chicken salad flavored with cilantro.

Wilder likes what he describes as its "herbaceous flavor. Nothing tastes like cilantro; nothing can compare. It's got such a distinctive flavor it can really be used as an accent." He prepares a ravioli flavored with lemon grass, cilantro, and Thai basil. He seasons vegetables and chicken with cilantro and likes to pair it with chiles.

Wilder combines his classic French "nouvelle" training with his love and appreciation for American Southwest ingredients. He was trained in the western United States and in the Bordeaux region of France, and moved to Tucson to be close to his wife's family. "I wanted to cook French food. The heart and soul of French cooking is the relationship between garden and chef. If you want to cook French in Tucson and feel compelled to use the ingredients around you, it means using cilantro," explains Wilder.

So cilantro is at the heart of his cooking. It's better fresh than cooked, he says, because it loses flavor in cooking. He recommends adding cilantro to hot foods at the end of the cooking.

He also maintains a large organic garden where he grows cilantro, mint, thyme, sage, pineapple sage, chives, garlic chives, tarragon, fennel, dill, a number of varieties of basil, and vegetables, including 27 varieties of tomatoes and dozens of types of cucumbers. For his menu, which changes daily, Wilder obtains other produce from a network of gardeners throughout southern Arizona. Wilder has been a Top Southwest Chef nominee of the James Beard Foundation several years in a row, was ranked among the top 12 chefs in the United States by the *Mobil Travel Guide,* was inducted into the Scottsdale Culinary Festival's Hall of Fame, and was named a Rising Star of American Cuisine by the James Beard Foundation in 1990.

Located on the grounds of the Westin La Paloma, the restaurant is ranked number one in the *Zagat Survey* as Arizona's favorite restaurant and one of the top five Tucson restaurants by *Tucson Lifestyle* magazine.

Wilder is the author of *Janos: Recipes and Tales from a Southwest Restaurant* (Ten Speed Press, 1990). In this book, he shares recipes as well as a history of his renowned restaurant.

Firecracker of Cilantro Pesto Gravlax

2 (1¼-pound) salmon fillets, skin on
2 tablespoons kosher salt
½ tablespoon sugar
1½ bunches cilantro
1 Anaheim chile, seeded and deveined
½ cup whole grain mustard

¼ cup olive oil
1 lemon, thinly sliced
1 lime, thinly sliced
1 orange, thinly sliced
Alfalfa or pepper sprouts

Sevruga caviar

Toast points

✤ Check the salmon to ensure that all bones have been removed (a pair of sterilized tweezers can be used to pull them out easily). Combine the salt and sugar, and rub the salt mixture into the flesh of the fish. In a food processor, make a pesto by puréeing the cilantro, chile, and mustard into a smooth paste. With the motor running, add the oil in a slow stream. Rub the pesto liberally into the flesh of the salmon. Shingle the citrus slices to completely cover one of the fillets. Sandwich the fillets together, skin side out, and wrap tightly in cheesecloth. Place the salmon in a shallow pan. Place another shallow pan on the salmon, and weigh the pan down with something weighing about 7 pounds (canned foods work well). Refrigerate for 4 to 6 days, turning the salmon daily and draining off any excess liquid.

✤ To serve, slice the gravlax into thin, skinless pieces. Wrap each slice around a small bunch of alfalfa sprouts, leaving the sprouts sticking out at the ends to resemble a firecracker. Top with sevruga caviar, and serve over toast points spread with a little of the pesto.

Yield: 60 firecrackers (as hors d'oeuvres)

✤ This variation of gravlax, the Scandinavian preparation of dry-cured salmon, brings out the southwestern flavors of cilantro and chiles for a fun and elegant appetizer. The gravlax is rolled around sprouts to form a "firecracker" and elegantly garnished with caviar.

✤ Spicy nuts would go well with this appetizer. Vodka, tequila, or a fruity wine, such as a spicy Gewürztraminer, would be a fantastic accompaniment.

Grilled Chicken with Cilantro Habanero Pepito Pesto on Pinto Bean Coulis with Exotic Mushroom and Smoked Poblano Flan

> ✣ Here's a rich, flavorful recipe using the world's hottest chile in a way that brings out its toasty flavor while modulating its heat. The coulis and flan are uniquely southwestern accompaniments.

Cilantro Habanero Pepito Pesto:
¼ cup shelled pumpkin seeds*
½ habanero chile
6 to 8 cloves garlic
½ bunch cilantro

2 ounces sun-dried tomatoes (about 16, not in oil)
¼ pound freshly grated Parmesan cheese (about 1 cup)
¾ cup olive oil
Salt and pepper

*Pumpkin seeds are available in health food stores and gourmet shops.

Pinto Bean Coulis:
4 cups dried pinto beans, washed and picked over
2 Anaheim chiles, peeled, seeded, and diced
1 bay leaf

1 medium yellow onion, diced
Salt and pepper
1 to 2 cups chicken stock (page 219)

Exotic Mushroom and Smoked Poblano Flan:
1 tablespoon fresh crushed garlic
½ cup olive oil
Salt and pepper
12 ounces portobello, shiitake, chanterelle, or
    other mushrooms

2 eggs
2 Anaheim chiles, peeled, seeded, and deveined
2 poblano chiles, peeled, seeded, deveined, and smoked*
1 cup heavy cream

*If you don't have a smoker, use regular poblano chiles; you just won't have the smoky flavor in your flan.

Grilled Chicken:
6 boneless chicken breasts with skin

✣ To prepare the pesto, toast the pumpkin seeds in a hot skillet to bring out their oils and flavor. In a very hot skillet, blacken the chile. Wearing gloves, remove the stem and seeds, and chop the chile coarsely. In a food processor, grind the pumpkin seeds with the garlic until the mixture is fairly fine but not powdery. Add the cilantro, and process until completely combined. Add the chile, sun-dried tomatoes, and cheese, and process. With the motor running, add the oil in a slow stream. Season with salt and pepper to taste. Set aside.

✣ To prepare the coulis, place the beans, chile, bay leaf, and onion in a saucepan with enough water to cover the beans by 2 inches. Bring to a boil. Simmer about 3 hours until the beans are almost cooked through. Add salt and pepper to taste. The beans will absorb quite a bit of salt at this point, so be generous. Continue cooking about another 30 minutes until the beans are quite soft and cooked through but still maintain their shape. Let the beans cool a bit, remove the bay leaf, and purée the bean mixture with enough chicken stock to reach the desired consistency. Strain the coulis, and set it aside.

✤ To prepare the flan, preheat a gas grill or wood barbecue. Mix the garlic, oil, salt, and pepper in a bowl. Toss the mushrooms in the oil mixture. Grill the mushrooms about 3 minutes, turning them constantly. Let the mushrooms cool a bit, and purée them in a food processor with the eggs and chiles. With the food processor running, slowly add the cream. Preheat the oven to 375°F. Grease 6 (4-ounce) ramekins or timbale molds. Divide the mixture equally among the 6 ramekins. Place them in a pan with enough boiling water to reach halfway up the ramekins, and bake them for about 12 to 14 minutes. Meanwhile, prepare the chicken. Unmold the flans, and serve them warm.

✤ To prepare the chicken, stuff about 2 tablespoons of the pesto under the skin of the chicken breasts. Grill the chicken until done.

✤ To serve, place about ½ cup of coulis on each plate. Place a chicken breast over the coulis, and a flan alongside.

Yield: 6 servings

Note: The pesto can be made ahead and stored in the refrigerator or freezer. Any remaining pesto can be used to season sauces, soups, and steamed or grilled vegetables.

✤ **Corn on the cob or fresh steamed or sautéed green beans would be great with this dish.**

clark frasier

chef/co-owner

Arrows
Ogunquit, Maine

Frasier says he and his partner, Mark Gaier, rely heavily on herbs from their garden for many of their dishes. A great favorite for him is Vietnamese coriander. They planted it for the first time about two years ago and have been using it in Thai and Vietnamese dishes.

"I first encountered Vietnamese coriander during one of our travels through Southeast Asia," says Frasier. "Since it was an herb I had never tasted before, I was intrigued by its similarities to cilantro and basil and challenged by its idiosyncrasies to cook with it at Arrows."

After returning to Maine, he says, they researched seeds and planted Vietnamese coriander in their herb and vegetable garden. The plant thrives in Maine's northern climate and grows back rapidly after being cut. "Balancing the rich but perfumed soapy character of this herb is a cooking challenge but one that yields some wonderful results. I have found that vinegars and juices, as well as some chiles, prudently used, will enhance foods and allow the coriander to shine. Vietnamese coriander is very versatile and has a lot of the character of cilantro and basil. The soapy flavor of cilantro is present and more pronounced. It has a rich flavor which mixes well in fresh curries along with parsley, serrano peppers, and coconut milk." Frasier uses Vietnamese coriander a lot for sauces and marinades. "You have to use it carefully," he says. "You have to realize that soapy flavor is there and work with it, not against it. In Asian cooking, balancing opposites — cool and spicy for instance — is essential." He offers these suggestions when working with Vietnamese coriander or any herb. "It is helpful to try to imagine the flavors of each ingredient in your mind. Ask yourself, What are the characteristics I want to taste? Always try to think about balance — what would go well with the other things in the dish? What works together texturally?"

Frasier developed an early interest in cooking. He traveled extensively, bringing back new ideas from Europe and Asia. He lived and studied in Beijing, China, for a year and a half, where he acquired expertise in the cuisine of China. Frasier also worked for two years as *chef tournant* at Stars Restaurant in San Francisco. Frasier was named a Great Regional Chef of the Northeast by the James Beard Foundation.

He and Gaier cure their own hams and fish and make all the desserts and breads for Arrows in house. The restaurant's name comes from the building's casement shutters, which were designed to protect against Indian attacks on the colonial building. Articles about Arrows and its chefs and gardens have appeared in *Bon Appétit, Food & Wine, Country Journal, Country Living Gardener, Boston* magazine, *Yankee* magazine, *Food Arts, USA Today,* and *The New York Times.*

Roasted Chicken with Vietnamese Coriander and Garlic

1 roasting chicken (about 4 pounds)
2 cloves garlic, minced
1 tablespoon corn oil
1 teaspoon kosher salt

1 teaspoon ground black pepper
4 sprigs Vietnamese coriander
2 tablespoons peeled, sliced ginger (about a 2-inch piece sliced ⅛-inch thick)

✦ Preheat the oven to 375°F. Wash the chicken and pat it dry. Mix together the garlic, oil, salt, and pepper. Rub the garlic mixture on the outside of the chicken. Place the Vietnamese coriander and ginger inside the cavity. Roast the chicken for 90 minutes. Let it stand 5 minutes before carving it.

Yield: 4 servings

✦ This recipe produces chicken infused with the flavor of Vietnamese coriander.
✦ Served with rice and bok choy, this chicken is a fast and wonderful dinner.

Vietnamese Coriander Marinade

3 tablespoons lime juice
1 bunch cilantro
1 cup coconut milk
1 serrano chile

1 teaspoon salt
½ bunch parsley
¼ cup rice wine vinegar
Leaves of 8 sprigs Vietnamese coriander

✦ Put the lime juice, cilantro, coconut milk, chile, salt, parsley, vinegar, and Vietnamese coriander in a blender, and blend until smooth.

Yield: about 2 cups

✦ This marinade is easy to make and very versatile. It can be used as a sauce as well as a marinade and works well with white fish, tuna, pork, and poultry.

Vietnamese Coriander Clear Dipping Sauce

1 clove garlic, minced
1 small serrano chile, finely chopped
2 tablespoons sugar
Leaves of 4 sprigs Vietnamese coriander, finely chopped

2 tablespoons lime juice
¼ cup rice wine vinegar
¼ cup Vietnamese fish sauce*

Vietnamese fish sauce is available in Asian stores.

✦ In a bowl, combine the garlic, chile, sugar, and Vietnamese coriander. Whisk in the lime juice, vinegar, and fish sauce.

Yield: about ½ cup

✦ Lime juice and rice wine vinegar provide a perfect balance to the coriander's opulent character. This sauce is also good as a marinade for chicken, quail, or white fish such as halibut or striped bass.

Vietnamese Coriander and Vegetable Salad

This light and tasty salad is perfect for hot summer nights and goes well with both meat and fish.

This salad is best served shortly after it has been made but can be kept in the refrigerator overnight in a sealed nonreactive container. On a sultry night, a well-chilled ale is a perfect accompaniment to this salad, or, if the occasion is more elegant, a light white wine from the Alsace region or a good Californian Sauvignon Blanc is a great match.

1 large carrot
1 large unblemished yellow summer squash
1 large unblemished zucchini
Ice bath
1 tablespoon chopped ginger
1 tablespoon chopped Vietnamese coriander plus
  Vietnamese coriander sprigs
1 tablespoon dark soy sauce
1 teaspoon kosher salt
1 teaspoon fresh cracked black pepper
1 teaspoon fish sauce*
1 teaspoon sesame oil
¼ cup sugar
¼ cup rice wine vinegar

Vietnamese fish sauce is available in Asian stores.

With a sharp knife or mandoline, cut the carrot, squash, and zucchini into ¼-inch wide matchstick strips. Use only the outside ½-inch of the squash and zucchini, avoiding the seeds. Next cut the carrots, squash, and zucchini into ¼-inch squares. In boiling water, blanch the vegetables until they are tender, and immediately chill them in an ice bath. Drain the vegetables.

In a stainless steel or glass bowl, mix the ginger, chopped Vietnamese coriander, soy sauce, salt, pepper, fish sauce, oil, sugar, and vinegar. Add the vegetables, and toss them with the coriander mixture. Garnish the salad with sprigs of Vietnamese coriander, if desired.

Yield: 4 to 6 servings

Note: It will take about 90 seconds to blanch the carrots and about 30 seconds to blanch the zucchini and squash.

dill

Anethum graveolens

ALTHOUGH MOST PEOPLE CONSIDER DILL a pickling spice, this tall feathery plant is not just for pickles. The leaves of this member of the parsley family enhance the flavor of many foods. The French use it in cakes and pastries, the Scandinavians in breads, potatoes, and seafood, and Polish chefs add dill to their soups and stews. Dill is sensitive to heat but is ideal for cold dishes such as dips, cottage cheese and other cheeses, and salads such as those using potato, cucumber, and egg.

Sprinkle dill over hot dishes at the end of the cooking time. Cooked potatoes, soups, sauces, fish, seafood, lamb, and omelets get a boost of flavor from dill. Try dill also with chicken, carrots, veal, and buttered vegetables. Whip up some dill butter to dollop onto grilled or poached fish.

Use dill seed to flavor cabbage, coleslaw, sauerkraut, onions, and breads, as well as sour cream and cream cheese. Dill seed was once known as the "meetin' seed" because mothers often carried some to church for the children to nibble on during long sermons.

Snipping dill's plumage with scissors preserves more of its flavor than cutting it with a knife. Snipped leaves or whole stems can be frozen, or stems and leaves can be infused in vinegar to use for marinades or salad dressings.

Dill is one of the herbs that's usually available in supermarkets nearly year round. It's a good thing, too, because while it's compatible with so many foods and its plumage makes a great garnish, it can be tough to grow indoors because of its long taproot.

The word "dill" is from the Norse word *dilla,* meaning "to lull." Dill was once considered a sleep aid and a charm against witches. To Romans, dill symbolized joy and pleasure.

jonathan m. cartwright

executive chef
⋙⋘

White Barn Inn
Kennebunkport, Maine

JONATHAN CARTWRIGHT MOST OFTEN USES DILL with Maine salmon. "It's a great herb to accompany salmon and other seafood from this area," says the New England chef who relies on the region's bounty of fresh ingredients for his menu.

There are so many wonderful herbs, he says, it's difficult to say that one is better than another. "But dill is a very nice flavored herb. It's also a beautiful herb on the plate. It's a great little branch to work with."

Cartwright likes dill's "great, distinct, clean flavor." He uses it mainly on fish, and he even includes it in a champagne sauce (see opposite) and with lobster. The most popular dill dish on the White Barn Inn menu is Maine salmon fillet cured in dill and citrus marinade (page 70).

Cartwright, a north London native, started cooking at a young age, helping his mother with special dinners. Even so, he says, "I wasn't hell-bent on becoming a cook." In fact, his first love was sports, particularly bicycling, which was very popular in Europe at the time. When he was offered a job cooking, he took it on the condition he could have Sundays off to pursue his biking.

Within a year, however, he traded his wheels for a toque and now bikes along Maine's rocky coastline purely for pleasure. Yet, he says, there is a parallel between biking and cooking.

"It's very sporting to be a chef. It's hard work, a lot of time on your legs, and there are a lot of challenging things going on in the kitchen."

His culinary talents have carried him through stints in the kitchens of the Horned Dorset Primavera in Puerto Rico and the Hotel Bareiss in Germany. He apprenticed at the Savoy Hotel in London, studying with Anton Edelmann, whom he accompanied to the Pierre Hotel.

After a two-year sous-chef position at the White Barn Inn, a member of the exclusive Relais & Châteaux hotel and restaurant group, Cartwright was named executive chef and now oversees the entire food and beverage operation of this five-diamond restaurant.

His signature dish is steamed lobster served on homemade fettuccine with julienne of carrot and a cognac sauce. The menu changes weekly, highlighting fresh Maine seafood and locally grown products, including herbs and vegetables from a small garden near the inn. There, despite Maine's short growing season, he grows dill, chives, flat-leaf parsley, and oregano.

The White Barn Inn is the recipient of the Distinguished Restaurants of North America Award, the only Maine restaurant to receive this honor. The restaurant was also inducted into the Fine Dining Hall of Fame of the *Nation's Restaurant News*.

Grilled Medallion of Maine Salmon with Seafood Medley, Vegetable Ribbons, and Dill Champagne Sauce

Seafood:

12 mussels

8 small hard-shell clams (preferably Mahogany clams)

1 cup white wine

4 large scallops (preferably diver harvested)

4 (5-ounce) salmon medallions

Salt and pepper

Dill Champagne Sauce:

1 bunch dill (½ bunch left whole, ½ bunch snipped)

1 clove garlic, diced

1 shallot, diced

1 teaspoon butter

1 cup reserved clam and mussel liquid

1 cup heavy cream

1 cup champagne

Salt and pepper

Vegetable Ribbons:

1 beet

1 carrot

1 celeriac

1 potato

1 tablespoon butter

Salt and pepper

✤ **This is one of my favorite dishes because it uses such a nice variety of seafood with lots of color, different textures, and flavors.**
✤ **I love to finish this dish off with some fresh dill oil, which gives it a Mediterranean accent.**

✤ To prepare the seafood, cook the mussels and clams in a heavy-bottomed saucepan with the white wine until the shells open, about 8 to 10 minutes. Strain the liquid, and reserve it for the sauce. Set aside the mussels and clams. Season the scallops and salmon medallions with some salt and pepper, and grill them to the desired doneness. (Salmon is best if not cooked to well done. A pink center is ideal.)

✤ To prepare the sauce, fry the whole dill, the garlic, and the shallots in the butter over low heat for about 3 minutes. Do not allow the butter or the garlic and shallots to brown. Add the reserved clam and mussel liquid, increase the heat to high, and reduce the liquid by half. Add the cream and half of the champagne. Reduce the sauce until it is thick enough to coat a spoon. Season the sauce with salt and pepper, and strain.

✤ To prepare the vegetable ribbons, cut the beet, carrot, celeriac, and potato into ribbons with a mandoline or potato peeler. Sauté the vegetable ribbons together in the butter until tender. Season with salt and pepper.

✤ To serve, reheat the sauce with the clams and mussels in it. Add the remaining champagne and the snipped dill. Place the vegetable ribbons in the center of the serving plate. Place the grilled salmon on the vegetable ribbons and the scallops beside them. Arrange the mussels and clams around the salmon, and spoon some of the sauce liberally between the seafoods.

Yield: 4 servings

(continued on next page)

Note: Mahogany clams are preferred for their delicate taste and beautiful shell color, but any small hard-shell clam can be substituted. Diver-harvested scallops are preferred because they are the largest and sweetest scallop and because they are harvested in an environmentally friendly way — by a diver handpicking each scallop from the ocean bed — rather than by dredging.

Dill-Scented Maine Lobster Cappuccino with Oyster and Dill Ravioli

Lobster Cappuccino:
3 pounds lobster shells
6 fresh tomatoes, halved
1 clove garlic
1 green stalk celery
1 onion
Fennel leaves from 1 fennel bulb

Several stalks dill and 4 tablespoons snipped dill
1 cup sweet white wine such as a muscatel
½ cup Pernod
1 tablespoon tomato paste
1 quart heavy cream
Salt and pepper

Ravioli Dough:
5 egg yolks
2 tablespoons olive oil

1 cup plus 1 tablespoon all-purpose flour
Salt

Ravioli Filling:
1 fennel bulb, finely diced
1 tablespoon butter
Salt and pepper

4 tablespoons snipped dill
8 oysters (preferably Pemaquid Bay oysters)

↠ To prepare the lobster cappuccino, preheat the oven to 350°F. In a roasting pan, mix the shells, tomato, garlic, celery, onion, fennel leaves, and dill stalks together, and roast for about 15 minutes. Remove from the oven, add the wine and Pernod, and flambé.

↠ Transfer the shell mixture to a large stockpot, cover with water, and add the tomato paste. Simmer for 3 hours. Strain, reserving the liquid. In a heavy-bottomed pan over high heat, reduce the reserved liquid by half. Add the cream, bring back to a boil, and season with salt and pepper to taste.

↠ To prepare the ravioli dough, process the egg yolks, oil, flour, and a pinch of salt in a food processor for about 30 seconds. Remove the dough, and knead it until it is smooth. Cover it with plastic wrap, and let the dough stand for about 30 minutes in a cool place. Roll the dough as thin as possible (if you have a pasta machine, use it on setting number one). Cut the dough into rounds with a 3-inch pastry cutter.

↠ Lobster cappuccino, a very popular soup at the White Barn Inn, is rich in flavor yet light and foamy. Without the ravioli it is also used as an intermediate course at our restaurant.

➤ To prepare the filling, cook the fennel in the butter until tender but not brown. Season with salt and pepper. Add the dill, and combine. Cool the fennel mixture before doing the next step.

➤ Place 1 oyster in the middle of each round of dough with about 1 tablespoon of the filling. Brush the edges of the dough lightly with water. Fold the dough over, and seal the edges by pressing them together. Pull the two points together, brush them with water, and squeeze them together. The ravioli will resemble a small pouch. Repeat.

➤ Cook the ravioli in boiling salted water for 3 minutes.

➤ In the meantime, reheat the lobster soup and add the 4 tablespoons snipped dill. Adjust the salt and pepper if necessary.

➤ To serve, use a submersible hand blender to foam the soup until it resembles a cappuccino, about 30 seconds. (Foaming with the hand blender is not absolutely necessary; foaming adds interest, not flavor.) Place 2 ravioli in each soup bowl, and pour in the soup.

Yield: 4 servings

Note: To obtain the 3 pounds of lobster shells, you will need about 4 (1½-pound) lobsters. You can freeze the shells from lobster dinners until you have accumulated enough to make the stock.

Variations: The lobster cappuccino may be served alone or with a purchased ravioli or cooked, diced lobster meat.

Timesaver Tips: Gourmet and mail-order stores carry lobster base, which can be used to make the stock quickly. When making stock from scratch, you can freeze the stock after straining it and finish the dish another day.

Maine Salmon Fillet Cured in Dill and Citrus Marinade with Orange-Scented Yogurt and Dill Sauce

Salmon:
2 pounds salmon fillets (preferably Maine salmon), boneless but with skin left on
1 tablespoon olive oil
2 juniper berries
¼ cup sea salt
¼ cup sugar

½ teaspoon crushed black pepper
2 lemons
2 oranges
2 tablespoons gin
1 bunch dill, snipped

Orange-Scented Yogurt and Dill Sauce:
½ bunch dill, snipped
¼ cup plain yogurt

Sliced cucumber

Juice and zest of 1 orange
Salt and pepper

Toast

➤ To prepare the salmon, rub the salmon with the oil, and place skin side down in a glass dish. Combine the juniper berries, salt, sugar, and pepper, and cover the oiled salmon with the mixture. Peel the lemons and oranges, and cover the seasoned salmon with the peelings. Squeeze the juice of 1 orange and both lemons into a glass, and add the gin. Stir the gin mixture, and pour it over the salmon. Marinate, refrigerated, for 12 to 24 hours. Remove the salmon from the marinade, and cover with the dill.

➤ To prepare the sauce, whisk together the dill, yogurt, orange juice and zest, and a little salt and pepper.

➤ To serve, slice the salmon, and place it on the sliced cucumber on a plate. Add some sauce, and serve the dish with toast.

Yield: 8 servings

➤ **Cured Maine salmon** is a favorite of mine because it is such a simple dish that is so versatile. It can be used as an appetizer, for canapés, or even as a special sandwich filling.

epazote

Chenopodium ambrosioides

LIKE CILANTRO, EPAZOTE IS USED in Mexican and South American cooking. Also like cilantro, people either love epazote or hate it.

Epazote's family name means "food of the Gods." The plant is also known as Mexican tea, Jerusalem oak, pigweed, and goosefoot, a term referring to its medium green leaves that resemble a goose's foot. Epazote is a highly aromatic plant with a strong mint and anise flavor that may be an acquired taste for some. But don't be put off by its aroma; epazote tastes milder than it smells, though the taste is a bit sharp with slight citrus overtones. Judy Miles, owner of the Miles Estate Herb & Berry Farm in Woodburn, Oregon, uses small quantities in her green salads. She says epazote gives mustard greens extra zip. She also makes a chicken soup that includes coriander and epazote.

If it is not available in your supermarket, epazote is certainly available from any good seed supplier and many herb nurseries. In some parts of the United States and in Mexico, it grows wild as a weed. According to Cheryl Alters and Bill Jamison in *The Border Cookbook,* epazote is often available in Mexican markets and health food stores, where it may also be called pazote.

Epazote is said to reduce flatulence and is frequently added to bean dishes. It's used with fish, in salsa, chili, and moles (thick chile sauces), and with corn, squash, and pork. Epazote also livens up soups and stews. Choose the tender young leaves; older leaves develop a bitter taste.

erasmo "razz" kamnitzer

chef/owner

Razz's Restaurant and Bar
Scottsdale, Arizona

*e*PAZOTE IS AN HERB THAT APPEALS to Razz Kamnitzer. "It has a distinct personality. It's pungent yet sweet; very strong but delicate and perfumy. Epazote reminds me of cardamom, but there's no way you can confuse it with any other herb. It tastes like a combination of sage, parsley, and mint."

A native of Venezuela and a seventh-generation chef of German descent, Kamnitzer became acquainted with epazote while growing up in South America. "When I was young, I remember my grandmother preparing beans and tamales that were always flavored with epazote."

Kamnitzer likes to use epazote in both cooked and raw relishes, and especially likes it with watermelon. Kamnitzer also substitutes it for basil in pestos. "When you make pesto with epazote, it's almost medicinal. When your chest is closed up [from a cold], epazote is like mentholated vapors."

His first job in hospitality was as the assistant manager of his father's Caracas restaurant, the Vegetarian Buffet. He studied at the National Hotel School of Lausanne in Switzerland and at the Culinary Institute of America in Hyde Park, New York. After graduating, he held executive chef positions in Florida and Wyoming before moving to Arizona.

Kamnitzer opened the French restaurant Auberge du Canal and later became chef de cuisine at Etienne's Different Pointe of View at the Pointe Hilton at Tapatio Cliffs. There he rebelled against the Hilton's purchasing practices and planted a 5,000-square-foot terrace garden that flourished in the desert landscape. The herbs, edible flowers, and exotic fruits and vegetables of that garden became integral ingredients of his cuisine.

In 1995, he and his wife Bobbi Jo Haynes opened their own restaurant, Razz's, in Scottsdale. At Razz's they serve contemporary international cuisine based on French techniques but also draw on the cuisines of Venezuela, Europe, Asia, and the Southwest. Among Kamnitzer's eclectic menu offerings are twice-roasted duck breast with lingonberry-orange sauce, and pabellon criollo (Venezuelan style black beans, spicy shredded beef, rice, and plantains).

This exuberant chef, with his ponytail and charismatic personality, often emerges from the kitchen to visit with his customers in dining rooms decorated with contemporary art.

He has appeared on the Food Network's *Ready... Set... Cook!*, *Chef du Jour*, *Dining Around*, and *Talking Food with Robin Leach* television programs. He also appears on *Cooking Under 10*, a biweekly television program featuring menus for two for under 10 dollars.

The Chefs Association of Greater Phoenix named Kamnitzer Culinarian of the Year in 1996, and he was inducted into the Arizona Culinary Hall of Fame in 1997. *The New York Times* and *Esquire* magazine both rated Razz's the Best New Restaurant of 1996.

Epazote Vegetable Pancakes with Black Bean Tropical Fruit Sauce

Epazote Vegetable Pancakes:

2 teaspoons baking powder
2 teaspoons sugar
2 tablespoons chopped epazote
1 cup all-purpose flour
1 cup Thai flour*
1 tablespoon sliced green onion
1 tablespoon snipped chives
1 teaspoon salt

Thai flour is also known as rice flour.

1 teaspoon pepper
3 eggs, beaten
2 cups milk
2 cups shredded mixed vegetables (carrots, zucchini, onions, celery, purple potatoes, parsnips, etc.)
¼ cup butter, melted
Oil

Black Bean Tropical Fruit Sauce:

2 cups julienned mixed vegetables (carrots, celery, and a variety of peppers)
1 small onion, sliced
1 cup cooked black beans
1 cup diced mixed fruit (mango, pineapple, and papaya)

3 tablespoons butter
3 tablespoons diced tomatoes
1 teaspoon chili paste
1 teaspoon chopped garlic
Salt and pepper

4 tablespoons chopped epazote

> ⟶ Epazote adds personality to the pancakes and is set off by the sweetness of the fruit sauce.
> ⟶ This dish makes a great summer supper on its own.

⟶ To prepare the pancakes, combine the baking powder, sugar, epazote, flours, green onion, chives, salt, and pepper in a mixing bowl. Make a well in the center of the flour mixture, add the eggs, milk, and mixed vegetables, and combine. Add the melted butter, and stir just until it is incorporated. Do not overmix.

⟶ Heat a small amount of oil in a skillet. Pour in the batter using a large spoon, and cook the pancakes for about 2 to 3 minutes or until they are golden brown on both sides. (Pancakes are ready to turn when dry bubbles form on top.) Remove the pancakes from the skillet, and keep them warm.

⟶ To prepare the sauce, place the mixed vegetables and onion in the same skillet over medium heat. Toss lightly for 1 minute. Add the black beans and mixed fruit, and cook for 30 seconds. Add the butter and tomato, chili paste, and garlic. Stir and continue cooking until the butter is incorporated. Season with salt and pepper.

⟶ To serve, pour the sauce over the pancakes, and top with the epazote.

Yield: 4 servings

Epazote and Mixed Flower and Cheese Ravioli with Tomato Epazote Broth

Epazote and Mixed Flower and Cheese Ravioli:

1 cup mixed edible flower petals
⅓ cup mascarpone cheese
⅓ cup ricotta cheese
4 tablespoons chopped epazote
1 tablespoon snipped chives
⅓ cup crumbled soft whole-wheat bread
   (crust removed)

½ teaspoon red chili paste
½ teaspoon salt
24 won ton wrappers
12 whole pansies
1 egg, beaten
2 cups water or vegetable stock (homemade, page 218;
   or canned)

Tomato Epazote Broth:

1 tablespoon chopped shallots
1 teaspoon olive oil
2 tablespoons chopped epazote
2 medium tomatoes, seeded and finely diced
   (about 1 cup)

1 teaspoon chopped garlic
2 cups vegetable stock, homemade (page 218)
   or canned
Salt and pepper

> ❧ The won ton wrappers form a translucent cover for the cheese and flower filling creating an exotic garnish for the broth. The epazote adds a delicate perfume.
> ❧ We serve this dish as an appetizer at Razz's.

❧ To prepare the ravioli, mix together the flower petals, cheeses, epazote, chives, bread, chili paste, and salt. Lay 12 won ton wrappers flat on a work surface. Place 1½ teaspoons of the cheese mixture in the middle of each won ton wrapper. Top with 1 whole pansy. Using a pastry brush, moisten the edges of the filled won ton wrappers with beaten egg, and cover with another won ton wrapper, sealing the edges with the fingers or the tines of a fork.

❧ To prepare the broth, in a saucepan sauté the shallots in the oil until they are transparent. Add the epazote, tomatoes, and garlic. Cook for about 2 minutes. Add the stock, and season with salt and pepper.

❧ To cook the ravioli, boil them in the water or vegetable stock for about 90 seconds.

❧ To serve, place 3 ravioli in each bowl, and fill each bowl with broth.

Yield: 4 servings

Shopping Tips: Won ton wrappers are available in different thicknesses at Asian shops and in some supermarkets. Choose the thinnest wrappers because they give the best appearance to this dish.

Lavandula

*i*F YOU'RE SURPRISED TO FIND LAVENDER in a culinary herb book, you aren't alone. I've observed a few raised eyebrows when serving my lavender herb bread and lavender pizzelles, or Ed Doherty's lavender ice cream (page 78). Really, lavender is more than just a pretty flower. It's not only lovely to look at, but also a treat to eat. Europeans, especially the French, have used lavender since about the 12th century. It was grown at Monticello by Thomas Jefferson, but used more for its beauty and aromatic properties than for cooking. A member of the mint family, lavender has a sweet aroma and a pleasantly pungent and slightly smoky flavor that teases your taste buds. Use lavender in jellies, baked goods, and beverages, as well as with lamb, fish, meats, and smoked foods. Add some sparingly to salads. Infuse it in vinegar and in honey, or brew up a pot of lavender tea.

Lavender is an herb you'll be unlikely to find fresh in your supermarket, but you will find it dried in many herb and gourmet shops. Just be sure you're buying culinary quality lavender, meaning that it's herbicide/pesticide free. Lavender is getting more attention as a culinary herb since being named the 1999 Herb of the Year by the International Herb Society.

An herb of the Mediterranean, lavender was served with most meals in ancient Greece and Rome and in Tudor and Elizabethan times in England. In fact, the Tudors felt compelled to plant lavender in their gardens in case Elizabeth I came to lunch. It seems she refused to eat lamb without lavender jelly.

ed doherty

executive chef

❧

Olive
Cherry Hill, New Jersey

*L*AVENDER IS THE HERB OF CHOICE for Ed Doherty, executive chef at Olive in Cherry Hill, New Jersey. "The lavender blossom is very versatile, adapting to many ingredients both savory and sweet," he says. It's "one of very few herbs that can take you through an entire menu from salad to dessert."

He first became acquainted with lavender about 10 years ago when his wife, Eileen, began growing it around their house. While she made sachets and potpourri, he took it to the stove. He once tossed a pinch of lavender into a lamb stew he was making at home for guests. They were amazed to learn the secret ingredient was lavender.

Doherty's romance with lavender really blossomed during his studies in France where he saw fields of the fragrant wild flowering shrub in Provence. "It reminds me of rosemary; it has the same menthol quality. It's a most amazingly intoxicating herb."

North Americans, he says, are not really used to lavender, but it is an important herb to the cuisine of Provence, Doherty's specialty. Lavender is one of the components of the classic blend, herbes de Provence. In the restaurant kitchen, he maintains a huge container of the blend, which he mixes himself, and uses it in ratatouille and to coat fish for grilling. He'll also toss lavender stems right on the grill when barbecuing, and the "sweet aroma just fills the air." Herbes de Provence also flavors his oven-dried tomatoes, lamb dishes, gratins, and a vegetable ragout. He says lavender complements fruits such as pears and finds its way into a number of desserts.

Doherty learned the basics of cooking from his mom, a home economics teacher. In fact, he quips, he was the only teenager on the block with his own set of knives and omelet pans. He later traveled to France and studied at La Varenne, where he learned from some of the finest chefs in Paris. He was executive chef at La Terrace, helped open the White Dog Cafe, and later moved on to the London Grille Restaurant, all in Philadelphia. While at the London Grille, he was inducted into Chefs in America, an honorary society for outstanding culinary achievement.

Before opening Olive for the Short Hills Restaurant Group in the fall of 1998, Doherty was executive chef at the acclaimed La Campagne, also in Cherry Hill, where he was delighted to discover a lavender field on the restaurant property.

Using fresh, local ingredients, he directs a "from scratch" kitchen that offers an eclectic menu of brasserie cuisine blending Mediterranean and American flavors.

The restaurant features a wood-burning brick pizza oven, an exhibition kitchen, an appetizer/seafood bar, a private dining room, and a lounge as well as an outdoor patio. The addition of an herb garden, including Doherty's beloved lavender, is a distinct possibility.

Lavender and Mustard Seed Crusted Salmon with Red Onion Marmalade and Balsamic Syrup

3 tablespoons olive oil
2 medium red onions, diced (about 1 cup)
1 large red pepper, diced (about 1 cup)
1 tablespoon fresh lemon juice
1 tablespoon honey
1 tablespoon maple syrup

¼ cup dry white wine
Coarse salt and freshly ground pepper
1 cup balsamic vinegar
3 tablespoons mustard seed
2 teaspoons dried lavender blossoms
4 (6-ounce) salmon fillets, boned and skinned

✦ In a sauté pan or skillet, heat 1 tablespoon of the oil over medium heat, add the onion and pepper, and cook, stirring often, for 15 minutes. Add the lemon juice, honey, maple syrup, and wine, and simmer for 5 minutes. Season to taste with salt and pepper. Keep warm. Meanwhile, preheat the oven to 450°F.

✦ In a saucepan, reduce the balsamic vinegar to 2 tablespoons of liquid. Reserve.

✦ Combine the mustard seed and lavender. Season the salmon with salt and pepper, and coat with the lavender mixture. Heat the remaining 2 tablespoons of oil in a nonstick sauté pan. Sear the salmon skin side up for 1 minute, turn, and sear for 2 minutes. Finish the salmon in the oven to the desired doneness.

✦ To serve, arrange the salmon on 4 warm plates. Top each fillet with marmalade and drizzle with balsamic syrup.

Yield: 4 servings

Note: Keep a close eye on the balsamic vinegar when you are reducing it. If it is overboiled, it will have a burnt taste.

✦ Here lavender lends its unique bouquet to a savory main dish.
✦ The salmon goes nicely with fennel roasted garlic risotto.

lavender/doherty

Lavender-Scented Tomato and Chèvre Gratin

6 Roma tomatoes (about 1 pound), seeded
  and quartered
2 sprigs thyme, stemmed
2 teaspoons dried lavender blossoms
1 sprig rosemary, stemmed and chopped
2 cloves garlic, minced

1 tablespoon extra virgin olive oil
Coarse salt and freshly ground black pepper
8 ounces chèvre
18 cured black olives (approximately), pitted
  and chopped

➤ The lavender blossom is very versatile and can be combined with both sweet and savory ingredients. In this savory example, lavender adds a floral touch to the earthy tomatoes.

➤ Serve this dish with toasted brioche.

➤ Preheat the oven to 200°F. Arrange the tomatoes in a single layer on a baking pan. In a bowl, combine half the thyme, lavender, and rosemary with the garlic, oil, and some salt and pepper. Sprinkle the herb mixture on the tomatoes. Bake the tomatoes for 1½ to 2 hours, or until they are meltingly soft.

➤ Preheat the broiler. Crumble 2 ounces of the cheese into each of 4 serving-sized, oven-proof baking dishes. Sprinkle the remaining herbs on the cheese, and top with the tomatoes and olives. Place the dishes under the broiler until the cheese has melted.

Yield: 4 servings

Lavender Ice Cream

6 large egg yolks
2 teaspoons vanilla
¾ cup honey

2 cups whole milk
1 cup heavy cream
1 tablespoon dried lavender blossoms

➤ Let the lavender in this floral dessert help cool off a hot summer night. Have fun with other lavender treats — try lavender honey, lavender tea, or lavender sorbet.

➤ At the restaurant, we serve lavender ice cream with a ginger-pistachio biscotti.

➤ Beat the yolks with the vanilla and honey until the volume has tripled. In a saucepan, bring the milk, cream, and lavender to a simmer over medium heat. Whisk one-third of the milk mixture into the egg mixture. Return the mixture to the saucepan, and cook, stirring constantly until the mixture coats the back of a wooden spoon. Strain, and cool over a bowl of ice water. Chill thoroughly, and freeze in an ice-cream maker following the manufacturer's instructions.

Yield: 1 quart

lemon balm

Melissa officinalis

Lemon balm's unassuming appearance in the garden may make you pass it by, but if, on the way, you brush against the leaves, their strong lemon scent will bring you back. Take some of those leaves into the kitchen and add a subtle lemony hint of mint to many dishes.

The green heart-shaped leaves with their scalloped edges make a great garnish for fruits and desserts. Use lemon balm, also known as lemon mint, anywhere a lemon flavor is desired — with fish, shellfish, chicken, lamb, herb butters, dips, salads, or vegetables. I often infuse a few stems in water, strain it, and use the water for cooking vegetables such as broccoli or asparagus. Lemon balm is compatible with borage, marjoram, thyme, or basil.

A tea made of lemon balm is said to be calming and relaxing. Use it alone or mix it with other herbs or black tea leaves for a soothing hot or cold drink. Lemon balm is an ingredient in the liqueurs Bénédictine and Chartreuse.

Old herbals recorded the use of lemon balm in Europe as early as 1551. Thomas Jefferson listed it among his garden herbs in 1794, and it's still found in the herb garden at Monticello.

Lemon balm is best used fresh though dried leaves can be used for teas and in potpourri. You can freeze leaves in a plastic bag for up to two months. You can also preserve lemon balm in vinegar or infuse it in water and freeze to use later in soups or to cook vegetables, poach fish, or stew chicken.

alfonso contrisciani

chef/co-owner
⋇⋇

Opus 251
Philadelphia, Pennsylvania

*Y*OU MIGHT SAY THAT OPUS 251, located in the Philadelphia Art Alliance, is where food meets art. Or, you might say food here is the art. Alfonso Contrisciani is the artist. Herbs, spices, and sauces are his palette, the plate, his canvas.

During the summer on the terrace at Opus 251, you'll see lemon balm in pots. If you accidentally brush against the leaves, you'll release a powerful citrusy scent. Contrisciani first started working with lemon balm while teaching at Johnson & Wales University. He planted it at the side of his house, and, by the next season, it had taken over the garden. So into the kitchen went lemon balm. "Lemon balm reminds me of basil and mint. It's a very strong herb; I have a lot of respect for the stronger herbs," says Contrisciani, whose culinary philosophy is to maintain simplicity within an elegant food style. He likes to bring out the true flavors and textures of foods while presenting them in exciting combinations.

Strong herbs such as lemon balm "can really accent a dish." They should be "used sparingly," he cautions. He uses lemon balm in desserts, to complement seafood or chicken, and in salads. He often snips the lemony scented leaves over a dish right before serving.

An early love of cooking propelled Contrisciani from dishwasher to a second cook position before high school graduation. He graduated from the College of Culinary Arts at Johnson & Wales University in Providence, Rhode Island, with high honors.

Following a 13-year stint in several Atlantic City hotels, he returned to his alma mater to teach regional American cuisine and served as executive chef/consultant for the Acoaxet Country Club in Westport, Massachusetts.

In 1996, he passed the 10-day American Culinary Federation examination to become the youngest of only 54 certified master chefs in the United States. He was the first Johnson & Wales graduate to become a certified master chef and also the first graduate to qualify as a member of the USA Culinary Olympics team. He was named captain of the 1992 Team USA Northeast and led the team in three competitions, garnering 27 international gold medals. He was named Chef of the Year by the Professional Chef's Association of South Jersey in 1993. He was a grand prize winner in the Pennsylvania Pork Producers Council pork recipe contest with his pecan-crusted pork mignonettes with a Jack Daniel's onion glaze.

Don't be surprised if your waiter breaks into song or entertains you with comedic charm. Members of the wait staff are actors, comedians, singers, and other musicians, and one is even a professional roller blader.

Sun-Dried Tomato Crusted Snapper with Fennel, Artichokes, and Lemon Balm

2 ounces sun-dried tomatoes
4 (6 to 8-ounce) red snapper fillets, descaled, skin on
Kosher salt and freshly ground black pepper
2 tablespoons canola oil
3 teaspoons minced shallots
½ teaspoon minced garlic
2 tablespoons olive oil

1 cup julienned fennel
¼ cup finely diced onion
1 cup quartered baby artichokes, cooked
¼ cup Chardonnay
¾ cup chicken stock (page 219)
4 tablespoons butter
¼ cup lemon balm leaves, sliced

→ Lemon balm adds a refreshing quality to artichokes, one of the hardest vegetables to pair with anything.
→ Serve this dish with toasted orzo or another pasta.

→ Preheat the oven to 225°F. Place the tomatoes on a baking sheet, and slow dry them in the oven for 2 to 3 hours. Grind the tomatoes into a fine powder in a blender or coffee grinder.

→ Preheat the oven to 350°F. Heat a skillet over high heat. Season the fish with salt and pepper, and coat it with the tomato powder. Add the canola oil to the skillet, and fry the fish, skin side down, for 3 to 5 minutes. Turn the fish, and sear the flesh side for 2 to 3 minutes or until it becomes a dark caramel color. Place the fish on a baking sheet, and bake for 10 to 12 minutes or until done.

→ In the same skillet, cook the shallots and garlic in the oil until they are lightly golden. Add the fennel, onion, and a little salt and pepper, and cook another 2 to 3 minutes over medium heat.

→ Add the artichokes and wine, and reduce the liquid by one-half. Add the chicken stock, and reduce the liquid by two-thirds. Whisk in the butter, and adjust the seasonings, if necessary. Add the lemon balm leaves, and combine.

→ To serve, pour some sauce onto the plate, and place a fillet on the sauce. Top the fish with artichokes, and pour more sauce over them.

Yield: 4 servings

Timesaver Tips: You can make the sun-dried tomato powder ahead of time and store it in an airtight container. The sun-dried tomato coating keeps the moisture in the fish and gives it an intense flavor and beautiful color.

Cinnamon Cured Pork Tenderloin with Stone Fruit Consommé and Lemon Balm and Black Pepper Fettuccine

Cinnamon Cured Pork Tenderloin:

1 cup brown sugar
2 tablespoons freshly ground black pepper
2 tablespoons ground cinnamon
3 teaspoons garlic flakes
3 teaspoons onion powder

¼ cup kosher salt
6 (6-ounce) portions pork tenderloin
2 teaspoons chopped garlic
2 teaspoons chopped shallots

Stone Fruit Consommé:

3 plums, cut into wedges
1 peach, cut into wedges
4 cups Chardonnay
2 cups granulated sugar

2 sprigs thyme
1 sprig rosemary
4 cups chicken consommé, homemade or canned

Lemon Balm and Black Pepper Fettuccine:

3½ cups bread flour
¼ cup semolina
1 tablespoon salt
4 eggs
½ cup water

2 tablespoons olive oil
1 egg white beaten with 1 tablespoon water
1 cup lemon balm leaves
2 tablespoons finely chopped lemon zest
3 teaspoons finely ground black pepper

※ To prepare the tenderloin, combine the brown sugar, pepper, cinnamon, garlic flakes, onion powder, and salt. Rub the tenderloin with the garlic and shallots, and then with the brown sugar mixture. Place the tenderloin in the refrigerator to cure for 24 to 36 hours.

※ To prepare the consommé, place the plums, peach, wine, sugar, thyme, and rosemary in the top of a double boiler, and simmer over low heat until the sugar dissolves and the fruit is soft. Add the chicken consommé, stir, and reserve.

※ To prepare the fettuccine, mix the flour, semolina, salt, eggs, water, and oil by hand or in a mixer until the dough is smooth and elastic. Roll out the dough at the thinnest setting on the pasta machine, dusting frequently with flour. Brush half the pasta sheet with the egg white mixture. Arrange the lemon balm leaves across the pasta sheet, and sprinkle them with the lemon zest and pepper. Cover with the remaining pasta sheet, and roll through the pasta machine again. Cut the pasta sheet into fettuccine.

※ To finish the dish, grill the tenderloin on a grill or under the broiler to the desired doneness. Cut the tenderloin on an angle into slices about ¼-inch thick. Cook the fettuccine in lightly salted water for about 2 to 3 minutes. Meanwhile, reheat the consommé.

→ To serve, place the fettuccine in a serving bowl, and arrange the tenderloin slices on top. Pour hot consommé over the tenderloin slices and fettuccine.

Yield: 6 servings

Note: If you don't have a pasta machine, roll the pasta dough as thin as possible with a rolling pin. Cut the pasta sheet by hand into irregular shapes (often called pasta rags). You can also use purchased fresh or dried pasta from gourmet shops or the supermarket. If you are using purchased or dried pasta, cook it first, and toss it with the lemon balm leaves, lemon zest, and pepper before assembling the dish. Use about ¼ cup sliced lemon balm per pound of cooked pasta. Note that freshly made pasta cooks much faster than dried pasta.

Blueberry Champagne Mousse with Lemon Balm

2 cups fresh blueberries
¼ cup champagne
⅛ cup granulated sugar
⅛ cup lemon balm sprigs (about 7 to 8)
   plus 6 lemon balm leaves

½ teaspoon lemon juice
3 egg yolks
¼ cup superfine sugar plus 3 tablespoons superfine
   sugar
1 cup heavy cream

→ In a heavy-bottomed saucepan, combine the blueberries, champagne, granulated sugar, lemon balm, and lemon juice. Simmer the blueberry mixture until it becomes a thick purée (about 15 to 20 minutes). Discard the lemon balm, and pass the blueberry mixture through a large-mesh strainer. Cool and reserve.

→ Combine the egg yolks and ¼ cup of the superfine sugar in a stainless steel bowl. With a hand beater or an electric mixer, whip until the egg mixture has tripled in volume. (The batter is the correct consistency when it forms ribbons that, when the beaters are lifted, quickly sink into the batter still in the bowl.) Gently fold in the blueberry purée. In a separate bowl, whip the cream and the remaining superfine sugar until the mixture stands in soft peaks, taking care not to overmix. Gently fold the cream mixture into the blueberry mixture. Pipe or spoon the mousse into small, chilled goblets, and refrigerate immediately.

→ To serve, garnish each goblet with a lemon balm leaf.

Yield: 6 servings

Note: You can buy a split of champagne, which holds 6.3 ounces, at many liquor stores. If you make this recipe and the Mexican mint marigold–champagne sorbet (page 131) at the same time, you will use nearly all of the champagne. The sorbet can be kept in the freezer for serving another day.

→ **Make this elegant dessert during the summer berry season. An easy but rich treat, this mousse is a grand finale for a special dinner.**

→ **Decorate each goblet with a rosette of whipped cream, a lemon balm leaf, and a cat's tongue cookie.**

lemon grass

Cymbopogon citratus

LEMON GRASS, A GRASS WITH A BULBLIKE BASE, resembles green onions, and emits a subtle scent of lemon and a hardy citrus flavor. Inside the grass stalks is the oil citral, which is also found in lemon peel. In fact, lemon zest is a satisfactory substitute for lemon grass, but you don't get quite the same texture or intensity of flavor. Adding a little grated fresh ginger makes the flavor of lemon zest more like that of lemon grass, but purists will say nothing can substitute for lemon grass.

Known as *takrai* in Thailand, lemon grass is used extensively in Thai and Vietnamese cuisine, but you'll find it popping up more and more in many restaurant dishes. Lemon grass is appearing in many grocery stores these days, and is always available in Asian markets and often in specialty stores. You can find dried as well as powdered lemon grass, but little of its scent or flavor remains. It's best to buy it fresh and freeze any that is left over.

The bulbous part of lemon grass is usually used, and even that has a rather tough texture. Like bay leaf, pieces of lemon grass should be removed from a dish before serving it, although a couple of stalks can make a dramatic garnish for a clear soup. Some recipes call for grinding lemon grass into a paste with a mortar and pestle.

Lemon grass blends well with other flavorings such as cilantro, ginger, garlic, shallots, chiles, and coconut. It's most often used with fish, and in soups, curries, marinades, and sauces. A touch of lemon grass will add zing to broccoli, cauliflower, and eggplant, and it also makes a pleasant lemony tea.

mai pham

*i*F YOU COULDN'T GUESS FROM THE NAME of her restaurant, Mai Pham is crazy about lemon grass. "I love it because there's nothing really like it," says the Vietnam-born chef. "It seems to be beautiful at blending ingredients together. It's floral; it's gingery. It brings together the zinginess of ginger and the tanginess of citrus. It adds a different dimension to a dish."

Pham uses lemon grass in two basic ways. She chops it very fine and adds it to marinades, or she infuses it into broths, stews, and curries. She suggests slicing lemon grass into two- or three-inch pieces and lightly bruising the pieces to release the aromatic oils before adding lemon grass to an infusion. Occasionally, she'll "chop it really fine and add it to salads as the Thais do."

Her affair with lemon grass is natural since Vietnamese cooks use it in just about everything, Pham explains. "Vietnamese cooking is wonderful," she says. "It's somewhat similar to Chinese cooking in that it's a rice-based cuisine and the same techniques of steaming and poaching are both used. At the same time, it's dramatically different in that Vietnamese cooking is more herbaceous and the flavors more lively." What makes it more lively, she says, is that Vietnamese cooks use "lots of lime juice." She says the lime juice is usually added later in the cooking process or in dipping sauces. "That's what gives Vietnamese dishes a very distinct delicate taste." Fresh vegetables and a generous helping of herbs are the foundations of Vietnamese dishes. She grew up in Thailand and likes to blend Thai and Vietnamese cuisines, creating her own style.

Since opening her first restaurant in 1988, she's been recognized as one of the preeminent Vietnamese chefs in the country. She first came to the United States after the fall of Saigon in 1975. She worked as a television reporter and anchor in Washington, D.C., after earning a degree in journalism from the University of Maryland. She was also a speechwriter for then California governor George Deukmejian.

Pham combined her journalistic skills and her expertise in the kitchen as author of *The Best of Vietnamese & Thai Cooking* (Prima Publishing, 1995). She also writes a food column for the *San Francisco Chronicle,* and her food articles have appeared in local and national publications.

Pham was named Businesswoman of the Year by the Sacramento Chamber of Commerce and was included in *Business Journal's* Women Who Mean Business. In 1996, she was named the YWCA Hospitality Woman of the Year. She received an honorary master's degree from the Culinary Institute of America in Hyde Park, New York, for her "entrepreneurial spirit, culinary leadership, and commitment to cooking education." She teaches at the Culinary Institute of America in St. Helena, California.

chef/owner

**Lemon Grass
Restaurant & Cafes**
Sacramento, California

Thai Hot and Sour Prawn Soup

1 tablespoon vegetable oil
1 teaspoon finely chopped garlic
½ teaspoon dried chile flakes
½ teaspoon chili paste
2 thin slices fresh or frozen, dried or powdered galangal
1 stalk lemon grass, bruised with the side of a knife
   and cut on the diagonal into 2-inch pieces
5 cups chicken stock, homemade (page 219) or canned
   (low-sodium)
1 cup water
2 kaffir lime leaves, cut into thirds

2 plum tomatoes, seeded and chopped
2 tablespoons fish sauce*
4½ teaspoons sugar
½ cup drained canned straw mushrooms or 3 ounces
   white mushrooms, quartered
½ pound raw prawns, shelled and deveined
5 basil leaves, chopped
5 sprigs cilantro, chopped
1 green onion, cut into 1-inch pieces
¼ cup fresh lime juice

Fish sauce is available in Asian stores.

> ✣ The leaves of the kaffir lime, an intensely aromatic lime used extensively in Thai cooking, give this soup a unique flavor. If kaffir lime leaves are not available, use lime zest.
> ✣ A stir-fry dish, a salad, and some steamed rice would make this soup a fabulous meal.

✣ In a large saucepan, heat the oil over medium heat. Add the garlic, chile flakes, and chili paste. Stir until fragrant, about 1 minute. Add the galangal and lemon grass, and stir until they are lightly browned, about 2 minutes. Add the chicken stock and water, and simmer for about 15 to 20 minutes. Bring the soup to a boil. Add the kaffir lime leaves, tomatoes, fish sauce, sugar, and mushrooms, and combine. Add the prawns, and cook just until they turn pink, about 2 minutes. (The prawns will continue to cook in the hot broth.) Remove the pan from the heat, and add the basil, cilantro, green onion, and lime juice. Serve immediately.

Yield: 4 servings

Lemon Grass Roasted Chicken

½ cup finely chopped lemon grass (3 or 4 stalks)
2 tablespoons finely chopped shallots (1 large bulb)
1 tablespoon finely chopped garlic (about 6 medium cloves)
1 tablespoon dried chile flakes
1 tablespoon soy sauce

1 tablespoon sugar
4½ teaspoons fish sauce*
1½ teaspoons kosher salt
1 chicken (3 to 4 pounds), rinsed and patted dry
2 tablespoons finely chopped cilantro
1 tablespoon vegetable oil

*Fish sauce is available in Asian stores.

> ✦ A last-minute basting with a lemon grass and cilantro paste gives this dish a wonderful aroma.

✦ In a nonreactive dish large enough to hold the chicken, combine all but 2 tablespoons of the lemon grass with the shallots, garlic, chile flakes, soy sauce, sugar, fish sauce, and salt. Add the chicken, turn it to coat it in the marinade, and put some marinade underneath the chicken skin. Pour any excess marinade into the cavity. Marinate the chicken in the refrigerator for at least 3 hours, preferably overnight. Bring the chicken to room temperature before cooking.

✦ Heat the oven to 350°F. Put the chicken, breast side down, on a rack in a roasting pan. Roast the chicken for 40 minutes. Turn it over, and roast until the chicken is cooked and nicely browned, 20 to 30 minutes. The sugar in the marinade may cause the pan juices to burn, but this won't affect the flavor. About 10 minutes before the chicken is done, combine the remaining 2 tablespoons lemon grass with the cilantro and vegetable oil, and baste the chicken with this mixture. The chicken is done when its juices run clear. Let the chicken stand for 10 minutes before carving it.

Yield: 4 servings

Recipes reprinted, with permission, from *The Best of Vietnamese & Thai Cooking: Favorite Recipes from Lemon Grass Restaurant and Cafes* by Mai Pham (Prima Publishing, 1995).

marty blitz

chef/partner

Mise en Place
Tampa, Florida

*M*ISE EN PLACE IS FRENCH FOR "everything in its place." At Mise en Place restaurant, Marty Blitz is in his place in the kitchen cooking up French Caribbean cuisine. He changes his menu weekly, and relies heavily on lemon grass.

"Lemon grass is very aromatic and has such a unique flavor that it can be used in endless ways," says Blitz, who, with his wife, Maryann, runs Mise en Place, Mise en Place Market (a gourmet shop), and 442, a sophisticated cocktail lounge. "Lemon grass is very lemony; a little goes a long way. If you drop a couple of stalks into a broth, you pick up on it very easily." Its versatility is a plus for lemon grass. "You can use it in desserts, in a variety of sauces, and it's a major ingredient in curry pastes, which we use as a baste for vegetables or fish and seafood." Lemon grass also makes a healthy tea, he says. He also suggests adding a couple of stalks when cooking rice to give the rice a subtle lemon grass flavor. Blitz also uses lemon grass in a carrot juice lemon grass vinaigrette that adds zip to his seared scallops.

Blitz says lemon grass is different from some of the other lemon herbs, such as lemon balm and lemon verbena. "Lemon balm is very subtle and lemon verbena is a very nice herb but lemon grass is unique." He always uses fresh lemon grass, although dried lemon grass can be used for tea, he says. Lemon grass grows well in warm climates.

Although he once had an extensive herb garden, Blitz no longer has time to care for it and now contracts with an organic farmer to provide what he needs. He does still have a few herbs around the house, including a hanging planter made for him from a 90-quart stockpot by one of his employees.

Born in New York and raised in Detroit, Blitz had an early love of cooking that made him at age 12, ride his bike to the local deli for a job. Learning classic recipes and techniques along the way, he eventually earned an American Culinary Federation apprenticeship under European trained master chef Milos Cihelka.

Blitz continued to study, practice, and collect recipes and cookbooks, resulting in the "ultimate food library." After four and a half years as head chef of RG's North in the Tampa Bay area, he opened Mise en Place Deli and Catering. The restaurant was "a new world style bistro" and was honored as Grand Winner, Central Florida/Gulf Coast Restaurants, in the *Zagat Survey.* Blitz was named a Rising Star in American Cuisine by the James Beard Foundation, and has represented Tampa at Coca-Cola's Taste of the NFL fundraiser for the past five years. His Cuban spiced shrimp with manchego cheese grits and Puerto Rican red bean salsa recipe was featured on the cover of *Cities' Cafe 1995*, the Taste of the NFL cookbook. He has also been chef/co-chair of the Tampa Bay Share Our Strength Taste of the Nation fundraiser. He has been featured on the Discovery Channel's *Great Chefs of the South* television program and was profiled in *Nation's Restaurant News.*

Udon with Lemon Grass, Cilantro, Shiitake Mushrooms, and Scallops

1 tablespoon peanut oil
16 large scallops
1 teaspoon chopped garlic
1 teaspoon finely chopped lemon grass
8 shiitake mushrooms, sliced
2 tablespoons dry sherry
1 tablespoon soy sauce

1 teaspoon rice vinegar
2 serrano chiles, seeded and finely chopped
4 tablespoons chopped cilantro
2 tablespoons finely sliced green onions
½ pound udon, cooked
1 tablespoon black sesame seeds*
4 sprigs cilantro

Black sesame seeds are sometimes available in gourmet shops. Toasted white sesame seeds can be substituted.

✤ Heat the oil in a hot wok or large frying pan. Sear the scallops, browning them on both sides. Remove the scallops, and set them aside. Add the garlic and lemon grass, and sauté until foamy. Add the mushrooms, and sauté for 1 minute. Deglaze the pan with the sherry, soy sauce, and vinegar. Cook for 1 minute, and return the scallops to the pan. Add the chiles, cilantro, green onion, and udon. Toss for 1 minute.

✤ To serve, garnish the dish with black sesame seeds and cilantro sprigs.

Yield: 4 servings

✤ Udon are thick, Asian noodles made from wheat flour and often used in soups and stews. Here they're spiced up with lemon grass and chiles.
✤ A nice, crusty, warm bread and grilled fresh vegetables would make great accompaniments to this dish.

Tomato Lemon Grass Salsa

2 stalks lemon grass, white part only, finely minced
2 Thai green or red chiles, finely chopped
1 large, vine-ripened tomato, coarsely diced
1 small red onion, finely diced
2 tablespoons chopped cilantro

2 tablespoons olive oil
2 tablespoons rice vinegar
1 tablespoon sesame oil
Salt

✤ In a mixing bowl, combine the lemon grass, chiles, tomato, onion, cilantro, olive oil, vinegar, sesame oil, and a little salt. Let the salsa stand for 60 minutes, and refrigerate.

Yield: 4 servings

Note: This salsa can be made up to 12 hours in advance.

✤ The lemon grass adds texture as well as flavor, creating a salsa with an Asian twist.
✤ Serve with grilled chicken or fish or as an hors d'oeuvre with crispy won ton chips. To make won ton chips, simply deep-fry cut pieces of won ton wrappers in hot oil.

Chardonnay Juice Mojo Red Snapper with Black Bean—Banana Sauce, Peach—Lemon Grass Salsa, and Habanero-Infused Oil

Habanero-Infused Oil:
2 habanero chiles, halved

1 cup olive oil

Chardonnay Juice Mojo Red Snapper:
1 red onion, cut into julienne
2 cups Chardonnay grape juice*
1 cup olive oil
4 tablespoons cider vinegar
2 tablespoons chopped cilantro

1 tablespoon chopped garlic
1 teaspoon chopped oregano
1 teaspoon chopped thyme
Salt and black pepper
4 (6-ounce) red snapper fillets, skin on

You can substitute white grape juice or a light white wine for the Chardonnay grape juice.

Black Bean—Banana Sauce:
2 tablespoons olive oil
2 bananas, sliced
1 white onion, chopped
1 habanero chile, chopped

1 tablespoon chopped ginger
2 cups cooked black beans with juice
Salt and pepper

Peach—Lemon Grass Salsa:
2 peaches, chopped
1 small red onion, chopped
4 tablespoons chopped cilantro
3 tablespoons olive oil

1 tablespoon chopped lemon grass
1 tablespoon lime juice
1 teaspoon chopped ginger
Salt and pepper

➤ To prepare the habanero-infused oil, warm the chiles with the oil, and let the mixture stand overnight. Strain, and set aside.

➤ To prepare the fish, combine the onion, grape juice, oil, vinegar, cilantro, garlic, oregano, thyme, salt, and pepper. Pour the mixture over the fish, and marinate for 2 hours, refrigerated.

➤ To prepare the sauce, heat the oil in a saucepan. Add the banana, onion, chile, and ginger, and sauté for 10 minutes. Add the black beans with juice. Season with salt and pepper. Purée the bean mixture with a submersible blender or in a food processor, and set the sauce aside.

➤ To prepare the salsa, combine the peaches, onion, cilantro, oil, lemon grass, lime juice, ginger, and some salt and pepper. Set aside.

➤ Mojo, a dish of Cuban origin, is traditionally made from sour oranges. This is a variation.
➤ This makes a hearty dish on its own. A good bread and a glass of wine would complete it nicely.

✦ To cook the fish, preheat the oven to 450°F. Heat a nonstick, ovenproof sauté pan over medium-high heat. Place the fish, skin side down, in the hot pan. Cook the fish on one side until it turns crispy. Turn the fish, and finish cooking it in the oven for 3 to 4 minutes or until done.

✦ To serve, spoon black bean sauce onto the plate, and place the fish on the sauce. Top with salsa, and drizzle on a small amount of the oil.

Yield: 4 servings

Note: Habanero-infused oil will keep for months in the refrigerator.

Poached Pear with Lemon Grass–Mirin–Star Anise Syrup and Raspberry Ginger Sauce

Poached Pear with Lemon Grass–Mirin–Star Anise Syrup:

4 whole star anise	1 cup sugar
2 stalks lemon grass, coarsely chopped	Juice of 2 lemons
2 cups water	4 pears, peeled
1 cup mirin	

Raspberry Ginger Sauce:

8 tablespoons sugar	1 pint raspberries
4 tablespoons water	½ teaspoon chopped ginger

Raspberries

✦ To prepare the pears, combine the star anise, lemon grass, water, mirin, sugar, and lemon juice in a saucepan. Bring to a simmer, add the pears, and poach them until they are tender, about 15 to 20 minutes. Remove the pears, and set them aside. Strain the syrup, and reduce it until it has thickened slightly.

✦ To prepare the sauce, place the sugar, water, raspberries, and ginger in a saucepan. Simmer for 5 minutes. Purée the raspberry mixture in a blender or food processor. Strain.

✦ To serve, spoon a couple of tablespoons of the sauce onto a plate. Place a pear in the center. Drizzle the pear lightly with syrup, and garnish with raspberries.

Yield: 4 servings

Note: Bosc pears are preferred for this recipe. Asian pears would also work well, or baby Seckel pears.

✦ **The combination of citrusy lemon grass, sweet mirin wine, anise, and ginger imparts a complex, yet delicate flavor to the pears. The raspberries add another fruity dimension along with a vibrant color contrast.**

✦ **This fruity dessert stands on its own, or you could add a couple of crunchy cookies or a scoop of ice cream.**

lemon verbena

Aloysia triphylla

*h*ERE'S YET ANOTHER LEMON-SCENTED HERB. This Rolls-Royce of the lemon herbs is a South American native discovered by Spanish explorers in Chile and Argentina during the 18th century. Lemon verbena has an intense lemon flavor and strong lemon scent. Sometimes called Spanish thyme, lemon verbena's lancelike leaves can be used as a substitute for lemon grass in Asian recipes. You can substitute lemon verbena in just about any recipe calling for mint to get a citrus, instead of a mint, flavor.

Use lemon verbena anywhere a lemon flavor would be welcome — with poultry and fish and in puddings, cookies, cakes, ice cream, and muffins. Try it with vegetables and in fruit salads. Brew a pot of lemon verbena tea. Infuse this herb in oil, butter, or broth to add a lemon scent and flavor to vegetables, soups, and casseroles. Infuse it in cream to use in desserts and custards, and in vinegar to use in marinades and dressings. The leaves make a lovely garnish but, like bay, can be a bit tough, so generally you'll want to chop them finely, or, if using whole leaves, remove them prior to serving. You can use lemon verbena in place of lemon peel; just chop the lemon verbena leaves finely.

Lemon verbena is another one of the herbs you probably won't find at the grocery store and may have to grow yourself.

It is the herb of enchantment; in the language of flowers it means "you have bewitched me." Spanish verbena, an essential oil, is distilled from the stems and has been used as an ingredient in colognes. In fact, you may remember that it was a favorite fragrance of Scarlet O'Hara's mother in *Gone with the Wind*.

Another fan of lemon verbena was Emperor Maximilian of Mexico who, along with Empress Carlotta, enlarged the gardens at Montezuma's palace. Since it was considered beneath an emperor's dignity to grow plants strictly for utilitarian purposes, he grew fragrant herbs instead. He so loved lemon verbena that he named it *yerba Louisa* after Carlotta's mother. Sweetened with honey, yerba Louisa tea is still a popular Mexican drink.

diane forley

$\mathcal{D}$IANE FORLEY ADMIRES LEMON VERBENA'S "lemony, perfumy quality. I love the aroma; it's very powerful and very soothing." She likes the idea that lemon verbena has both culinary and medical uses, and she has fond memories of sipping lemon verbena tea after dinner while visiting relatives in Guatemala. It's an attractive plant, too, says Forley, who especially likes the shape of its leaf.

She takes advantage of lemon verbena's versatility in the kitchen. "Right now we're using it in crème brûlée; we're making verbena syrup, even verbena-flavored vodka. We've also used it for chicken."

Located amid brownstones in the heart of Gramercy Park, Verbena offers a garden retreat. Large glass panels at the entrance contain cross-sections of vegetables as well as pressed herbs. Potted plants replace cut flower arrangements, and, during the summer, large market umbrellas shade tables in a courtyard garden that serves as a chef's inspiration. A collection of herbs, including thyme, basil, sage, lemon verbena, mint, and rosemary, grow here and find their way into dishes such as butternut squash ravioli flavored with roasted oranges and sage, a signature dish. Also growing here are nasturtiums, sweet peas, and other edible flowers Forley likes to use in her kitchen. She offers classes on herbal folklore and edible flowers.

Forley's interests include nutrition and food history. Her senior honor's thesis at Brown University — *The History of Gastronomy in 19th-Century France, Examined Through the Works of Balzac and Flaubert* — incorporated her interests in food and literature.

She has trained with noted chefs both in the United States and in France. As a high school student, Forley apprenticed with Michel Fitoussi at the Palace Restaurant in New York. She rejoined Fitoussi after graduation from college, and then became pastry chef at the newly opened Gotham Bar and Grill. The following year she joined the opening team at the Adrienne with Jacques Chibois and Jean-Michel Diot. She further refined her skills working each station of the kitchen at the River Cafe with David Burke. Forley studied in France with Michel Guérard of Eugénie-les-Bains, Jose Lampreia at Maison Blanche, and Alain Passard at L'Arpège. Upon her return to New York, she was both sous-chef and pastry chef at Petrossian, helped open the Park Avenue Café, and created intensely flavored Italian dishes and handmade breads and desserts at Oggi Domani.

Just eight weeks after opening Verbena, Forley received a two-star review from *The New York Times*. Verbena was also named one of the top new restaurants in the country by *Esquire* magazine. *New York Magazine*, *New York Newsday*, *Village Voice*, and *Paper Magazine* have all praised Verbena and its chef/owner.

chef/owner
❖

Verbena
New York, New York

Lemon Verbena Crème Brûlée

1½ cups heavy cream
½ cup milk
2 tablespoons lemon verbena leaves (about 2 dozen large leaves), bruised and crushed

½ cup plus 2 teaspoons sugar
¼ vanilla bean, split
6 egg yolks
Ice bath

➤ Heat the cream and milk to lukewarm in a medium saucepan. Remove from the heat. Add the lemon verbena, and allow the mixture to steep about 20 minutes to infuse the lemon verbena flavor.

➤ Preheat the oven to 300°F.

➤ Add ¼ cup of the sugar along with the vanilla bean to the cream mixture, place it over low heat, and bring it to just under a boil. Remove the cream mixture from the heat. In a bowl, whisk together the egg yolks and the remaining ¼ cup of sugar. Slowly whisk the milk mixture into the egg mixture. Cook, stirring frequently, over medium heat until the egg mixture has thickened.

➤ Strain the egg mixture immediately into a bowl placed over an ice bath. Pour the egg mixture into 4 (4-ounce) custard cups. Place the custard cups in a baking pan, and add enough boiling water to reach halfway up the sides of the custard cups. Bake until set, about 30 to 35 minutes. Chill thoroughly.

➤ Just before serving, sprinkle the surface of each custard with ½ teaspoon of the remaining sugar. Use a kitchen blowtorch to brown the sugared surface, or place the custards on a bed of cracked ice and place them under the broiler to brown.

Yield: 4 servings

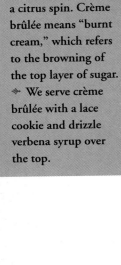

➤ Here's a traditional crème brûlée with a citrus spin. Crème brûlée means "burnt cream," which refers to the browning of the top layer of sugar.
➤ We serve crème brûlée with a lace cookie and drizzle verbena syrup over the top.

Lemon Verbena Madeleines

¼ pound butter (½ cup)
2 tablespoons lemon verbena leaves (about 20 large leaves), crushed
½ cup sugar

½ cup all-purpose flour
½ cup almond flour
6 egg whites
1 tablespoon honey

❖ Melt the butter over low heat until foam begins to form, and add the lemon verbena. When the butter begins to brown, remove it from the heat. Let the butter mixture stand for about 15 minutes. Strain, and set aside.

❖ Butter and flour the madeleine pans. Mix together the sugar, all-purpose flour, and almond flour. In a separate bowl, beat the egg whites with a whisk until they are frothy. Add the flour mixture, and stir until the dry ingredients are incorporated. Stir in the infused butter and then the honey. With a pastry bag, pipe the madeleine batter into the molds, filling them about half full. (You can also carefully spoon the batter into the molds.) Refrigerate for 60 minutes before baking.

❖ Preheat the oven to 325°F. Remove the madeleine pans from the refrigerator, and bake about 10 minutes or until the madeleines are lightly browned. Unmold the madeleines, and cool them.

Yield: 24 (2 by 3-inch) madeleines

Note: Almond flour is available in specialty shops. You can also make your own by processing whole almonds in a food processor until finely ground. About 6 tablespoons almonds will yield ½ cup almond flour. Add 2 teaspoons of the sugar while processing to keep the almonds from clumping. If using miniature madeleine pans, adjust the baking time.

❖ Madeleines, a French sponge cake baked in small, shell-shaped molds, are usually eaten as cookies and are often served with tea. This is the treat made famous by Marcel Proust in *Swann's Way*: "She sent out for one of those short, plump little cakes called 'petites madeleines,' which look as though they had been molded in the fluted scallop of a pilgrim's shell."

❖ We serve these madeleines as an accompaniment to petit fours.

colin cameron

pastry chef

Esplanade Restaurant
Portland, Oregon

COLIN CAMERON DISCOVERED LEMON VERBENA by accident. The plant caught his attention while he was shopping for herbs for his herb garden. One taste and he was hooked. He was delighted to find "such a clean flavor." While lemon verbena has a strong lemon flavor, he says, it's not just lemon. "It has a real sharp, clean flavor profile unlike sage and some other herbs that have a rounder, almost muddy profile."

This taste discovery led him to experiment with lemon verbena and incorporate it into his eclectic dessert menu. "It's something I like — finding interesting variations on things. I like to be able to surprise customers with something a little unexpected." Lemon verbena, he says, helps him do that. "You get a strong lemon component but it's not really lemon."

Cameron's signature desserts are a triple chocolate terrine with red and black raspberry sauces and a crème brûlée tangerine torte. His real passion, however, is ice cream, and he wasted no time creating a lemon verbena ice cream (page 99).

As he discovered lemon verbena by accident, Cameron also came by his craft almost by accident. He graduated from the University of California at Berkeley with a degree in English literature. After graduation, he worked in a variety of jobs. During this time, he became interested in cooking and baking and enjoyed giving dinner parties for friends, sometimes including a decorated cake.

"On the advice of a friend who'd seen one of my primitive cakes, I began taking courses in cake decorating — still very much an amateur — though I eventually began producing and selling wedding cakes." (Incidentally, he says, he valued that friend's advice so highly that he married her.) Later he enrolled in the baking program at Clark College in Vancouver, Washington. Before graduation, he was offered a pastry chef position at the then newly renovated Heathman Hotel and later also produced desserts for the Greenwood Inn in Beaverton, Oregon. He joined Esplanade, located in the RiverPlace Hotel, in 1986 and has been happily creating desserts ever since.

Cameron was a guest chef at the American Institute of Wine and Food's Fifth Annual Conference on Gastronomy in California's Napa Valley. He's also actively involved with Chef's Night Out, the Portland version of Share Our Strength's Taste of the Nation, an annual event to benefit the hungry. His recipes have been published in *PGE Chef's Night Out Cookbook, Restaurant Hospitality* magazine, *Wine Country International Magazine,* and the Sunday magazine of the *Seattle Times.*

The cuisine at Esplanade features northwestern regional ingredients prepared in ways that draw on a variety of influences such as Pacific Rim, Mexican, and South American. The restaurant's dark woods, oil lamps, and subtle wall decoration create a subdued elegance without an overly formal atmosphere, and diners can enjoy a view of the Willamette River.

Mascarpone and Lemon Verbena Mousse with Huckleberry Coulis

Mascarpone and Lemon Verbena Mousse:

2½ cups plus 2 tablespoons heavy cream

2 tablespoons chopped lemon verbena leaves

1½ teaspoons granulated gelatin

1½ tablespoons champagne, Triple Sec, or
   pear eau-de-vie

12 ounces mascarpone (Italian-style cream cheese),
   at room temperature

Huckleberry Coulis:

2 pints fresh huckleberries or blueberries*

⅔ cup sugar

2 tablespoons water

You could also substitute any strongly flavored berry such as raspberries or blackberries.

Crisp cookies (optional)

Mint sprigs (optional)

Whipped cream (optional)

❧ To prepare the mousse, heat 2 cups of the cream to scalding with the lemon verbena. Remove from the heat, and steep for 60 minutes. Strain the cream through cheesecloth or a fine-mesh strainer to remove the leaves. Refrigerate the cream until it is cold before proceeding with the rest of the recipe.

❧ Soften the gelatin in the liquor (water may be substituted for the liquor). Scald the remaining cream and whisk it into the softened gelatin until it is dissolved. Set the gelatin mixture aside to cool. Meanwhile, prepare the coulis.

❧ To prepare the coulis, place the huckleberries, sugar, and water in a small saucepan, and simmer until the berries are very soft. Press the berry mixture through a fine-mesh sieve (or multiple layers of cheesecloth) to remove the seeds. Refrigerate until needed.

❧ Finish preparing the mousse: when the gelatin mixture has cooled to the point that it begins to thicken, rapidly fold it into the mascarpone. Whip the verbena-infused cream until it forms soft peaks, and fold it into the mascarpone mixture.

❧ To serve, use a pastry bag with a large star tip to pipe the mousse onto cooled dessert plates or into cooled serving cups. Pour chilled coulis next to the mousse, and garnish with a crisp cookie, a mint sprig, and a little whipped cream, if desired.

Yield: 8 servings

Note: The mousse may be refrigerated until you are ready to serve it.

❧ The deep purple of the huckleberry coulis, so dark it is nearly black, is a wonderful visual counterpoint to the very pale yellow of the mousse, and consequently this dessert doesn't require much dressing up when you serve it.

❧ For a slightly more sophisticated presentation, place the mousse in flexible molds and freeze. Before serving, unmold the mousse by dipping the molds into cool water and inverting them onto the serving plates. Serve the mousse when it is fully thawed.

Honeyed Lemon Verbena—Cornmeal Shortcakes with Stone Fruit Compote

Honeyed Lemon Verbena—Cornmeal Shortcakes:
3⅓ cups cake flour
1½ cups yellow cornmeal
2 tablespoons sugar
1¾ tablespoons baking powder
1 teaspoon salt

4 tablespoons chopped lemon verbena leaves
10 tablespoons cold butter, cut into chunks
1 tablespoon strong-flavored varietal honey
2 cups half-and-half

Stone Fruit Compote:
5 to 6 large peaches, nectarines, plums, or any combination, peeled and pitted

1 cup sugar
1 to 2 tablespoons Triple Sec

Whipped cream or ice cream

✦ For this recipe, I like to use Oregon locust honey, which is strongly floral and, to me, reminiscent of a summer walk in a forest.

✦ To add a really decadent touch, drizzle a little of the same honey used to make the shortcakes over the top.

✦ To prepare the shortcakes, sift together the flour, cornmeal, 1½ tablespoons of the sugar, and the baking powder and salt. Stir in the lemon verbena. Using a pastry knife or food processor, cut in the butter until the mixture is the texture of coarse cornmeal.

✦ In a separate bowl, whisk the honey into the half-and-half. Add the cream mixture to the flour mixture, and stir just until the liquid is absorbed. Do not knead or mix the dough after it comes together. The dough should be very soft and sticky at this stage.

✦ Preheat the oven to 375°F.

✦ On a well-floured surface, roll out the dough about 1 inch thick. Cut it with a 3½-inch round cookie or biscuit cutter. Rework the scraps as necessary, letting the dough stand briefly each time you roll it out. Brush the tops of the shortcakes with water, and sprinkle them with the remaining sugar. Place the shortcakes on a baking sheet, and bake them until they are golden brown and done in the center, about 15 minutes. Cool.

✦ To prepare the compote, slice or chop the peaches into large pieces. Place them in a bowl, and sprinkle them with the sugar and liqueur. Stir briefly, and let stand for at least 30 minutes before serving.

✦ To serve, split the shortcakes in half horizontally. Place the bottom half in a shallow bowl, ladle on some compote, and top with whipped cream. Place the top half of the shortcake on the whipped cream.

Yield: 8 shortcakes

Note: Any honey may be used in this recipe (or the honey may be replaced by an equal amount of sugar added to the dry ingredients), but strong-flavored varietal honeys, made from only one variety of flower, will give a more distinctive result than the mild-flavored honeys found in supermarkets. Varietal honeys are worth seeking out; each has its own distinctive flavor, which varies from type to type. Experiment until you find one you especially like.

Lemon Verbena Ice Cream

1 quart half-and-half
2 tablespoons chopped lemon verbena leaves
½ teaspoon vanilla

12 large egg yolks
1 cup plus 2 tablespoons sugar

✦ Scald the half-and-half with the lemon verbena and vanilla. Remove the half-and-half mixture from the heat, and let it steep for 60 minutes. Strain the half-and-half mixture through cheesecloth or a fine-mesh strainer to remove the leaves. Return the half-and-half to the stove and scald again.

✦ While the half-and-half is heating, combine the egg yolks with the sugar, and whip the egg mixture on high speed until it has tripled in volume and is very pale in color. Remove the half-and-half from the heat, and gradually whisk it into the egg mixture, stirring rapidly. Cook the egg mixture in the top of a double boiler, stirring constantly, until the egg mixture is thick enough to coat the back of a wooden spoon. Remove from the heat, and cool. Refrigerate the egg mixture at least 3 hours, preferably overnight. Process in an ice-cream maker following the manufacturer's instructions.

Yield: about 1½ quarts

✦ **This recipe is, essentially, one for French vanilla ice cream in which lemon verbena is substituted for the vanilla. This herb, combined with the egg yolks, results in a lovely, pale yellow ice cream without the use of any artificial coloring.**
✦ **Scoop the ice cream into bowls, and top with fresh raspberries or blackberries that have been lightly mashed with a little sugar.**

lovage

Levisticum officinale

Lovely as it may be, lovage is another herb little used by North American cooks. Lovage has also been neglected by poets and painters and appears to have little folklore associated with it, although it was a popular medicinal herb during the 14th century. The ancient Romans and Greeks chewed lovage seeds in the belief that they aided digestion. Lovage was also included in love potions, earning it the nickname "love parsley."

Lovage is a native of southern Europe and grows wild in the mountains of northern Greece and in the south of France. The tall stalks of this herb can be used as an aromatic, green filler in flower arrangements and as a background plant for shorter herbs in the kitchen garden. Lovage is also known as garden lovage, and Italian lovage.

The French call lovage "false celery" because its flavor strongly resembles that of celery with a hint of parsley. I often use lovage leaves in soups, stuffings, and salads when I've run out of celery. Some people like lovage soup; others use it in place of lettuce in sandwiches. It makes a nice seasoning for stir-fried foods and can flavor beans, peas, and lentils, as well. A few leaves blended into tomato juice add flavor, and the leaves and stems can be used to make herb vinegar. Lovage makes a nice celery-flavored herb butter that can be used to flavor steamed vegetables or rice.

The entire plant, in fact, is edible. The roots are sometimes cooked as a vegetable, and the seeds, often called celery seeds, can flavor breads, sauces, dressings, and cheese spreads much as poppy seeds do. The stems are hollow and make a novel straw for that tomato juice cocktail. Lovage dries fairly well but loses some flavor.

michael smith

"LOVAGE IS ONE OF THE MOST intensely flavored herbs growing in my kitchen garden," says Michael Smith. "As a chef, I'm intently focused on creating boldly flavored cuisine, and lovage easily plays a role in that quest."

He first started using lovage after singer Theresa Doyle, a well-known member of the Maritime music scene and a frequent guest of the inn, gave him a cutting. "As soon as I chomped on one of those leaves, I declared it celery times ten. It's very aromatic; as a seasoning, I consider it on par with the classic bay leaf."

Smith first embarked on the path to a career in art, but soon the kitchen became his studio and the plate his canvas. He delights in designing dramatic dishes that highlight the bounty of Prince Edward Island, which he calls a "chef's paradise." His menu is heavily influenced by local ingredients, including more than 100 varieties of herbs, along with edible flowers and greens growing in his own kitchen garden. "I look at the herb garden as a wine cellar; I like width and depth in what's available." Of course, that garden includes lovage. "In the garden, its presence is particularly distinctive as it often grows over six feet tall," says Smith. "It has an unmistakable earthy pungency that is reassuringly familiar to most palates while simultaneously exotic. It works well with most ingredients native to Prince Edward Island and is often highlighted on my menu." In addition to herbs, Smith relies on vegetable extracts for flavor rather than cream and other dairy products.

The inn, perched on a hill overlooking Bay Fortune, is a 1911 New England style frame house. Despite the artistic style of its chef, the atmosphere of the inn is deliberately unpretentious. "We strive to take fine dining off its pedestal and make it appreciated by everyone." His menu is straightforward, highlighting familiar ingredients while eschewing fancy cooking terms.

Smith operates an open kitchen: he encourages diners to visit his kitchen, freely dispenses recipes, and offers a customized tasting menu. "I invite guests to join me in the kitchen, and we create a menu based on the freshest ingredients of the day," he says. He also offers a one-day cooking class in which he teaches guests "about the mechanics of tasting and how it influences your cooking. We learn what flavors are and what the components are." The class leads into a seven-course tasting at the chef's table.

The inn was awarded one of just 12 three-star ratings in Anne Hardy's *Where to Eat in Canada*. Smith and the inn have received praise from *USA Today*, *The Boston Globe*, *The Globe and Mail*, *Canadian House & Home*, and *Foodservice and Hospitality*.

Smith is the author of *Open Kitchen: A Chef's Day at The Inn at Bay Fortune* (Callawind Publications, 1998).

chef/co-owner

The Inn at Bay Fortune
Bay Fortune,
Prince Edward Island

Parmesan Crusted Salmon with Tomato Lovage Compote

2 large, vine-ripened tomatoes, diced
4 tablespoons extra virgin olive oil
½ cup minced lovage
½ cup minced red onion
½ teaspoon hot sauce
½ teaspoon sea salt
Juice and zest of 2 lemons, zest minced

1 egg
2 tablespoons milk
1 cup fine bread crumbs
½ cup grated aged Parmesan cheese
4 (6-ounce) salmon fillets, skin off
4 tablespoons olive oil

→ In a large bowl, gently toss the tomato, extra virgin olive oil, lovage, onion, hot sauce, salt, and lemon juice and zest until completely combined. Set aside, and let stand for 60 minutes.

→ Whisk together the egg and milk until combined thoroughly. In a separate bowl, combine the bread crumbs and cheese.

→ Pat the salmon fillets dry with paper towels. Dip each fillet into the egg mixture, drain briefly, and dredge in the bread crumb mixture. Use your hands to pat the coating onto the fish.

→ In a large nonstick skillet, heat the olive oil over high heat. Carefully add the fillets, and sauté them until they are evenly browned. Turn the fillets, and brown the other side until the fish is cooked. Serve immediately with the tomato lovage compote.

Yield: 4 servings

Note: Take the time to find excellent Parmesan cheese for this recipe; the results will reward your efforts. You may need to adjust the heat of the pan as the fish cooks. Don't let it brown too quickly, or the salmon won't cook evenly.

North Side Scallop and South Side Clam Chowder with an In-Between Potato Crab Cake

This dish has several components that all need to be ready at the same time. Here are some timing hints that will ensure your success:

❧ Prepare the chowder and refrigerate it overnight.

❧ Form the crab cakes, and refrigerate them for at least 1 hour, or up to 1 day.

❧ Coat the crab cakes, which can be stored for several hours.

❧ When you are almost ready to serve this dish, reheat the chowder and brown the crab cakes.

❧ At the last moment, add the clams to the chowder and heat them through, and pan sear the scallops.

South Side Clam Chowder:

5 pounds littleneck clams in the shell (about 60)	2 cups heavy cream
¼ cup water	1 cup white dry vermouth
1 cup chopped onion	1 cup lovage leaves
¼ pound butter (½ cup)	1 teaspoon Tabasco
4 cloves garlic, minced	½ teaspoon salt
1 cup shredded potato	Ice bath

❧ Place the clams in a large pot with a tight fitting lid. Add the water, and steam the clams over medium heat until they open and heat through, about 10 minutes. Remove the meat from the shells, and reserve it in the refrigerator. Strain the remaining liquid through cheesecloth or a coffee filter. Reserve 1 cup of the clam liquid.

❧ In a thick-bottomed saucepan, sauté the onion in the butter until cooked through and translucent. Add the garlic, and cook a few minutes longer. Add the potato, cream, vermouth, and reserved clam liquid. Bring the soup to a simmer, cover it, and cook for 20 minutes over low heat, stirring occasionally.

❧ In batches, process the soup with the lovage in a blender until completely puréed. Add the Tabasco and the salt, and adjust the seasoning to taste.

❧ Pour the chowder into a storage container, and cool it rapidly by immersing it in an ice bath, stirring the chowder frequently as it cools. Refrigerate overnight.

❧ Just before serving, gently reheat the chowder, stirring frequently. Add the clam meat, and heat it through.

❧ *Every seaside inn should have a signature chowder; this is ours. It's named after the source of the fish we use in our remote location. The intense, celery-like flavor of the lovage is the key to this chowder.*

Note: A variety of clams, including canned, work in this recipe. When steaming fresh clams, don't overcook them. When the shells open, the clams are almost done. Only another minute is needed to cook them through; any longer and they will become rubbery. Leaving the clam meat whole makes the chowder look more interesting when it is served. Be sure to taste the chowder before serving it, and add salt, if necessary. The clams will add some salinity, but more may be needed. Cooling the chowder quickly will preserve the light green color that the herb purée gives.

Potato Crab Cake:

1 pound baking potatoes, peeled and diced (about 3 cups)

3 eggs

1 pound fresh lump crab meat, well drained (about 2 cups)

½ cup snipped chives

1 teaspoon salt

1 teaspoon freshly ground white pepper

1 tablespoon water

1 cup all-purpose flour

1 cup instant mashed potato flakes

4 tablespoons butter

◆ Preheat the oven to 350°F. Lightly grease a baking sheet.

◆ Steam the potato until tender. Pass it through a food mill, or mash it lightly with a fork. Spread the potato on the baking sheet, and dry in the oven for 10 to 15 minutes, stirring occasionally. Let the potato cool for several minutes.

◆ In a large bowl, whisk 2 of the eggs lightly until slightly frothy. Add the mashed potato, crab, chives, salt, and pepper, and stir until completely combined. Form the mixture into 6 cylinder-shaped cakes, about 3 inches tall by 2 inches wide. Refrigerate for at least 1 hour, or up to 1 day.

◆ Whisk together the remaining egg with the water. Roll the crab cakes in the flour, then dip them in the egg mixture, and finally roll them in the potato flakes. They may be stored in the refrigerator for several hours until you are ready to cook them.

◆ Preheat the oven to 400°F. Heat the butter in a skillet over medium heat, and brown the crab cakes evenly, about 5 minutes. Place them in the oven, and continue heating for 5 minutes.

Note: The moisture content of potatoes varies. Drying the potato is necessary to help the crab cakes bind. Feel the potato as it dries; it will feel dry to the touch when done. Try using a mold to form the crab cakes. They should be tall enough to protrude from the chowder when you serve it. As you are coating the crab cakes, take the time to shake off the excess flour and allow the egg mixture to drain from them. This will help the coating adhere and prevent it from falling off as you fry the crab cakes. Use one hand to handle the cakes when they are dry and the other when they are wet: you won't coat your fingers, and the cleanup will be faster.

North Side Scallops:

4 tablespoons butter

¾ pound large sea scallops, patted dry

Salt and freshly ground black pepper

✦ Heat the butter until frothy in a hot skillet. Place the scallops in the butter and sear until the edges are crispy and slightly brown. Season the scallops lightly with salt and pepper. Turn them over, and turn off the heat.

Garnishes:

Chive oil

Lovage leaves

✦ To serve, pour the chowder into 6 warm, wide, shallow soup bowls. Place a crab cake in the center of each, and add a seared scallop. Garnish with some chive oil and lovage leaves, and serve immediately.

Yield: 6 servings

Recipe reprinted, with permission, from *Open Kitchen: A Chef's Day at The Inn at Bay Fortune* by Michael Smith (Callawind Publications, 1998).

✦ **Although fresh lovage may be hard to find, its effect makes the search worthwhile. As with most chowders, the flavor of this one benefits greatly from being stored overnight.**

john zenger

executive chef
❧❧
Esplanade Restaurant
Portland, Oregon

*i*T AMUSES THIS CHEF THAT LOVAGE IS "a kind of a culinary pun. It tastes like celery; it looks like celery; it smells like celery but it isn't. I get a kick out of that," chuckles Zenger.

He became aware of the "breadth and variety of the world of food" at a young age. He was born of Oregon natives in Managua, Nicaragua, where his father served as a Foreign Service officer. The senior Zenger's job took the family all over Latin America and Africa where the young Zenger often accompanied his mother, an avid cook, to local food markets.

It wasn't food he first studied, however, but linguistics. He left Oberlin College after abandoning his linguistic studies and next turned to food. He honed his culinary skills in various Portland area restaurants and a sushi bar in San Francisco. He moved to chef positions at two small bistros, one in Ohio and one in Vermont, before taking advanced placement at the New England Culinary Institute of Montpelier in Vermont in 1987.

After a stint running the kitchen at a small resort in Antigua, Zenger decided he'd "had enough of the roving life and returned to roost in Portland, taking a line position with the RiverPlace (then Alexis) Hotel." There he spent the next two years working up to the sous-chef position in which he assisted the restaurant's two previous chefs not only with the nuts and bolts side of kitchen operations but also by contributing to the tone of the menus and to the direction of restaurant and banquet service.

Somewhere in this period, lovage became one of his favorite herbs. "It's not an all-purpose herb," he says, adding that "it was a challenge for me to come up with ways to use it where it showed itself well. It has a big flavor that tends to be a bit astringent. It's kind of like cilantro — it doesn't appeal to everybody. It's an acquired taste. You can't just pluck some off the bush and eat it like you can with some herbs."

Lovage is a favorite of Zenger's, though, because of the things it does very well. "I love the plant; I like how enormous it is. I find it real decorative. It's a great garnish. It's like parsley in that it holds up well under heat lamps or when placed on hot plates. It's really nice in cocktail sauce; it stands up well to all those flavors." He likes it with duck and feels its ability to show off the sweet elements of other foods enables him to create enticing dishes even with otherwise bland ingredients.

He has been the executive chef at Esplanade in the RiverPlace Hotel since 1995. He participates in a number of culinary charities including Share Our Strength, a national hunger relief organization; Operation Frontline, an educational program for people at risk of hunger; and the American Heart Association and the Edgefield Children's Center.

The RiverPlace Hotel is a Mobil four-star/AAA four-diamond property and has been included in *Gourmet* magazine's Top Tables list. *Condé Nast Traveler* named the RiverPlace Hotel to its 1998 Gold List, citing it as one of the top hotels in the world.

Sturgeon with Black Butter and Caperberries with Wild Rice—Lovage Griddle Cakes

Wild Rice—Lovage Griddle Cakes:

6 cups water
1 pound wild rice
1 tablespoon salt plus a little extra
2 cups all-purpose flour
1 tablespoon kosher salt
1 tablespoon sugar

3 eggs
1 cup milk
1 bunch green onions, thinly sliced
1 tablespoon chopped lovage leaves
Pepper
2 tablespoons butter

Sturgeon with Black Butter and Caperberries:

2½ pounds fresh sturgeon* (preferably Columbia River sturgeon), cut into 6 portions
Salt and pepper
Rice flour
2 to 3 tablespoons peanut oil

1 pound butter (2 cups)
24 caperberries,** rinsed
Juice of 2 lemons
1 bunch chives, snipped
½ bunch parsley, chopped

If sturgeon is not available, you could substitute any firm-fleshed white fish such as swordfish, ono, cod, catfish, or tuna.

**You can use capers as a substitute for the caperberries. Use only 2 teaspoons capers per person.*

✢ To prepare the griddle cakes, combine the water, rice, and 1 tablespoon of the salt in a large pot. Bring to a boil, reduce the heat to a simmer, and cook until the rice grains have softened and are beginning to explode and all the water has been absorbed. Remove from the heat. If any water remains, let the rice drain in a colander for several minutes. Spread the rice on a cookie sheet and refrigerate until cold, about 2 hours.

✢ While the rice is cooling, make the batter. Combine the flour, kosher salt, and sugar in a large bowl. Make a well in the center of the flour mixture, add the eggs, and beat them with a whisk, incorporating the flour a little at a time. If the mixture becomes too thick, add a little of the milk. When the mixture is smooth, add the rest of the milk, the onion, and the lovage. Season with salt and pepper. Thin the batter with a little milk, if necessary, to achieve a consistency like that of heavy cream. Stir the rice into the batter.

✢ In a heavy skillet, cook spoonfuls of the batter in the butter. Keep the griddle cakes hot.

✢ To prepare the fish, season the sturgeon with salt and pepper, and dredge it in rice flour. Wipe out the skillet used for the griddle cakes with a paper towel. Add the peanut oil and heat it over medium heat. Sauté the fish for 4 minutes on each side. Keep the fish warm while finishing the sauce.

✢ This is a popular lunch menu dish; it just flies out the door. The sturgeon provides a nice textural counterpoint to the rice. The pancakes can be really bland, so we looked for something assertive. Lovage's ability to show off the sweet elements of other foods fits the bill.

✢ A watercress salad simply dressed with a red wine vinaigrette or a simply prepared fresh, green vegetable such as asparagus, broccoli, or green beans would make an outstanding accompaniment.

❧ To prepare the sauce, melt the butter in the same skillet over medium heat, allowing the butter to brown. Add the caperberries and lemon juice. Remove from the heat, and add the chives and parsley.

❧ To serve, arrange 2 griddle cakes in the center of each of 6 dinner plates. Place the fish on top, and spoon some of the sauce over each griddle cake. Serve piping hot.

Yield: 6 servings

Three-Way Duck Consommé with Lovage and Apple Wood Smoked Bacon

This is an involved and time-consuming recipe, which is most easily made over the course of two days. It's probably best to save this one for a special occasion or a formal meal.

Day one: Start early! Bone the ducks, make confit of the legs, make the stock, assemble the raft for use the following day, and marinate the breast meat.

Duck Confit:

2 whole ducks	6 sprigs rosemary
1 pound (about 2 cups) kosher salt	6 whole cloves
Olive oil, if needed	1 head garlic, split
6 bay leaves	

❧ Bone the ducks: remove the legs and breast meat whole from the birds, leaving the carcass intact. If you're unsure of how to do this, ask your butcher to do it for you. Reserve the necks and giblets for the duck stock.

❧ To prepare the confit, salt the legs very heavily, using the entire pound of salt. Let stand for 2 hours. The salt extracts the water from the legs, leaving the flavorful solids behind.

❧ Preheat the oven to 275°F. While the legs are in the salt, render the fat from the ducks: remove the skin from 1 breast, and reserve it and both breasts, one with skin and the other without. Trim and save all other skin left on the carcasses and any fat from the cavity of each. Reserve the carcasses for the duck stock. Place all skin and fat in a large saucepan, cover with water, and cook over high heat until the water has evaporated and all that remains are the cracklings and the liquid, yellow fat.

❧ **This recipe is the duck equivalent of the old story about how "every part of the pig is used except the squeal." Here, every part of the duck but the quack is processed and cooked differently and everything ends up being used in the soup.**

lovage/zenger

✦ Rinse the salt off the legs, and pat them dry with paper towels. Place the legs in a roasting pan, and strain the yellow fat over them. If the fat does not cover them fully, add olive oil until the legs are submerged. Add the bay, rosemary, cloves, and garlic. Place the pan in the oven for 4 to 5 hours; there should be no resistance when the legs are pierced with the point of a paring knife. Carefully remove the legs from the fat, and reserve 1 leg for the garnish. Transfer the other 3 legs to a nonreactive (stainless steel, not aluminum) crock. A tall Mason jar also works well. Strain the fat over the legs in the crock, covering them completely. The fat acts as a seal, so be sure no meat protrudes above the fat.

Note: These legs will keep, refrigerated, for about 6 months, so the next time you need confit for something, you won't need to go through all this! These legs are intensely flavored and can be used to make a nice garnish. Crisp them in a skillet with no oil. Once crisped, shred the meat and use it as you would bacon bits — over green salads or for soups. The fat can also be used in sautés as you would olive oil.

Timesaver Tip: You can buy prepared duck confit from some gourmet shops.

Duck Stock:

6 sprigs thyme
4 bay leaves
2 stalks celery, diced
1 carrot, diced
1 onion, diced
2 teaspoons peppercorns

1 tablespoon butter
Reserved duck carcasses, necks, and giblets
2 to 3 pounds chicken backs and necks
1 cup dry white wine
2 gallons water

✦ Preheat the oven to 350°F. In an ovenproof pan, sauté the thyme, bay, celery, carrot, onion, and peppercorns in the butter for a few minutes; do not brown.

✦ Add the duck carcasses, necks, and giblets and the chicken backs and necks to the pan, and roast for 60 minutes. Transfer everything to a large (10 to 12-quart) stockpot. Deglaze the roasting pan with the wine, being careful to scrape the pan well to loosen any bits stuck to the bottom. Add the contents of the pan to the stockpot with the water, and bring to a boil over high heat. Reduce the heat, and simmer for about 4 hours, occasionally skimming the particles and fat that accumulate on the surface. Strain through a fine-mesh strainer, reserving the liquid and discarding the solids. Skim all the fat from the surface of the stock, clean the stockpot, and return the stock to it. Boil vigorously over high heat until the stock has been reduced to 1 gallon. Allow the stock to cool, and refrigerate it overnight. Store it in the stockpot if you have room in the refrigerator because the stock will be cooked in the same stockpot again tomorrow.

(continued on next page)

> ✦ **Lovage loves duck. The astringent celery overtones of the herb perfectly balance the sweet richness of this meat.**

lovage/zenger

Raft:
1 bunch lovage
Reserved skinless breast from 1 duck
1 leek, split
1 carrot

6 egg whites and shells
2 tablespoons soy sauce
¼ cup dry sherry

✦ Remove the leaves from the lovage stems, and reserve the leaves for the garnish. Dice the breast, and cut the lovage stems, leek, and carrot into 1-inch sections. Put the diced duck, lovage stems, leek, and carrot in a food processor, and process until the mixture has the texture of chunky peanut butter.

✦ Add the egg whites, soy sauce, and sherry, pulsing the processor to combine them. Transfer to a bowl, crush the egg shells into the egg mixture, and refrigerate overnight.

Duck Breast Marinade:
1-inch piece ginger, thinly sliced
2 tablespoons hoisin sauce*
2 tablespoons sake or white wine
1 tablespoon honey

1 tablespoon rice vinegar
1 tablespoon soy sauce
Reserved breast with skin from 1 duck

Hoisin sauce, which is made from soybeans, garlic, chiles, and various spices, is available in Asian markets and many supermarkets.

✦ Combine the ginger, hoisin sauce, sake, honey, rice vinegar, and soy sauce in a glass dish or sealable plastic bag. Add the breast, and turn it to coat it on all sides. Marinate the breast overnight in the refrigerator.

Day two: Clarify the stock, cook and assemble the garnishes, and enjoy the fruits of your labor.

✦ To clarify the stock, heat it until the natural gelatin that settled on the top has melted and the stock is once again liquid but still cool. Add the raft, stirring to combine it well with the stock. Continue heating the stock, gently stirring it and scraping the bottom of the stockpot every few minutes, until the liquid feels like bath water to the touch (about 120°F on an instant-read thermometer).

✦ At this point, stop stirring; the proteins in the raft will start to coagulate at this temperature, and it is essential that they not be broken apart as they do. As they coagulate, the proteins trap any sediment or impurities in the stock. This whole, rather ugly looking mess then floats to the surface of the stock, hence, the name "raft," carrying with it all the particles that cloud the stock, and leaving a crystalline brown liquid below.

⤖ Once the raft has formed, allow the stock to simmer, but not boil, for 30 minutes or so. Turn off the heat, and allow the stock to settle for a few minutes. Carefully remove a window from the center of the raft. Ladle the consommé out through this window. If bits of the raft are breaking off, strain the consommé.

Note: If you don't need 8 servings of the consommé, any remaining consommé freezes beautifully. You can serve it at another time according to the directions given below, or reduce it by one-third to one-half and combine it with pan drippings from a roasted chicken to make a flavorful sauce.

Garnishes:

Reserved lovage leaves
6 ounces smoked bacon, preferably apple wood
    smoked bacon*

Reserved marinated duck breast
Reserved duck leg

*Apple wood smoked bacon is available at many farmer's markets, by mail order, and from gourmet shops. You could substitute any sweet smoked bacon such as maple smoked bacon.

⤖ Cut the lovage leaves into chiffonade, and set aside.

⤖ Cut the bacon into matchstick-sized pieces, and gently sauté them until crisp. Drain the bacon, and set it aside. In the same pan, sauté the marinated breast until it is cooked to medium. When it is cool enough to handle, slice the duck breast thinly. Set aside.

⤖ Crisp the leg in a skillet with no oil. Once the leg is crisp, remove it and discard the skin. Shred the leg meat finely.

⤖ To serve, arrange the bacon, sliced breast meat, and shredded leg meat in soup bowls. Sprinkle the lovage over the top. Serve the consommé from a soup tureen or pour it from a silver teapot over the garnishes.

Yield: 8 servings

⤖ **This dish can really stand on its own, and, since you sweated over a stove for two days to make it, you want to show it off. It's an excellent first course for a formal meal and also makes a nice lunch. For lunch, you could add a light and neutral baguette, if you wish.**

marjoram

Origanum majorana

*n*ATIVE TO PORTUGAL AND POPULAR throughout Europe, marjoram's sweet aromatic scent and spicy flavor are also well liked across North America. In addition, marjoram is a common ingredient in Greek, Polish, Italian, Mexican, French, Austrian, and Scandinavian cooking.

The early Romans believed that Venus gave marjoram its delightful scent to remind mortals of their own beauty. At times, the herb has been used to make love potions, and many herbal bridal bouquets include marjoram. In Greek, the word for marjoram comes from the words *oros,* meaning "mountain," and *ganos,* meaning "joy," and is loosely translated as "joy of the mountain."

Also called sweet marjoram and sometimes knot marjoram, marjoram has a mild taste that is sweeter than that of its cousin, oregano. It can be hard to tell the two plants apart, and they're often interchanged. Marjoram leaves are oval shaped and hairy and are a light green color on the top side but a grayer shade on the underside. They are smaller and lighter in color than oregano leaves.

A little marjoram can go a long way so use it with a light touch in bean soup, vegetable marinades, and salad dressings. Marjoram is often used in the same way as oregano in tomato sauces, with beef, pork, and fish, and with vegetables such as eggplant, potatoes, carrots, and lima beans. It goes well with bay, thyme, and basil and, because it is a common flavoring for sausage, has earned the title "sausage herb."

Toss some marjoram into green salads, sprinkle some into stuffings, and add some to vinegar for a Mediterranean touch in your dressings and marinades. Marjoram, mint, and lemon balm are a popular combination for herb tea.

zov karamardian

chef/owner

Zov's Bistro
Tusten, California

bORN IN ISRAEL OF ARMENIAN DESCENT, Zov Karamardian says she "pretty much grew up with marjoram." Her mother used it in her daily cooking. "It has a minty character to it; it's like a secret herb you can use to flavor many things. It's full bodied; its strong taste goes a long way."

Marjoram is among her "very, very favorite herbs." Her other top picks are rosemary, tarragon, and flat-leaf parsley.

Zov is short for her Armenian name, Zovak, which means "whirlpool in the ocean." Whirlpool in the kitchen is more like it. Zov opened Zov's Bistro in 1987 after many years of running a popular catering business from her home. First offering lunches, Zov's Bistro was so popular she soon added dinner service. She also operates an adjoining bakery that *Gourmet* magazine named among the Best Bakeries in Southern California. Zov also offers cooking classes with guest chefs. Culinary talents run in Zov's family. Her mother was well known for her voluntary community cooking, and her grandmother was a professional chef in Turkey.

Healthy eating and fresh ingredients are the trademarks of Zov's Bistro, which serves an eclectic blend of California cuisine and Mediterranean and Middle Eastern dishes. Zov has been known to make a 50-mile trek to the Los Angeles produce market during the early morning hours to ensure getting the freshest fruits, vegetables, and herbs.

Despite an out-of-the-way location, Zov's Bistro draws notable people such as Bette Midler and Chuck Norris. Best-selling author Dean Koontz has written of Zov's Bistro and even dedicated his novel, *The Dark Rivers of the Heart,* to Zov and her husband. In fact, Koontz has said, "If aliens ever try to abduct me, I will refuse to go — unless Zov caters the mother ship."

Karamardian received the Gold Award from the Southern California Restaurant Writers, and Zov's Bistro was nominated for Restaurant of the Year by the same organization. She was honored with the 1997 Pacesetter Award by the Roundtable for Women in Foodservice, and received a Profiles in Excellence Award from the Executive Women's Forum. Zov's Bistro has consistently earned top ratings in the *Zagat Survey,* and Zov has been featured in *Gourmet, Bon Appétit, Sunset Magazine,* and *Nation's Restaurant News.* She has also appeared in various television programs on the Food Network. One of her pet projects is to visit inner-city high schools weekly to encourage students to pursue a restaurant career.

She is active in culinary organizations such as Les Dames d'Escoffier, Women Chefs and Restaurateurs, the International Association of Culinary Professionals, the American Institute of Food and Wine, and the Southern California Culinary Guild.

Grilled Eggplant Appetizer with Marjoram–Kalamata Olive Topping

→ This is a two-part recipe for a hearty appetizer with robust flavor. The olive topping can be made ahead.

Marjoram–Kalamata Olive Topping:
½ bunch marjoram, chopped
½ bunch rosemary, chopped
½ bunch thyme, chopped
2 cups kalamata olives, pitted

2 ounces anchovies in oil
1 cup olive oil
½ cup sliced garlic
¼ cup coarse black pepper

Grilled Eggplant Appetizer:
2 eggplants, cut into ¼-inch rounds
¼ bunch rosemary, chopped
2 tablespoons crushed garlic
1 tablespoon salt

1 tablespoon black pepper
1 tablespoon dried thyme
Juice from ½ lemon

→ To prepare the olive topping, preheat the oven to 400°F. Combine the marjoram, rosemary, thyme, olives, anchovies, oil, garlic, and pepper in a baking pan, and bake for 20 to 25 minutes. The topping will be bubbly and aromatic. Keep warm while preparing the eggplant.

→ To prepare the eggplant, increase the oven temperature to 450°F. Combine the eggplant, rosemary, garlic, salt, pepper, thyme, and lemon juice in a large mixing bowl. Mark each side of the eggplant on a grill, and bake for about 10 minutes or until tender.

→ To serve, spread a spoonful of the olive topping on each eggplant slice. Serve immediately.

Yield: 4 servings

michael olson

*I*T WAS ONCE A COMMON SIGHT to see Michael Olson pedaling from farm to farm in search of the freshest produce. Today, he drives a car and has cultivated more than 100 local suppliers to keep his kitchen stocked with the freshest ingredients.

"When I first moved from the city to the country, I didn't have a car," explained the Saskatchewan-born chef. "Biking was a good way to get to know the area."

As a founding member of the Knives and Forks Chef's Federation, he has worked to promote the use of organically grown farm produce throughout the province.

One local grower, for instance, now delivers fresh herbs, still in potting soil, with roots attached, three times a week. The herbs, displayed on the wall, serve as décor in the restaurant as well as adding a great aroma to the air and fresh flavor to the food.

There's no comparison between using "these living herbs and those that were alive a couple of weeks ago. It's not even close," insists Olson.

Marjoram is among those herbs always present in Olson's kitchen. "Marjoram is very interesting. You can use it simply, but it's complex at the same time. It has a smell that makes me think of sunshine. It can be a warm weather herb; it takes very well to any vegetable or vegetable salad."

Although oregano and marjoram are related, Olson prefers marjoram to oregano because "where oregano has a heat, almost a peppery bent to it, marjoram is quite a bit softer. It has an aroma with a background of eucalyptus or sage. Although it's not as coarse as sage, it does have that sort of bent to it."

There's a garden at On The Twenty, but it's mostly for aesthetic purposes, says Olson. He does, however, grow some herbs at home. He designed a huge barbecue in his yard, and grows a number of herbs right by the barbecue, he says, "so we can pluck them right from the ground to season our food."

As a teen, Olson's passion for hockey took him to Japan to play the sport. It was while working in a Japanese health food store that he learned to appreciate simple foods and freshness, the cornerstones of Japanese cuisine. He studied science at the University of Saskatchewan before eventually enrolling in the culinary program at George Brown College of Applied Arts and Technology in Toronto. He trained under a number of Toronto chefs and cooked in several prestigious restaurants in Ottawa and in Oakville, just outside of Toronto. In 1989 in Toronto, he opened Liberty, a restaurant that earned Olson a reputation for his culinary creativity. He has competed in culinary competitions in the United States, Switzerland, Ireland, and Vancouver, British Columbia.

executive chef

On The Twenty
Jordan, Ontario

marjoram/olson

Corn and Pepper Chowder

6 ears corn, shucked
¼ cup diced carrots
¼ cup diced celery
1 small onion, diced
Olive oil
3 cups water

½ cup julienned basil leaves

2 green or red peppers or a combination, diced
  (about 2½ cups)
1 teaspoon butter
1 teaspoon chopped marjoram
1 teaspoon chopped thyme
Salt and pepper

> ❧ The marjoram offsets the otherwise sweet flavors of the corn and peppers, giving this popular chowder a heady, meadow-like aroma.
> ❧ Serve a rustic bread and a wine like Riesling or Gewürztraminer with this chowder.

❧ Cut the kernels from the corn, and reserve both the kernels and the cobs. Sauté the diced carrots, celery, and onion in a stockpot with a small amount of olive oil until the vegetables are soft but not brown. Add the corn cobs and water, and cook for about 20 minutes. Strain and reserve the stock.

❧ In a medium saucepan, cook the peppers in the butter, covered, over low heat until soft but not brown. Add the stock and cook for 20 minutes.

❧ Place one-third of the mixture in a blender or food processor, and purée. Return the mixture to the saucepan. Add the marjoram and thyme, and season with salt and pepper.

❧ To serve, garnish the chowder with the basil.

Yield: 6 servings

Lemon Marjoram Roasted Chicken

1 (4-pound) chicken
1 lemon, sliced
½ large bunch marjoram

1 medium onion, sliced
Salt and pepper

> ❧ Marjoram lends a full-bodied base to this roasted chicken with sharp lemon tones.
> ❧ Serve with a green salad and roasted potatoes. This chicken goes great with Chardonnay; choose one that's not too heavily oaked.

❧ Preheat the oven to 350°F. Gently loosen the skin from the chicken breasts with your fingers. Slip a lemon slice and a small sprig of marjoram in between the skin and the chicken. Fill the chicken cavity with the remaining lemon and marjoram, and the onion. Season with salt and pepper. Roast the chicken for 60 minutes or until the juices run clear.

Yield: 4 to 6 servings

Marjoram and Roasted Garlic Mushroom Salad

2 tablespoons olive oil
8 ounces mixed mushrooms such as portobello,
    shiitake, cremini, or oyster mushrooms, sliced
4 cloves garlic, roasted (page 222)
1 teaspoon chopped marjoram

Salt and pepper
1 green onion, chopped
2 tablespoons balsamic vinegar
4 cups mixed salad greens, including a sharp-flavored
    green such as radicchio

✦ Heat the oil in a large sauté pan over medium-high heat. Add the mushrooms, and sauté them until they are three-quarters of the way cooked. Squeeze the roasted garlic from its skin. Add the roasted garlic and the marjoram, season with salt and pepper, and stir gently. Add the onion and balsamic vinegar, and cook another 2 minutes.

✦ To serve, place some of the warm mushroom mixture on the mixed salad greens.

Yield: 4 servings

Note: Other sharp-flavored greens that could be used include curly endive, escarole, Belgian endive, and frisée. What you're looking for here is a range of flavors — sweet, lemony, sharp — which cannot be provided by just one type of lettuce or a vinaigrette.

✦ Marjoram adds a sweet scent to the otherwise woody aroma of the mushrooms. It goes well with the caramelized sugars in the roasted garlic.
✦ Serve this dish as an appetizer or a salad. A light-bodied red wine like Gamay would be a good accompaniment.

Peach Marjoram Salsa

4 ripe peaches, peeled and pitted
1 red pepper, seeded and halved
4 sprigs basil
2 sprigs marjoram
2 sprigs mint

2 sprigs thyme
2 tablespoons olive oil
Juice of 1 lemon
Salt and pepper

✦ Place the peach, red pepper, basil, marjoram, mint, thyme, oil, lemon juice, and a little salt and pepper in a food processor, and process until the peach is in ¼-inch dice.

Yield: about 2 cups

✦ Peach pairs with the soft edge of marjoram to provide a good foil for grilled fish or poultry.
✦ Serve this salsa over grilled rainbow trout or salmon, or with any light-fleshed, sea-going fish such as halibut or sea bass. It's also great with grilled chicken, quail, or partridge.

Roasted Tomato Marjoram Vinaigrette

12 plum tomatoes, halved
1 tablespoon sugar
Salt

2 cups olive oil
½ cup plus 2 tablespoons balsamic vinegar
1 tablespoon chopped marjoram

✤ Preheat the oven to 275°F. Place the tomatoes on a cookie sheet, and season them with the sugar and a little salt. Bake the tomatoes in the oven for 90 minutes until they are dry. Let the tomatoes cool.

✤ Place the tomatoes, oil, vinegar, and marjoram in a blender or food processor, and purée. Check the seasonings. Store the vinaigrette in the refrigerator.

Yield: about 2½ cups

Note: If the vinaigrette separates, purée it again.

✤ This vinaigrette captures the essence of summer flavors. Make a batch of roasted tomatoes and freeze some for future use.
✤ Use this vinaigrette as a dressing over a mesclun salad.

Peach, Ice Wine, and Marjoram Vinaigrette

2 ripe peaches, peeled, pitted, and sliced
1 shallot
½ cup plus 2 tablespoons olive oil

¼ cup ice wine
2 tablespoons white wine vinegar
1 teaspoon chopped marjoram

✤ Place the peaches, shallot, oil, ice wine, vinegar, and marjoram in a food processor, and purée until smooth.

Yield: about 1 cup

✤ The high acidity and fruitiness of ice wine mean that a little goes a long way.
✤ Use this vinaigrette to dress flavorful greens such as arugula or radicchio.

Mentha

*e*UROPEANS BROUGHT BOTH PEPPERMINT and spearmint, the two most popular culinary mints, with them to the New World. Here they enjoyed drinking tax-free mint tea, evading England's notorious tea tax. The Romans are credited with bringing the plant to Britain.

Mint is still popular, both as a tea and as a flavoring. Hundreds of varieties of mint are used in cuisines around the world, such as those of India, the Middle East, and Greece.

Peppermint is most often used to flavor candy, gum, tea, water, and the mint julep. This species also adds zip to peas, carrots, new potatoes, and custards.

Spearmint, also known as garden mint, is a tad milder in flavor than peppermint and is used in wheat or other grain salads such as tabbouleh and in fruit salads, jellies, chutneys, and sauces. Add spearmint to eggplant, lentils, and cream soups or to veal or lamb. This herb is often a partner of both yogurt and cucumbers, as well as peas and new potatoes. Infuse spearmint in vinegar, and make a snappy mint vinaigrette for your summer greens. Both peppermint and spearmint are often paired with chocolate.

There are a number of other varieties of mint, many of which have culinary uses. Consider growing apple mint in your garden for a strong apple-mint flavor and fragrance. Use it for tea and fruit salads. Pastry chefs often use chocolate mint to create delightful goodies, and pineapple mint has, as its name suggests, a subtle pineapple flavor and scent.

The leaves and flowers of mint are edible, though the flowers have a more subdued flavor. Add a purple contrast to salads by tossing in some mint blossoms. Mint is compatible with a number of other herbs, especially basil, parsley, tarragon, dill, and lemon balm. Like other herbs, mint is best used fresh, but unlike many herbs, it retains much of its flavor when dried. Mint can also be frozen.

Mint's versatility, flavor, fragrance, and healthful attributes prompted the International Herb Association to name mint the 1998 Herb of the Year. Mint contains vitamins A and C, as well as iron, calcium, and riboflavin, and is considered an aid to digestion, accounting for the practice of serving mints or mint tea after dinner.

Its origin, according to Greek mythology, was brought about by Pluto, god of the Underworld, who loved a nymph named Minthe. Persephone, his jealous wife, turned Minthe into the homely mint plant.

tracy pikhart ritter

chef/owner

Whistling Moon Cafe
Sante Fe, New Mexico

*T*RACY PIKHART RITTER APPRECIATES the versatility of mint. "It's a very aromatic herb. Mint can be used in appetizers as well as entrées, for savory dishes or sweet." It has such a wide variety of uses, she explains, that she's used mint as long as she's been cooking. Mint enhances other flavors in a dish or adds another flavor focus.

"It's a very ancient herb; it's always been used for teas and in a variety of cuisines all over the world. You'll find it everywhere. It's a flavor that people recognize," says Ritter.

Her favorite mint has always been spearmint. She uses it in meat dishes, with vegetables such as carrots, and with fruits. It flavors her yogurt sauce (see opposite) and chutneys, including her cilantro mint chutney. She uses it in tabbouleh (see opposite) and in pestos. She makes a sun-dried tomato mint pesto to flavor lamb. She even makes mashed potatoes with mint and cumin. Actually, she says, she uses mint with just about everything.

Her home herb garden includes three or four different mints, as well as a couple of basils and oregano, thyme, sage, flat-leaf parsley, and chives.

Ritter likes to harvest the mint plants she grows roots and all and store them in a glass of water in the refrigerator. If you buy mint from the grocery store, she advises that you shake it to remove grit and moisture, pack it loosely in paper towels, and store it in the vegetable bin in the refrigerator. Mints are pretty hardy, she says, and will keep for about a week.

Ritter was formerly the executive chef at Santacafe in Santa Fe, and during her time there, her culinary creations were featured in *Bon Appétit*, *Art Culinaire*, and *Wine & Spirit*. Santacafe garnered *Zagat Survey*'s Best Restaurant in New Mexico Award during her reign in the kitchen. She was also a guest chef at the Hotel Istana in Malaysia, where she demonstrated southwestern cuisine during the America's Cup.

Previously, Ritter worked as a recipe developer for a consulting firm, as the executive chef at the Golden Door Fitness Resort in Escondido, California, and as a consulting chef for the Cunard cruise line. She also taught French culinary techniques at the New York Restaurant School in New York, and has appeared in television programs on the Food Network.

Whistling Moon Cafe features Middle Eastern and Mediterranean cuisine. The restaurant is especially known for its salade Niçoise made with fresh tuna. The vegetarian grape leaves have a filling of pine nuts, currants, pomegranate molasses, and a number of exotic spices. A side order of spicy coriander-cumin fries is highly recommended, and a favorite dessert is the chocolate soufflé cake.

Tabbouleh with Mint

3 cups boiling water
1 cup bulgur
5 teaspoons canola oil
¾ teaspoon salt
¾ teaspoon black pepper

⅛ cup lemon juice
¾ cup chopped parsley
¾ cup chopped tomatoes (about 1 medium)
¼ cup chopped green onions
⅛ cup chopped mint

✦ Add the boiling water to the bulgur, and let stand for 30 minutes. Meanwhile, mix together the oil, salt, pepper, and lemon juice. Set this dressing aside.

✦ In a separate bowl, mix together the parsley, tomatoes, onion, and mint.

✦ If the bulgur has not absorbed all the water after 30 minutes, wait another 10 minutes, or drain the liquid and discard it. Add the bulgur and the reserved dressing to the tomato mixture, and combine.

Yield: 4 servings

Mint Yogurt Sauce

1 cup yogurt
1½ tablespoons chopped mint
½ tablespoon chopped parsley
½ tablespoon snipped dill

¾ teaspoon lemon juice
¾ teaspoon minced garlic (2 to 3 cloves)
¾ teaspoon salt
¼ teaspoon black pepper

✦ In a bowl, combine the yogurt, mint, parsley, dill, lemon juice, garlic, salt, and pepper.

✦ Chill the sauce in the refrigerator for at least 60 minutes. Refrigerated, the sauce will keep as long as a week.

Yield: about 1 cup

✦ Tabbouleh is a traditional dish of the Middle East. It's often a staple in vegetarian diets.

✦ Serve this tabbouleh warm as a side dish to accompany meat and poultry or at room temperature as a vegetarian dish with other vegetables such as eggplant.

✦ This refreshing sauce is a typical recipe of the Middle East, where it is called *cacik* (pronounced ca-SEEK).

✦ Use this sauce over grilled meat, lamb, and chicken. We use it on chicken kebabs topped with tomatoes and cucumbers. It's also tasty as a dressing over a cucumber and onion salad.

scott mason

executive chef/
managing partner
❧❧
Ketchum Grill
Ketchum, Idaho

*i*T'S MINT'S REFRESHING TASTE AND VERSATILITY that Scott Mason enjoys. Mint is readily available, he says, and grows prolifically in a part of his garden where nothing else will grow. He also grows lavender, sage, thyme, oregano, marjoram, tarragon, chives, basil, and summer savory.

Mason especially likes mint with lamb, and makes a mint pesto (see opposite) to flavor it. He also makes a mango and mint salsa for chicken, a tomato and mint salad, and an apple and mint salad. He considers mint highly compatible with all other herbs. He's particularly sweet on his pastry chef's mint ice cream (see opposite). His pastry chef, incidentally, is his wife, Anne.

As a young boy, perched atop a stepstool at his grandmother's side, Mason helped prepare family breakfasts. His first restaurant job was as a busboy at a steakhouse in his home town of Eugene, Oregon. "The guys back there [in the kitchen] were having a lot more fun than we were out on the floor," remembers Mason. To Mason, who studied biology at the University of Oregon, the fun is in "creating food and presentations that are balanced both to the eye and the palate." Food won over biology, and Mason went on to study and apprentice at a number of restaurants, including Norberts in Santa Barbara and San Ysidro Ranch in Montecito, California, where he met Anne.

The pair stashed their toques for three months while they toured the restaurants and markets of Europe. Stints in various kitchens followed before they settled in the mountains of central Idaho. At the helm of Freddy's Taverne d'Alsace, a seasonal restaurant, Mason gained expertise in Alsatian cuisine. In the off-season, he apprenticed in four restaurants in Paris and Alsace.

Freddy's Taverne d'Alsace is now Ketchum Grill. The restaurant's new American menu treats diners to updated versions of classic dishes. The house burger, for instance, is topped with fontina or Gorgonzola cheese, house-made ketchup, caramelized onions, and is served on a bun baked in the restaurant's kitchen. Ice cream, offered in a number of exotic varieties, is another example of a classic dish prepared creatively.

Snow Country Magazine named Ketchum Grill as one of the "8 best ski town restaurants" with "food rivaling Manhattan's best." The American Dairy Counsel chose Mason as one of the 21 Premier Chefs of America 1997. The Ketchum Grill was awarded *Wine Spectator*'s Award of Excellence and has been recognized by *Town & Country* magazine, the *Chicago-Sun Times,* and *Mountain Living Magazine,* as well as a number of other publications.

Mint Pesto

1 clove garlic
1 cup mint leaves
⅛ cup freshly grated Parmesan cheese

⅛ cup toasted pine nuts
¼ cup extra virgin olive oil
Kosher salt

✢ In a food processor fitted with a sharp cutting blade, process the garlic, mint, cheese, and pine nuts until smooth. Scrape the sides of the processor, and process again. Transfer the pine nut mixture to a storage container, and stir in the olive oil and a pinch of salt.

Yield: about ¾ cup

Fresh Mint Ice Cream

½ bunch mint
¾ cup sugar
1 cup heavy cream

1 cup half-and-half
½ tablespoon crème de menthe

✢ With a sharp knife, coarsely chop the mint to release the mint oils. Place the mint and sugar in a large, heavy-bottomed saucepan. Add the cream, and place the saucepan over medium heat. Heat the mint mixture to a boil, and stir until the sugar has dissolved. Remove from the heat. Add the half-and-half, and stir. Chill the cream mixture, covered, in the refrigerator overnight.

✢ Strain the cream mixture, and discard the mint leaves. Add the crème de menthe to the cream mixture, stir, and freeze it in an ice-cream maker following the manufacturer's instructions.

Yield: about 1 quart

✢ Toasting the pine nuts deepens the flavor and complements the mint, creating an earthy taste and aroma.
✢ This is an excellent sauce for leg of lamb or lamb chops grilled over wood.

✢ Here's an excellent end to a large meal. I find this ice cream very refreshing, and it doesn't have the odd green color of store-bought mint ice cream. By not using eggs for the custard, a lighter taste is achieved.
✢ Try this ice cream with chocolate chip cookies as an ice cream sandwich, or with your favorite brownies.

mexican mint marigold

Tagetes lucida

*h*ERE'S AN HERB OF MANY NAMES. Its most common nickname is Texas tarragon because it mimics tarragon and thrives under the Texas sun. Mexican mint marigold is also known as sweet marigold, probably in reference to the yellow, marigold-like blossoms that crown the plant in late summer. The English refer to it as winter tarragon, and in Mexico it's known as cloud plant.

Whatever you call it, Mexican mint marigold has a licorice flavor that does resemble tarragon and is sometimes used as a substitute for it. True tarragon aficionados, however, will tell you it doesn't have the same refined character as tarragon. They may be right. There is a difference. Mexican mint marigold has a more earthy flavor and more robust aroma. Still, it makes an acceptable tarragon substitute, although you may want to use a little less of it. Texas chefs and many gardeners like it because it's easier to grow than tarragon and can take the scorching southern heat better.

Mexican mint marigold is native to the mountains of Mexico and Guatemala. The botanical name of the genus, *Tagetes,* comes from "Tages," the name of an Etruscan deity believed to be the grandson of Jupiter; *lucida* means "bright" or "shining," a reference to the plant's bright flowers. In Texas and other warmer places, you may find Mexican mint marigold in supermarkets and produce stands. In more northern areas, you'll probably have to grow your own.

Mexican mint marigold brightens up poultry, gives a zip to green salads, sauces, eggs, and tomatoes, and adds zest to fish and shellfish. Latin Americans brew tea from its leaves.

david garrido

executive chef

Jeffrey's
Austin, Texas

$\mathcal{D}$AVID GARRIDO TEACHES HIS COOKS that "all food should have fresh herbs." He says, "herbs do something incredible to foods; they're big enhancers of flavor." Mexican mint marigold is one of his favorite herbs. Garrido started using Mexican mint marigold about 10 years ago while working for Bruce Auden in San Antonio, Texas. "Bruce would bring in anything exotic or different he could find. Every day, I knew when I came to work I'd find something new. It made my job fun."

He says Mexican mint marigold is great with rice, especially risottos. He sprinkles it into mashed sweet potatoes and tosses some in seafood. What makes it so interesting, he says, is that it has "a really complex flavor." He uses it a lot in salsas and finds it blends very well with fruits. He likes it with papaya or mango, and with jícama. He likes to combine it with chiles to make sauces.

The son of a Mexican diplomat, Garrido was born in Canada, grew up in Mexico, Puerto Rico, and Costa Rica, and was schooled in Switzerland. He trained under Stephan Pyles at Routh Street Cafe and later helped Pyles open Star Canyon restaurant in Dallas.

Along with Mexican mint marigold in his garden, he grows Mexican oregano, lemon grass, all kinds of thyme, sage, rosemary, and dill.

Garrido has been chairman of the Taste of the Nation, which raised over $100,000 for Share Our Strength, a national hunger relief organization. After winning awards at the Hill Country Wine & Food Festival, he was invited to cook at the James Beard House in New York. He was also invited to participate in a benefit for the Make a Wish Foundation, hosted by *Bon Appétit* magazine.

Garrido is the founder of Food for Thought, a fundraising project for Communities in Schools. As a representative for Chefs Collaborative 2000, Garrido works on the Adopt-a-School project to teach kids about sustainable foods. He was nominated for Five Who Care, a local television station's recognition of community service.

Garrido was named winner of *Chef Magazine*'s National Maple Leaf Farms Duckling Contest in the Best Appetizer category. He has been featured in *Food & Wine*, and *Bon Appétit,* and has developed a line of hot sauces. Garrido and his partner, Ron Weiss, recently assumed operations of the Fresh Planet Café inside the Whole Foods Market's flagship store in Austin.

Garrido is also co-author of *Nuevo TexMex* (Chronicle Books, 1998).

Peanut–Mexican Mint Marigold Crusted Tuna with Cilantro Lemon Sauce

Peanut–Mexican Mint Marigold Crust:
1 cup Mexican mint marigold leaves
½ cup unsalted peanuts

¼ cup all-purpose flour

Cilantro Lemon Sauce:
4 cloves garlic, sliced
2 serrano chiles, sliced
½ leek (white part only), diced
1 tablespoon butter

Juice of 1 lemon
¾ cup heavy cream
½ cup yogurt
Leaves of ½ bunch cilantro

Tuna:
4 (4-ounce) very fresh tuna steaks
Salt
¼ cup yogurt

1 tablespoon water
4 tablespoons olive oil

> ✦ The crunchiness of the crusted tuna creates a surprising contrast with the tart sauce.
> ✦ Serve this dish with a salad or rice.

✦ To prepare the crust, combine the Mexican mint marigold, peanuts, and flour in a food processor, and process until well mixed. Reserve the peanut mixture for the tuna.

✦ To prepare the sauce, in a medium sauté pan, sauté the garlic, chile, and leek in the butter over medium heat for 3 to 4 minutes. Add the lemon juice, and simmer for 2 minutes until the juice is completely reduced. Add the cream and yogurt, bring to a boil, and simmer for 4 minutes or until the liquid is reduced by one-quarter. Transfer the sauce to a blender. Add the cilantro, and purée until smooth. Strain the sauce, and set it aside in a warm spot.

✦ To prepare the tuna, season it with salt. Combine the yogurt and water. Coat the tuna with the yogurt mixture, and then with the reserved peanut mixture, making sure the tuna is completely covered. In a large sauté pan, cook the tuna in the oil at medium heat for 2 minutes on each side for each inch of thickness or until it reaches the desired doneness.

✦ To serve, place a tuna steak on each plate, and spoon some sauce around it.

Yield: 4 servings

Pecan Chicken Salad with Chipotle and Mexican Mint Marigold

1 teaspoon plus 1 tablespoon olive oil
4 boneless chicken breasts
1 large tomato, halved
1 ancho chile, soaked in hot water for 10 minutes
1 chipotle chile, soaked in hot water for 10 minutes
2 tablespoons brown sugar
2 tablespoons water

½ carrot, finely diced
¼ large onion, finely diced
½ stalk celery, finely diced
1 cup mayonnaise
½ cup pecans, roasted and chopped
3 tablespoons chopped Mexican mint marigold
½ teaspoon sea salt

> ✤ You could grill the chicken breasts and blend the sauce the day before so that this dish is quick to prepare on the day of serving.
> ✤ Serve with fresh country bread and a Sauvignon Blanc.

✤ Lightly oil the chicken breasts with the 1 teaspoon of olive oil, and grill them until done. Allow the chicken breasts to cool, dice them, and reserve. Grill the tomato about 3 minutes on each side. Remove the tomato from the grill when the tomato is bubbly and the skin comes loose. Discard the skin.

✤ In a blender, combine the tomato, chiles, brown sugar, and water. Purée the tomato mixture until smooth, and strain it to remove the seeds. Transfer the tomato purée to a saucepan, and simmer for about 4 to 6 minutes until it has been reduced to ½ cup. Set the tomato purée aside.

✤ In a medium-sized sauté pan over medium heat, sauté the carrot, onion, and celery in the remaining oil for about 5 minutes, stirring the vegetables several times. They should be crunchy but not have a raw flavor.

✤ In a stainless steel bowl, combine the sautéed vegetables, reserved chicken, tomato purée, mayonnaise, pecans, and Mexican mint marigold, and season with a little salt.

Yield: 4 servings

Summer Pasta with Apricot–Mexican Mint Marigold Sauce and Vegetables

Pasta:
⅓ pound capellini

1½ tablespoons olive oil

Apricot–Mexican Mint Marigold Sauce:
2 shallots, sliced
1 teaspoon olive oil
½ cup Sauternes or white wine
½ cup water

1 teaspoon sugar
Juice of 1 lemon
Sea salt
4 fresh apricots, peeled and pitted

Vegetables:
2 baby beets, peeled and quartered
2 baby cocktail artichokes, trimmed and quartered
2 baby turnips, peeled and quartered
½ cup julienned basil
4 baby carrots

2 tablespoons chopped Mexican mint marigold
4 baby sunburst squash, cut in half
4 baby zucchini, cut in half lengthwise
1 medium red onion, finely chopped (about ½ cup)
1½ tablespoons extra virgin olive oil

⤖ To prepare the pasta, cook the capellini in a large pot of boiling salted water for 2 to 3 minutes until slightly soft. Transfer the pasta to a container of ice water to stop the cooking. Drain, and toss the pasta with the olive oil to keep it from sticking. Set the pasta aside.

⤖ To prepare the sauce, in a medium saucepan, combine the shallot and oil. Cook over medium heat for about 1 minute or until the shallot is translucent. Add the Sauternes, water, sugar, lemon juice, and some salt. Bring to a boil, and cook for 2 minutes. Transfer the shallot mixture to a blender, add the apricots, and purée until smooth, about 1 minute. Set the sauce aside in a warm spot.

⤖ To prepare the vegetables, cook the beet, artichoke, and turnip in a pot of boiling water for about 20 minutes or until they feel tender when speared with a knife. Set the beet mixture aside. In a sauté pan over medium heat, combine the basil, carrot, Mexican mint marigold, squash, zucchini, onion, and oil, and cook for 30 seconds. Add the reserved pasta, and cook for about 2 minutes until the pasta is hot. (If the pasta was refrigerated, allow an extra minute or two for reheating.)

⤖ To serve, divide the pasta among 4 plates, place some of the beet mixture on top, and spoon the sauce around the pasta.

Yield: 4 servings

Timesaver Tip: The capellini can be cooked up to 1 day ahead and kept refrigerated.

⤖ For this sauce, you do not cook the apricots, and so their refreshing qualities are preserved. I always recommend using ripe fruit. You may substitute peaches or mangoes for the apricots in the sauce.
⤖ Serve with a good sourdough bread and a green salad with a balsamic vinaigrette, and to drink, maybe a Riesling or very fruity Chardonnay.

Couscous and Wild Mushrooms with Guajillo–Red Pepper–Mexican Mint Marigold Sauce

Wild Mushrooms:

1 pound wild mushrooms, such as portobello, shiitake, chanterelle, or cremini mushrooms
2 cloves garlic, chopped
2 shallots, sliced in half
2 sprigs basil
1 sprig rosemary

1 sprig thyme
2 tablespoons extra virgin olive oil
½ cup white wine
Juice of ½ lemon
½ teaspoon sea salt

Guajillo–Red Pepper–Mexican Mint Marigold Sauce:

2 shallots, chopped
2 sweet red peppers, cut into small pieces
1 guajillo chile
1½ teaspoons chopped Mexican mint marigold

1 teaspoon olive oil
¾ cup white wine
1½ teaspoons sugar
1 teaspoon sea salt

Couscous:

1 cup couscous

Sea salt

➤ Choose your favorite mushrooms for this dish. The sauce adds a colorful touch of flavor.
➤ Serve this dish as an appetizer followed by fish or game.

➤ To prepare the mushrooms, preheat the oven to 375°F. Rinse the mushrooms lightly in cold water. In a stainless steel pan, mix the garlic, shallot, basil, rosemary, and thyme. Place the mushrooms on top of the garlic mixture. In a bowl, combine the oil, wine, and lemon juice. Sprinkle the oil mixture on top of the mushrooms, and season with the salt. Cover the pan with foil, and bake for 30 minutes. Strain the mushrooms, and set them aside in a warm place. Keep the mushroom liquid hot for the couscous.

➤ To prepare the sauce, in a medium-sized sauté pan, sauté the shallot, red pepper, chile, and Mexican mint marigold in the oil for 1 to 2 minutes. Add the wine, sugar, and salt, and bring to a boil. Cook the shallot mixture for 2 minutes, and transfer it to a blender. Purée the shallot mixture until smooth. Strain the sauce, and set it aside in a warm place.

➤ To prepare the couscous, place it in a stainless steel bowl and pour 2 cups of the reserved hot mushroom liquid over the couscous. (If you do not have 2 cups of mushroom liquid, add enough water or chicken or vegetable stock to equal 2 cups.) Cover, and let stand for 4 minutes. Uncover, separate the couscous grains gently with a fork, and season with sea salt.

➤ To serve, divide the couscous among 4 plates. Place the mushrooms next to the couscous, and spoon some sauce around it.

Yield: 4 servings

jay moore

executive chef
❋

Hudson's on the Bend
Austin, Texas

*i*F IT'S A WALK ON THE WILD YOU SEEK (culinarily speaking), Hudson's on the Bend is the place for you. While the restaurant is known for its wild game dishes, Jay Moore has made his reputation pursuing his passion, classic and nouvelle sauces.

Hudson's on the Bend food has been dubbed "hill country cuisine." The restaurant features many varieties of game grilled over pecan wood or smoked in a limestone smokehouse, which is in the midst of an extensive herb garden.

The herb garden includes lemon grass, marjoram, oregano, sage, pineapple sage, rosemary, and a 25-foot bay tree. Edible flowers such as lavender, yucca, nasturtiums, begonias, and hibiscus grow there too, as does Mexican mint marigold.

"I like the flavor and sweetness [of Mexican mint marigold] as opposed to tarragon," says Moore. He also likes its ability to thrive in the Texas heat. "Tarragon wilts here," he adds. He uses Mexican mint marigold in place of tarragon in many soups and sauces, and in veal stock.

The garden began as small raised beds, but Moore and Hudson's on the Bend owner Jeff Blank eventually converted the whole yard into an organic garden. It provides not only fresh ingredients for the kitchen but also a pleasant atmosphere where diners can enjoy coffee, dessert, and cigars at garden tables.

Moore began as a self-taught chef and eventually attended the Culinary Institute of America. Moore and the restaurant have been featured in *The New York Times, Cooks* magazine, *Nation's Restaurant News, The Dallas Morning News,* the *Fort Worth Star-Telegram, Texas Monthly, Chili Pepper Magazine, Men's Journal,* and *Field & Stream.*

Moore participates in fundraising dinners for Share Our Strength, Aids Services of Austin, and the Austin Symphony. He's also active in the Texas Food and Wine Festival, where he won the People's Choice Award for rattlesnake cakes with chipotle cream.

Known as the most romantic restaurant in Austin, Hudson's on the Bend is located about 30 minutes outside of Austin overlooking Lake Travis. The restaurant was named one of the Top 50 Restaurants in America by *Condé Nast Traveler* magazine.

Moore and Blank conduct cooking classes in which they teach game cooking to local hunters and their spouses. In addition, Moore has developed a line of sauces, Hudson's on the Bend Gourmet Sauces, so home cooks can recreate some of his flavors for their meat, game, poultry, and fish dishes. The sauces, such as Mexican mint marigold honey mustard, are featured in the *Texas Parks and Wildlife Christmas Catalogue* and are available in many Texas, as well as national, gourmet shops.

Although Hudson's on the Bend specializes in game, the menu includes a number of fish and seafood dishes, as well as veal, pork, and beef.

Corn Pudding with Mexican Mint Marigold

¾ cup all-purpose flour
¼ cup sugar
2½ tablespoons baking powder
1 teaspoon salt or seasoned salt
¾ teaspoon cayenne
5 whole eggs
1 (8-ounce) can creamed corn

5 tablespoons butter, melted
½ cup heavy cream
1 pound corn kernels, fresh or frozen
½ Anaheim chile, seeded and cut into ¼-inch pieces
½ green pepper, seeded and cut into ¼-inch pieces
½ red pepper, seeded and cut into ¼-inch pieces
2 tablespoons chopped Mexican mint marigold

✤ Preheat the oven to 375°F. Mix together the flour, sugar, baking powder, salt, and cayenne. In another bowl, mix together the eggs, creamed corn, butter, and cream. Combine the flour mixture with the egg mixture. Stir in the corn kernels, chile, green and red peppers, and Mexican mint marigold.

✤ Butter an 18 by 12-inch sheet cake pan and dust it with flour. Pour the batter into the pan, and bake for 40 to 45 minutes or until the pudding is golden brown and firm.

Yield: 8 servings

> ✤ Corn pudding is a little like spoon bread and cornbread; it serves as a starchy side dish. Our version spices things up a bit with peppers and Mexican mint marigold.
> ✤ The Mexican mint marigold adds a light flavor to this corn pudding, making it a good accompaniment for fish, chicken, or pork.

Mexican Mint Marigold–Champagne Sorbet

1¼ cups sugar
1 cup water
1 egg white
¾ cup white wine

½ to ¾ cup minced Mexican mint marigold
½ cup champagne
½ cup white dry vermouth
Juice and zest of 2 limes

✤ Combine the sugar and water in a medium-sized saucepan, and bring to a boil to dissolve the sugar. Set the sugar water aside until it is cool. Add the egg white, wine, Mexican mint marigold, champagne, vermouth, and lemon juice and zest, and combine. Place the mixture in an ice-cream maker, and freeze following the manufacturer's instructions.

Yield: 1 quart

Variations: You could substitute any combination of mint, lemon basil, thyme, dill, basil, and sorrel for the Mexican mint marigold.

Shopping Tip: You can buy a split of champagne, which holds 6.3 ounces, at many liquor stores. If you make this recipe and the blueberry champagne mousse with lemon balm (page 83) at the same time, you will use nearly all of the champagne. The sorbet can be kept in the freezer for serving another day. The mousse is best served the day it is made.

> ✤ This tasty sorbet has long been a tradition with our special dinners. We've also served it as a summer dessert.
> ✤ Place a small scoop of the sorbet in a champagne glass, and drizzle with champagne. Add a pecan sandy cookie, and you have a sumptuous summer dessert.

Jay and Jeff's Unbreakable Mexican Mint Marigold Béarnaise Sauce

9 extra large egg yolks
3 dashes hot sauce
2 tablespoons mixed herb vinegar*
1 teaspoon salt

Juice of 1½ lemons
1 pound butter (2 cups), melted, kept hot
½ cup Mexican mint marigold leaves

Herb vinegar is available in supermarkets and gourmet shops and from Hudson's on the Bend, or you can make your own.

❧ Blend the eggs, hot sauce, vinegar, salt, and lemon juice in a blender for 3 to 4 minutes at high speed. With the blender still on high, add the hot butter very slowly, 1 tablespoon at a time. The heat from the butter will cook the eggs. If the sauce becomes too stiff, add 1 to 2 tablespoons of warm water to thin it. Add the Mexican mint marigold leaves, and blend for 15 to 20 seconds. Either serve the sauce immediately, or keep it warm until needed.

Yield: about 3 cups

Note: At Hudson's on the Bend, we store this sauce in a thermal pitcher that has been heated with warm water. The sauce may become too stiff after sitting for 30 minutes or more. If it does, add 1 to 3 tablespoons water — just enough so that the sauce can be poured with a ladle. A blender is recommended for making this sauce, but a food processor will do.

Variations: For hollandaise sauce, omit the Mexican mint marigold. For Maltese hollandaise sauce, substitute ½ cup blood orange juice and 2 tablespoons lemon zest for the lemon juice.

Green Gazpacho with Mexican Mint Marigold

30 tomatillos, husked
3 cloves garlic
Leaves of 2 bunches cilantro
2 cucumbers, peeled and seeded
Juice of 4 limes

Mexican crema or sour cream
Pico de gallo

2 tablespoons sugar
½ cup chopped Mexican mint marigold leaves
½ cup virgin olive oil
⅜ cup sherry vinegar
Salt

12 shrimp, smoked or boiled

❧ Place the tomatillos, garlic, cilantro, cucumber, lime juice, sugar, Mexican mint marigold, oil, vinegar, and a little salt in a food processor, and purée. Chill thoroughly.

❧ To serve, garnish the gazpacho with Mexican crema, pico de gallo, and shrimp.

Yield: 4 servings

oregano

Origanum

OREGANO IS ANOTHER CONFUSING HERB. There are at least 20 species of *Origanum*, but often the same species is of different intensity and flavor when cultivated in different environments. For instance, *O. vulgare,* which has a pungent flavor when grown in the Mediterranean region, is much less flavorful when grown in cooler climates says Robin Siktberg, a horticulturist with The Herb Society of America. For this reason, the species is generally considered to be an ornamental oregano and is shunned as a culinary herb throughout North America.

Greek oregano (*O. vulgare* hirtum) is very flavorful and is preferred for cooking because of its strong peppery flavor with hints of balsam and clove. This species is a hardy perennial with gray-green hairy leaves and tiny white flowers. You'll sometimes find oregano labeled Greek oregano or as "grown in Greece," but most often it's simply labeled oregano.

When you are choosing plants for your kitchen garden, taste the leaves of different varieties until you find the one you like best. Incidentally, you may want to do the same thing if you use commercially dried oregano. Some commercial oreganos are actually a blend of two or three varieties, and some may even include thyme and marjoram, which are both related to oregano. A number of plants, such as *Lippia graveolens,* commonly sold as Mexican oregano because of its oregano flavor, are not in the *Origanum* genus at all but are used in Spanish and Mexican cooking in the same way as oregano is used.

Native to the Mediterranean and Asia, oregano is also cultivated in Spain, Europe, and both North and South America.

Oregano, which is in the mint family, is especially tasty with tomato-based dishes. Oregano's pungent, peppery flavor embellishes mushrooms, broccoli, eggplant, peppers, spinach, summer squash, and tomatoes, making it especially useful to the vegetarian cook. Its spicy flavor lends itself well to salt-free diets. Lamb, egg, and cheese dishes are also flavored with oregano. Try it with poultry, fish, and beef, too. Stir some into salads, sauces, and marinades, as well as into dressings, butters, bread doughs, and vinegars. Oregano is good in soups and stews. Pair oregano with other herbs such as garlic, thyme, basil, and parsley. Marjoram is a reasonable substitute for oregano, although you'll need to use a bit more marjoram to get the same intensity of flavor.

kim miller

executive chef

Belleview Biltmore Resort & Spa
Clearwater, Florida

*I*N KIM MILLER'S OPINION, OREGANO is underrated. While rosemary, thyme, and tarragon are roasted, toasted, and stewed, too often oregano merely tops off pizza. For the life of her, Miller doesn't know why. "It's not like rosemary where when you put it in a dish that's all you taste. Oregano has a nice subtle flavoring. It's one of my most favorite herbs."

Her favorite way to use oregano is in moussaka, a Greek dish of eggplant and lamb. She also uses oregano to make her blends for dishes such as herb crusted rack of lamb. At home, oregano flavors her herb roasted chicken and a generous helping of oregano seasons her light version of ratatouille (page 136), a recipe she created while executive chef at Bern's Steakhouse.

Fresh oregano tastes "kind of light and fragrant with somewhat of a buttery richness," says Miller. The difference between fresh and dried oregano, she says, "is like drinking instant coffee versus brewing it fresh."

Miller has demonstrated her culinary artistry to royalty and heads of state, to diners at Bern's, and to guests of the Belleview Biltmore Resort & Spa. She has worked at the Airodrome Hotel in Croydon, England, the private Tyrellis Wood Golf Club in Surrey, England, and the world renowned cancer facility, The Royal Marsden hospital. She was also executive chef for the English government and for dignitaries associated with Queen Elizabeth. Miller arrived in the United States after being selected from more than 160 applicants for 10 places in the culinary program of Professor Greg Parker in Coral Gables, Florida, and was placed at the Pier House Resort and Spa, Key West, Florida. She also served as executive chef at the Marriott Hotel in Fort Lauderdale and was executive chef at Maritana Grill at the Don Cesar Beach Resort, the only four-diamond restaurant in the St. Petersburg area.

In her native England, Miller earned several degrees — two in cooking, one in health and hygiene, and another in the training and teaching of culinary arts.

Now executive chef at the newly renovated Belleview Biltmore Resort & Spa in Clearwater, Florida, she oversees a staff of 50 and three dining areas. It's her goal to "bring good food to everybody." That includes home cooks. "I'm not of the school that says 'that's my recipe and I'm not going to share.' If people enjoy what I'm preparing, I'm happy to share [recipes] with everybody."

Only the second female chef for Interstate Hotels, Miller has traveled around the United States and Canada, winning several culinary competitions and teaching her culinary skills to other company executive chefs.

She has won awards in the Broward County Healthy Hearts Cook-Off and in the Culinary Olympics of Canada.

Crispy Herb Roasted Pork

Citrus Marinade:

1 tablespoon chopped cilantro
1½ teaspoons cornstarch
½ cup grapefruit juice
½ cup sour orange juice*

¼ cup orange juice
¼ cup chopped garlic (about 12 cloves garlic)
⅛ cup chopped onion

Sour oranges, sometimes called bitter oranges or Seville oranges, can often be found in Cuban or Latin markets. You can make your own sour orange juice by adding the juice of 1 lemon to the juice of 2 oranges.

Pork:

1 (2½ to 2¾-pound) boneless pork loin or any other pork cut such as pork tenderloin

Herb Rub:

1 tablespoon chopped oregano
¼ tablespoon chopped parsley
¼ teaspoon chopped thyme
¼ teaspoon snipped chives

¼ teaspoon freshly ground black pepper
⅛ teaspoon salt
2 tablespoons olive oil

> ➤ I've given pork a Cuban twist with a citrus marinade and topped it off with an herb rub in which oregano predominates. The rub adds a surprisingly buttery flavor with light earthy undertones.
> ➤ The ratatouille with oregano (page 136) is a good accompaniment to this dish.

➤ To prepare the marinade, blend the cilantro, cornstarch, juices, garlic, and onion in a blender or food processor.

➤ To marinate the meat, place the pork in a nonreactive pan, and pour the marinade over the pork. Cover and marinate at least 8 hours in the refrigerator or, preferably, overnight.

➤ Preheat the oven to 350°F. Remove the pork from the marinade, and let drain while preparing the herb rub.

➤ To prepare the herb rub, combine the oregano, parsley, thyme, chives, pepper, and salt. Stir in the oil.

➤ To finish the meat, rub the herb mixture over the pork on all sides. Bake the pork until the temperature taken with a meat thermometer reaches 165°F and the juices run clear, about 20 minutes per pound for the pork loin. The cooking time may vary depending on the cut of pork used.

Yield: 6 servings

Ratatouille with Oregano

1½ tablespoons olive oil

1 medium onion, cut into medium dice
(about ½ cup)

1 small eggplant, cut into medium dice (about 1 cup)

1 medium zucchini, cut into medium dice
(about ½ cup)

2 medium tomatoes, cut into medium dice
(about 1 cup)

1 medium yellow squash, cut into medium dice
(about ½ cup)

3½ tablespoons finely chopped oregano

Salt and pepper

❧ Heat the oil in a sauté pan. Add the onion, and sauté until the onion is soft. Add the eggplant, and sauté until soft. Add the zucchini, and cook for 1 to 2 minutes. Add the tomato, squash, oregano, and some salt and pepper. Cook, covered, for about 2 to 4 minutes. Adjust the seasonings, if necessary.

Yield: 4 servings

Variation: Other vegetables such as peppers can be included, and the quantities of each vegetable can be adjusted depending on taste and what's available.

❧ Here is my version of a traditional ratatouille without the customary heavy tomato sauce. This recipe keeps it light and allows oregano's earthy flavor to come through.

❧ Ratatouille makes a wonderful vegetarian dish, and it's also great with all kinds of meat and fish. I like to serve ratatouille over pan seared grouper. It's also good with chicken. Pour ratatouille over cooked chicken breasts, top with Parmesan or mozzarella cheese, and melt the cheese under the broiler.

costas spiliadis

*M*ANY RESTAURATEURS PLACE VASES filled with fresh flowers on the tables. Never one to follow the crowd, Costas Spiliadis adds a new twist by placing potted plants, delivered fresh every day, on his tables. And not just any plants will do — his pots sport oregano plants. And not just any oregano will do, either. It must be authentic Greek oregano. It's so authentic, Spiliadis carried the seeds from Crete himself. "I love the oregano that is found on the island of Crete. It has a stronger aroma and is less bitter than any other I've tasted." If you want to try Spiliadis's favorite oregano at home, you'll probably have to grow it yourself. The variety to buy is *O. kaliteri.*

When you are seated at Milos, you're instructed to pluck oregano leaves from the table-top plant and swirl them in a saucer of olive oil for your bread dipping pleasure. Even the olive oil is Greek. Long before olive oil was trendy, Spiliadis insisted on olive oil in his kitchen; extra virgin olive oil, of course, pressed to his specifications from the olives of his sister's olive groves in Greece.

When people first encountered the oregano plants on the tables, says Spiliadis, "they wondered what the hell it was all about. They would feel it and make a wonderful discovery. They saw it and tasted it, not in a package, but in its natural form."

There are two main reasons Spiliadis likes oregano. "The first and most important reason is that I grew up in a country where oregano grew all over; it grows wild in the mountains, in the countryside, virtually everywhere."

The second reason is that "oregano best complements the tastes of Greek cuisine. Whether used with lamb, fish, or vegetables, it brings out the best in these foods."

Spiliadis says oregano's taste is sharp and peppery, with the capacity to wake you up. "It's explosive; it takes over your palate." Yet, he says, it also has a delicate side.

Oregano's understated flavor typifies the simplicity and balance present in the kind of food he serves at Milos. Stronger flavored herbs such as tarragon and sage would totally overwhelm and conceal the subtle nuances of these foods, says Spiliadis.

He's been called obsessive, even a madman, for his insistence on serving only the freshest food. When he first opened the Montreal Milos in 1980, he made the 750-mile round trip to New York twice a week in a borrowed car because the fish available to him locally didn't meet his standards.

Spiliadis first left his native Patras, Greece, to study sociology at New York University. He moved to Montreal for post graduate work at Concordia University. In both Montreal and New York, Milos serves as a cultural center where poetry readings, art exhibits, and musical performances take place. Spiliadis is a member of Montreal's Hellenic community and has received the Deka Award for Hospitality from the Montreal Greek Board of Trade.

chef/owner
⇝⇜
Milos
Montreal, Quebec
⇝⇜
Milos
New York, New York

Milos Special

Tzatziki Dip:
2 cloves garlic, chopped
½ cucumber, seeded and diced
4 teaspoons extra virgin olive oil
1 cup goat's milk yogurt*

½ tablespoon snipped dill
½ tablespoon white wine vinegar
Salt and pepper

*Purchase yogurt with a thick consistency, or drain thinner yogurt by hanging it in cheesecloth until much of the liquid drains away.

Vegetables and Cheese:
Canola oil
1 medium zucchini, sliced paper thin
½ medium eggplant, sliced paper thin
All-purpose flour

½ cup roughly chopped oregano
Salt
1 (2 by 6-inch) slice Kefalograviera cheese

❧ Eggplant, zucchini, and Kefalograviera cheese are all common ingredients in the Greek diet. What makes this dish special is how these ingredients are combined. Although fried, this dish is light, crisp, and delicate. The chopped oregano adds the finishing touch.

❧ Together, this appetizer, Greek salad (see opposite), and shrimp spetsiota (see opposite) make a wonderful meal. Add some rustic bread if you wish.

❧ To prepare the dip, place the garlic, cucumber, oil, yogurt, dill, vinegar, and a little salt and pepper in a food processor, and purée until smooth. Refrigerate the dip while preparing the vegetables.

❧ To prepare the vegetables, place enough oil in an electric skillet or a frying pan to reach a depth of 1 inch, and preheat the oil to 350°F. Place the zucchini and eggplant slices in some warm water in a pan deep enough to hold them separate from each other. Using only a few of the vegetable slices at a time, shake off the excess water and dredge the slices in flour, shaking off any excess. Dip the slices back in the water, and then drop them carefully into the hot oil. Fry the vegetable slices until crispy and golden brown. Using a slotted spoon, remove the vegetable slices and place them on paper towels to drain. Sprinkle the vegetable slices with some of the oregano and a little salt.

❧ Replenish the oil and preheat it, if necessary. Dip the cheese slice in water and then in flour, repeating this procedure three times. Fry the cheese slice in the oil until golden brown. Remove the cheese slice, and cut it into 4 to 6 pieces, depending on the number of people being served.

❧ To serve, arrange slices of zucchini, eggplant, and cheese on a plate with the tzatziki dip beside.

Yield: 4 to 6 servings

Note: Kefalograviera cheese is similar to Gruyère cheese but is made with sheep's milk. Tzatziki is a yogurt-based dip popular as a Greek appetizer.

Shrimp Spetsiota

3 tablespoons extra virgin olive oil
2 onions, finely chopped
3 ripe tomatoes, peeled, seeded, and chopped
1 cup dry white wine
Salt and pepper

1 pound jumbo shrimp, peeled and deveined
½ pound feta cheese
3 tablespoons chopped flat-leaf parsley
3 tablespoons chopped oregano

➤ In a large sauté pan, heat the oil. Add the onion, and sauté for a few minutes until the onion is lightly golden. Add the tomato, and cook over moderate heat until somewhat reduced, about 5 minutes. Add the wine and a little salt and pepper, and cook the tomato sauce for 2 to 3 minutes. Add the shrimp, and cook, turning them periodically, just until they are done, about 5 minutes. Turn off the heat. Crumble the cheese over the shrimp and sauce, and stir. The residual heat of the sauce will melt the cheese. Sprinkle on the parsley and oregano, and serve.

Yield: 4 servings

➤ This is an adaptation of a traditional dish from the Greek island of Spetses. Tomatoes are always part of the recipe, and the short cooking time helps maintain the freshness of the tomato sauce.

➤ Serve this dish with a Greek salad (see below) or lightly grilled mixed vegetables.

Greek Salad

½ English seedless cucumber, sliced
½ green pepper, thinly sliced
½ large sweet Spanish onion, sliced horizontally
1 teaspoon red wine vinegar
2 large, vine-ripened tomatoes, cut into chunks
1 tablespoon chopped oregano

1 teaspoon chopped flat-leaf parsley
1 teaspoon chopped purslane*
4 tablespoons extra virgin olive oil
Salt and pepper
8 to 10 kalamata olives
4 slices feta cheese, cut into chunks

Arugula may be substituted for the purslane in this recipe.

➤ In a bowl, mix the cucumber, pepper, onion, and vinegar. Add the tomato, oregano, parsley, purslane, oil, and a little salt and pepper. Toss the mixture gently, but well. Top with olives and cheese, and serve.

Yield: 4 servings

➤ This is an authentic Greek salad in which the quality of the ingredients makes all the difference. Feta cheese is a classic Greek sheep's milk cheese and is often paired with olives. If necessary, you could substitute good quality dried oregano. Our oregano is dried immediately after being harvested right at the farm.

parsley

Petroselinum

PARSLEY WAS THE FIRST FRESH HERB I ever cooked with. I became obsessed. Parsley here, parsley there, parsley in and on everything. You know how it is with firsts. "What's the green stuff?" asked my husband. "Hey, what's with all the green stuff?" queried the kids.

There was very good reason for my obsession. Parsley is readily available, and its clean, fresh, slightly peppery flavor has the ability to unite many different flavors. It adds a touch of color to otherwise colorless dishes, and is chock-full of nutrients such as vitamins A, C, several B vitamins, calcium, and iron.

Parsley is a member of the carrot family and one of the ingredients in the classic seasoning blends fines herbes and bouquet garni. According to folklore parsley symbolizes both revelry and victory.

You'll find curly-leaf parsley and flat-leaf, or Italian, parsley. The curly-leaf variety is used most often as a garnish, while many cooks prefer the flat-leaf variety for its stronger flavor.

Eventually I branched out to include a wide variety of herbs in my cooking, but parsley still holds a special charm for me. There's still "green stuff" everywhere.

nora pouillon

*N*ORA POUILLON, CHEF/OWNER OF NORA and Asia Nora, both in Washington D.C., shares my passion for parsley. She shuns the curly parsley, however, in favor of the Italian, or flat-leaf, variety.

Many chefs are hard pressed to pick one herb as a favorite. Pouillon has "a favorite herb for favorite dishes." Yet, if when stranded on a desert island she could have just one herb, it would be parsley. "It goes with everything and contains a lot of nutrients. I put it in nearly everything — mashed potatoes, salads, stews — so many things." She grows parsley along with basil, lemon thyme, rosemary, tarragon, and cilantro in a garden next to the restaurant.

Recently *Fitness Magazine* honored Pouillon as one of America's healthiest chefs, and her unique, organic lifestyle was the topic of a feature article in Japan's top food and living magazine. The American Tasting Institute named her 1996 USA Chef of the Year. Her cookbook, *Cooking with Nora,* was published in 1996 by Park Lane Press. The cookbook features seasonal organic menus, wine suggestions, nutritional information, "Nora's Notes," and recipes created especially for the home kitchen. Both Nora and Asia Nora were named among the 20 Top Tables in Washington by *Gourmet* readers. In 1997, Pouillon was named Chef of the Year by the International Association of Culinary Professionals (IACP).

Organic before organic was in, Pouillon searched for local organic farmers to provide ingredients for her menu, which changes daily. Pouillon's commitment to healthy eating doesn't end at her kitchen door. A former consultant for Fresh Fields, the Maryland-based chain of natural food stores, she developed flavorful, low-fat dishes for the prepared foods counter. She serves on the board of directors of Public Voice for Food and Health Policy, an advocacy group promoting legislation for healthy foods. The Vienna-born chef is also a founding board member of Chefs Collaborative 2000, an organization promoting closer ties between chefs and farmers. She also worked with the U.S. Department of Agriculture to improve the quality and flavor of school lunches.

Decorated with American folk art, Nora opened in 1979 featuring organic (pesticide-free produce and hormone-free meats) multi-ethnic cuisine. The restaurant has been praised for its high quality and healthy approach to eating. Pouillon later opened Asia Nora on M Street where she creates her own artful interpretation of dishes from all across Asia.

chef/owner

Nora
Washington, D.C.

Asia Nora
Washington, D.C.

Parsley Sauce

5 to 6 shallots
6 anchovy fillets
3 tablespoons capers
2 bunches flat-leaf parsley, roughly chopped
1½ to 2 cups water

1 tablespoon white wine vinegar
1 tablespoon chopped garlic
½ teaspoon red chile flakes
¼ to ½ cup olive oil
Salt and black pepper

→ Preheat the oven to 350°F.

→ Remove the outer skin from each shallot. Place the shallots in an ovenproof baking pan. Cover the pan, and roast the shallots until very soft, about 30 to 40 minutes.

→ Place the roasted shallots, anchovies, capers, parsley, water, vinegar, garlic, and chile flakes in a blender, and purée until smooth. Slowly add the oil until the parsley mixture has the consistency of sauce. Season with salt and pepper.

Yield: 4 cups

Persian Lamb and Parsley Ragout

4 tablespoons butter
16 green onions, chopped
4 large bunches flat-leaf parsley, chopped
3 tablespoons canola oil
3 pounds trimmed lamb shoulder, cut into 1-inch cubes
Salt and freshly ground pepper

Water or beef stock (page 217)
1 lemon, quartered
Juice of 2 lemons
1 cup dried red kidney beans, soaked overnight, or
  2 (16-ounce) cans, slightly drained

→ In a heavy 4-quart pot, heat the butter, add the onion and parsley, and cook until the parsley is dark green. Set aside.

→ In a large skillet, heat the oil, add the meat, and brown it lightly (you may have to do this in batches). Season with salt and pepper. Combine the meat with the reserved parsley mixture in the pot. Add enough water to cover the meat, and the lemon juice and quarters. Cover, and simmer until the meat is almost tender, about 60 to 90 minutes. Add the kidney beans, and adjust the seasonings. Continue cooking until the beans are soft and the lamb is tender.

Yield: 8 to 10 servings

Variation: This ragout can also be made with beef. A vegetarian version can be made by substituting portobello mushrooms for the meat.

rosemary

Rosmarinus officinalis

*i*TALIAN BUTCHERS OFTEN INCLUDE A rosemary sprig with meat purchases so customers will remember to keep coming back to their shop. You can remember rosemary because it's a very robust and hardy herb. It has long been associated with loyalty, remembrance, and love and is often seen at funerals and weddings. Early Romans would always place rosemary in bridal wreaths and present sprigs of it to wedding guests. In Victorian times, a sprig of rosemary was always included in the bridesmaid's bouquet. During the Middle Ages, people believed that if you tapped another person with a blooming rosemary sprig, that person would fall in love with you. Rosemary is one of the many herbs Shakespeare mentioned in his writings. In *Hamlet,* Ophelia remarks, "There's rosemary, that's for remembrance."

Rosemary's name is derived from the Latin *ros,* meaning "dew," and *maris,* meaning the "sea," resulting in a literal translation of "dew of the sea." This name is certainly appropriate for an herb that thrives along the coastal hills of the Mediterranean.

Rosemary resembles pine needles in appearance and smell. It has a spicy flavor that's also a bit peppery. It's a really pungent herb and, therefore, generally is used sparingly. Rosemary also has a tough texture that's easier to swallow if the leaves are finely chopped. Since it is less delicate than many other herbs, it holds up well to the long cooking times of soups, stews, and stocks. Whole sprigs can be simmered and then removed from the dish at serving time. Rosemary also retains its flavor better than most herbs when dried or frozen. In Provence, it's an ingredient of bouquet garni.

Rosemary is a good seasoning for poultry, fish and shellfish, beef, pork, lamb, and veal. It flavors marinades, dressings, lentils, eggs, and breads. Some people even use it to add a sweetness and spice to fruit salads and cakes, jams, jellies, and wine. Try combining rosemary with mild herbs such as parsley, chervil, and chives.

trish morrissey

executive chef

❧ ❧

Philadelphia Fish & Company
Philadelphia, Pennsylvania

*R*OBUST ROSEMARY IS A FAVORITE HERB of Trish Morrissey. She remembers rosemary as a staple, along with basil, in her mother's garden. "It's really fragrant and totally infuses in anything," she says. Its sweet, piney scent transforms any meat into an aromatic and tasty treat. Morrissey especially likes to use it in mashed parsnips, gratins, and marinades. It's also compatible with potatoes, beans, bean soup, and chicken.

Because of its pungent flavor, a little rosemary goes a long way. One-eighth to one-quarter teaspoon will season a dish for four people.

Rosemary, a member of the mint family, is also a great garnish. Morrissey suggests removing all but the top few leaves from a stem and using the stem as a skewer for shrimp or vegetables. "It looks really neat and adds a lot of flavor," she says. Since rosemary is actually a perennial shrub, its stems are quite sturdy. Mince the leaves you removed from the stems finely, and sprinkle them around the edge of plates. Whole stems can be placed upright in most anything to add height. You can, by the way, use both the leaves and the flowers for either cooking or garnishing.

Before joining Philadelphia Fish & Company, Morrissey was the first female chef at the dining room at The Ritz-Carlton in Philadelphia. During her reign there, the Ritz-Carlton dining room was awarded the Distinguished Restaurants of North America Award and was named one of Philadelphia's Top 20 Tables by *Gourmet* magazine two years in a row. She joined The Ritz-Carlton as a pastry apprentice while still attending The Restaurant School in Philadelphia, where she earned an associate degree in culinary arts.

In 1997, Morrissey received the PANACHE award, presented to women for achievement in the hospitality field by the Philadelphia Delaware Valley Restaurant Association. She was also inducted into the Philadelphia chapter of Les Dames d'Escoffier. Recently, she was awarded second prize for her grilled honey-glazed center-cut pork chop with crabmeat poblanos and polenta in the Pennsylvania Pork Producers Council recipe contest.

A self-described "hands-on executive chef crazy for detail," Morrissey "finds true pleasure in creating perfect basics with a twist." She gives traditional dishes that twist by adding an ethnic touch or by incorporating unusual or exotic ingredients. Born in Carlisle, Pennsylvania, she has lived in Italy, Germany, Panama, California, and northern Virginia. Yet the greatest influences on her culinary creations, she says, come from her mother and grandmother and their Moroccan, French, and Italian style of cooking.

Philadelphia Fish & Company is known for its innovative and trendsetting ways and serves fish from all over the world, with an emphasis on fresh and seasonal seafood. Philadelphia Fish & Company was the first Philadelphia restaurant to own a smoker. The restaurant is located in the heart of the Old City section of Philadelphia.

Grilled Tuna on Penne Tossed with Rosemary, Roasted Garlic, and Roasted Red Pepper Sauce

2 heads garlic, top half cut off
1½ cups chicken stock (page 219)
¼ cup white wine
1 pound penne
1 small jar roasted red peppers or 2 peppers, roasted, seeded, and skinned

1 tablespoon chopped rosemary plus 6 rosemary sprigs
6 (5-ounce) tuna steaks
Salt and pepper
Cooking spray

> ❧ This is a healthy, low-fat dish that tastes great.
> ❧ A green salad or grilled mixed vegetables would be excellent with this dish.

❧ Preheat the oven to 350°F. Place the garlic in a small ovenproof roasting pan. Add ½ cup of the chicken stock and the wine. Cover with foil, and bake in the oven for 30 to 40 minutes or until the garlic is soft. (Toward the end of the baking time, bring a large pot of salted water to a boil for the pasta.) Remove the garlic from the oven, and set aside.

❧ Cook the pasta in the boiling water for about 10 to 12 minutes. Meanwhile, preheat an outdoor grill or stovetop grill pan, prepare the sauce, and grill the tuna.

❧ To prepare the sauce, use a knife to remove the garlic from the skins; it should pop out easily. Place the garlic in a blender with the roasted pepper, remaining chicken stock, and chopped rosemary. Pulse the blender until the sauce is blended but slightly chunky. Pour the sauce into a saucepan, and warm it over low heat. Season the sauce with a little salt and pepper. Keep the sauce warm.

❧ To prepare the fish, sprinkle the tuna steaks with some salt and pepper. Spray them with cooking spray, and grill them until they are medium rare or cooked to your preference.

❧ To serve, drain the pasta, and toss it in a bowl with the sauce. Divide the pasta into 6 bowls, and top each with a tuna steak. Garnish each bowl with a sprig of rosemary.

Yield: 6 servings

Grilled Portobello Sandwiches with Rosemary

2 sprigs rosemary
6 large portobello mushrooms
2 tablespoons extra virgin olive oil
1 tablespoon balsamic vinegar

Salt and pepper
12 thick slices hearty sourdough bread
6 slices Havarti cheese

➤ This is a new twist for your ordinary grilled cheese sandwich.
➤ This hearty sandwich could be served for lunch on its own or with a green salad or French fries.

➤ Remove the rosemary leaves from the stems, and reserve the leaves. Remove the stems and dark underside of the mushrooms with a knife. Place the mushrooms in a dish, and drizzle them with the oil and vinegar. Sprinkle the mushrooms with the reserved rosemary and a little salt and pepper. Marinate the mushrooms for at least 60 minutes.

➤ Preheat an outdoor grill or stovetop grill pan. Grill the mushrooms for 3 minutes on each side. Meanwhile, toast the bread. Place a mushroom and a slice of cheese between 2 slices of bread, wrap the sandwich in foil, and heat on the grill or in the oven until the cheese melts. Serve the sandwiches hot.

Yield: 6 servings

Rosemary and Potato Frittata

1 tablespoon vegetable oil
1 medium onion, sliced
3 medium potatoes, boiled and diced
1 tablespoon chopped rosemary or 1 teaspoon dried rosemary

10 eggs, beaten
½ cup freshly grated Parmesan cheese
½ teaspoon salt
½ teaspoon cracked pepper

➤ This is great comfort food. A frittata is an Italian version of an omelet. Where an omelet has ingredients folded inside the egg, a frittata has the ingredients mixed throughout, and the slow baking results in a firmer texture.
➤ Nothing is better on a cold day than a frittata with a bowl of hot soup. A green salad is another good accompaniment.

➤ Preheat the oven to 375°F. In a large, ovenproof frying pan, warm the oil. Add the onion, and sauté for 5 minutes. Add the potato and rosemary, and stir until combined. Add the eggs and Parmesan cheese. Stir slowly, and add the salt and pepper. Cook for 5 minutes, stirring each minute. Place the frying pan in the oven, and bake the egg mixture for 15 to 20 minutes or until firm but not dry. Remove the frying pan from the oven, place a plate over the frying pan, and invert to transfer the frittata to the plate.

Yield: 6 servings

Rosemary Roasted Chicken

1 (6-pound) chicken
4 tablespoons minced garlic
4 tablespoons minced rosemary or 2 tablespoons
  dried rosemary

1½ teaspoons salt
1 teaspoon cracked black pepper
¼ pound butter (½ cup), softened

➤ Preheat the oven to 375°F.

➤ Rinse the chicken in warm water. Mix the garlic, rosemary, salt, pepper, and butter until well combined. Smear the butter mixture under the skin of the chicken breast and legs, as well as inside the cavity. Place the chicken on a rack over a roasting pan. Tuck the wings under, and tie the legs together. Place the pan in the oven, and bake about 60 minutes or until cooked through. Remove the pan from the oven, and let stand 10 minutes before carving the chicken.

Yield: 6 servings

➤ This recipe is simple but good. My mom taught me how to roast chicken when I was a young girl, and this is the recipe.

➤ Serve this fragrant dish with fresh seasonal vegetables and mashed potatoes.

richard chamberlain

chef/owner

Chamberlain's Prime Chop House
Addison, Texas

WHEN RICHARD CHAMBERLAIN ENROLLED in home economics class in high school, he did so to meet girls. No one knew (not even Chamberlain himself) that 20 years later he'd be grilling up Texas beef in his own restaurant.

Chamberlain relies extensively on fresh herbs to create the refined flavors that are the foundation of his reputation. Although he confesses to having a favorite herb for different seasons, he often counts on rosemary, especially in winter. There's rosemary on his portobello mushroom appetizers drizzled with homemade Worcestershire sauce, in his veal, lamb, and chicken dishes, and in some wild game dishes. "We use rosemary in just about every soup we make. It also fries very well; whole sprigs can be used to add interest and flavor."

"As a flavoring, I like it because, from a meat standpoint, it's very versatile." And, he says, rosemary blends very well with other traditional meat seasonings such as peppercorns and garlic.

Rosemary shrubs surround the restaurant, and so the herb is easily accessible to Chamberlain. In the Texas climate, rosemary and many other herbs stay green all winter. He also grows mint, chives, and, in summer, basil. Overall, he says, he likes rosemary's "big and bold flavor; it's a perfect match for steakhouse cuisine."

Chamberlain studied culinary arts at El Centro College in Dallas, simultaneously serving an apprenticeship at The Mansion on Turtle Creek. Later, while executive chef at San Simion Restaurant in Dallas, he was selected as one of the Rising Stars to Watch by *Food & Wine* magazine. He has worked as executive sous-chef under Dean Fearing at The Mansion on Turtle Creek and at the Hotel Bel-Air in Los Angeles.

Prior to opening Chamberlain's, he spent three years as the executive chef of the Little Nell Hotel in Aspen, where he received national attention for pioneering American Alpine cooking. During that time, Chamberlain was nominated by the James Beard Foundation as the Best Chef in the Northwest and was featured in national publications including *Connoisseur, Dossier, Ski, Destinations, Harper's Bazaar, Food & Wine, Esquire*, and *W Magazine*.

While keeping with the traditional fare of a chop house by offering veal, lamb, and pork chops, the menu at Chamberlain's also includes seafood. Shortly after opening in 1993, Chamberlain's was named one of the country's top new restaurants by *Bon Appétit* magazine. In addition, it was rated the best steak house in Dallas by *The Dallas Morning News* and *The Dallas Observer*. In 1997, *Texas Monthly* named Chamberlain's one of the top 10 steakhouses in the state and the best steakhouse for epicures. *Gourmet* magazine readers rated Chamberlain's among the 20 Top Tables in the Dallas/Fort Worth area.

Whiskey Braised Venison with Creamy Garlic Polenta

Whiskey Braised Venison:

10 cloves garlic
¾ cup diced carrot (about 2 large carrots)
¾ cup diced onion (about 1 medium onion)
½ cup diced celery (about 1 medium stalk)
½ cup diced mushrooms (about 3 to 4 medium mushrooms)
¼ cup olive oil
1 cup balsamic vinegar

4 pounds venison stew meat
2 bay leaves
2 cups whiskey
1 teaspoon black peppercorns, crushed
½ teaspoon thyme leaves
4 cups veal stock (page 218)
1 tablespoon chopped rosemary

Creamy Garlic Polenta:

5 cloves garlic
¼ cup olive oil
5 ears corn (choose ears that are heavy for their size)
4 cups chicken stock (page 219)
3 cups fine yellow cornmeal

4 cups heavy cream
3 tablespoons snipped chives
¾ cup grated Parmesan cheese
Salt and white pepper

> ✤ In some areas of North America, rosemary is an evergreen shrub and thrives all winter, making this a wonderful fall and winter dish.
>
> ✤ Try grilled portobello mushrooms as a prelude to this hearty, rustic dinner.

✤ To prepare the venison, place the garlic, carrot, onion, celery, mushrooms, and oil in a large, heavy-bottomed saucepan over medium-high heat. Sauté the vegetables until they are golden brown. Add the vinegar, and simmer until the liquid has been reduced by half. Add the venison, bay leaves, whiskey, peppercorns, and thyme. Simmer for 10 minutes, and add the veal stock and rosemary. Cover, and simmer until the meat is tender, about 4 hours.

✤ Remove the venison from the saucepan, and set the venison aside. Strain the cooking liquid, removing the cooked vegetables and setting them aside. Continue simmering the cooking liquid until it has been reduced to one-quarter of its original volume. Return the venison and the vegetables to the sauce in the saucepan, and keep warm.

✤ To prepare the polenta, preheat the oven to 325°F. Place the garlic and oil in a small, ovenproof sauté pan. Bake the garlic until it is soft but not burned, about 10 minutes. Set the garlic and oil aside.

✤ Cut the corn kernels off the cobs, and reserve the corn kernels. Place the cobs and chicken stock in a saucepan over medium-high heat, and simmer for 20 minutes. Remove the cobs, and slowly add the cornmeal while stirring. Reduce the heat to medium-low, and simmer, stirring occasionally, for about 45 minutes. Set the cornmeal mixture aside.

(continued on next page)

❧ In a separate saucepan, combine the reserved garlic and oil, reserved corn kernels, and cream, and simmer for 8 minutes. Purée the cream mixture in a blender or food processor. Add the cream mixture to the cornmeal mixture, and stir. Add the chives, cheese, and a little salt and pepper.

❧ To serve, remove the bay leaves from the venison mixture. Place some of the polenta in the center of a plate. Top with some venison, and spoon some vegetables and their sauce all around.

Yield: 8 servings

Flaming Beef on Rosemary Skewers

6 woody sprigs rosemary, 7 to 9 inches long
12 ounces beef sirloin strip, cut into 6 pieces
12 ounces beef tenderloin (filet mignon), cut into 6 pieces
3 large portobello mushrooms, sliced
2 medium red onions, cut into eighths
2 red peppers, cut into ½-inch chunks
Salt and fresh cracked pepper
¼ cup olive oil

2 shallots, finely chopped
½ tablespoon peppercorns
7 tablespoons brandy
½ cup chicken stock, homemade (page 219) or canned
2 tablespoons butter
1 tablespoon chopped parsley
1 tablespoon lemon juice
Cooked rice

❧ Using the rosemary sprigs as skewers, arrange the pieces of meat, mushroom, onion, and red pepper on the rosemary sprigs. If your rosemary sprigs are not firm enough, use a metal skewer to pierce the ingredients, and insert the rosemary sprigs through the hole made by the skewer. Season with salt and pepper.

❧ Heat a sauté pan over medium-high heat. Add the oil, and sear the kebabs on both sides for 1 minute. Add the shallot, peppercorns, and brandy, and ignite. When the flame burns out, add the chicken stock, bring it to a simmer, and simmer for 1 minute. Add the butter, parsley, and lemon juice, and remove the pan from the heat. Remove the kebabs. Stir the sauce to incorporate the butter.

❧ To serve, lay the kebabs over some rice, and either drizzle the sauce over the top or serve the sauce in individual cups for dipping.

Yield: 6 servings

❧ Rosemary sprigs are not only used as seasoning but also as skewers. This dish is exciting to prepare and has an attractive presentation.

lili sullivan

VITAL TO THE TORONTO RESTAURANT SCENE for the past 14 years, Lili Sullivan, former sous-chef of the Auberge du Pommier and chef of Chapeau, is a strong supporter of organic farming and regional and seasonal cooking. She is also a consultant specializing in menu and recipe development.

Sullivan uses rosemary a lot both at home and at The Rebel House. "I like to use rosemary in pastas. It goes great with any chicken (smoked or fresh) as well as salmon or even just a grilled vegetable and chèvre pasta. It's a perfect pairing for lamb and also enhances beef or veal."

She says that even though rosemary is a strong-flavored herb, it combines well with just about anything. "Rosemary mixed into a Dijon mustard is excellent brushed on poultry, pork, or lamb before grilling. I also like to brew a little rosemary in my tea." In the evenings, Sullivan and her husband enjoy a pot of tea brewed from any of a variety of herbs, including basil, rosemary, lemon grass, or chamomile, and like experimenting with different herb combinations.

As an executive member of the Women's Culinary Network, she has appeared on radio and television and published a CD-ROM on baking. She earned a diploma in culinary management from George Brown College of Applied Arts and Technology in Toronto.

Chef at The Rebel House for the past three years, Sullivan prepares traditional Ontario recipes, some from pioneer cookbooks, using fresh ingredients from regional markets. "In fact, The Rebel House concept is to showcase the best of traditional Ontario recipes and new, fresh-market cuisine using seasonal and indigenous fare." The beef on the menu is Black Angus from Alberta, and the lamb is produced in Ontario. She also incorporates local cheeses into the menu and gets her maple syrup and honey from a local farm. The Rebel House features beers from Ontario microbreweries that use natural ingredients. Sullivan likes to cook with beer as well. Her house salad dressing, for instance, is made with raspberry wheat ale from an Ontario microbrewery, the Kawartha Lakes Brewing Company. The restaurant's wine list is all-Ontarian.

chef

The Rebel House
Toronto, Ontario

Rosemary and Leek Bread Pudding

1 clove garlic, minced
1 leek, white part only, halved lengthwise and
   sliced thin
3 tablespoons butter
2 tablespoons finely chopped rosemary
2 cups whole milk

2 cups heavy cream
½ loaf sourdough or French bread, broken into chunks
1 teaspoon salt
½ teaspoon white pepper
2 eggs

> This is a savoury, that is, a dish served as an appetizer or with other dishes. Adding the rosemary to the hot leek mixture releases the flavor and aroma of the herb. The pudding will rise up and get puffy on top but will then fall as it cools.

> This bread pudding makes an excellent alternative to starches such as potatoes, rice, or pasta. This dish would go well with almost any roast meat, including poultry, beef, game, or venison as well as roast pork or even grilled chops. It would also work well as a light entrée (call it a mock soufflé), served with a green salad or maybe some nice grilled or roasted vegetables.

❧ Preheat the oven to 350°F. Butter an 8-inch glass baking dish. (A glass dish allows you to see when the pudding is nicely browned all around.)

❧ In a small saucepan, sauté the garlic and leek in 2 tablespoons of the butter until the vegetables are soft but light in color. Stir in the rosemary, and remove the saucepan from the heat. Cool the leek mixture to room temperature.

❧ Whisk together the milk and 1 cup of the cream. Place the bread chunks in a bowl, pour the milk mixture over them, and let stand for about 15 minutes. Sprinkle the leek mixture over the bread mixture. Season with the salt and pepper.

❧ Whisk the eggs with the remaining cream, and stir into the bread mixture until well blended. Pour the batter into the baking dish. Dot the top with the remaining butter. Bake for 45 to 60 minutes or until the pudding is set on top and golden brown all around.

Yield: 4 to 6 servings

Note: You can substitute a lighter cream or evaporated milk for the heavy cream if you prefer, but the flavor will not be the same. Use only fresh rosemary for excellent results. The pudding can be refrigerated for 1 or 2 days before baking.

Rosemary Lemon Shortbread

½ pound unsalted butter, softened to room
    temperature (1 cup)
½ cup superfine sugar

2 teaspoons finely minced lemon zest
1½ cups all-purpose flour
¼ cup finely chopped rosemary

❧ Preheat the oven to 350°F. Line cookie sheets with parchment paper. In a medium-sized bowl, cream together the butter and sugar. Stir in the lemon zest, flour, and rosemary. Mix until the ingredients combine to form a soft dough.

❧ Drop the dough from a teaspoon onto the cookie sheets. Flatten the cookies with a fork or the bottom of a glass that has been dipped in flour. Bake for 15 to 18 minutes until the edges of the cookies are golden brown.

Yield: 56 cookies

Variation: You could also bake these cookies in one square pan as for Scottish shortbread. You will need to increase the baking time according to the pan size and the thickness of the dough.

❧ This shortbread is a delicious variation of the classic shortbread. These cookies are very delicate. Store them in an airtight container in a cool place. They also freeze very well.

❧ These cookies go great with a glass of milk or a nice pot of tea, and are the perfect accompaniment for a light mousse such as lemon- or berry-flavored mousse. You could also pair these cookies with some fresh fruit salad or even a light-flavored soufflé; again lemon or berry flavors would work best.

sage

Salvia

*S*AGE HAS A LONG HISTORY; it was planted in nearly every kitchen garden during colonial times. Thomas Jefferson also included sage in his gardens at Monticello. A medieval legend is that sage flourishing in the garden was an indication of the wealth of the household.

The ancient Romans believed sage helped prolong life and considered it a sign of immortality. Its name, in fact, comes from the Latin *salvere,* meaning "to save." It's been reported that the Chinese valued sage so much they once traded two cases of Chinese tea for a single sage leaf.

Native to the northern Mediterranean where it grows wild along the coast, sage comes in hundreds of varieties including tricolor sage, purple sage, golden sage, and pineapple sage.

While many of us think of sage only when stuffing our Thanksgiving turkey, sage actually lends its robust camphor-like flavor to a wide variety of foods. Italians use it in veal piccata, saltimbocca, and osso buco. Sage is frequently used with fatty foods, such as pork, duck, and sausage, in bean dishes, and with poultry and game. The famous English Derbyshire cheese is flavored with the greenish-gray leaves of sage. Add some to your own herb butters or cheese spreads and dips. Some folks savor a spot of sage tea, especially good when made with the fruity pineapple sage. Sage is a good companion to mushrooms, tomatoes, and eggplant. It is another strong herb, so use it sparingly.

Fresh sage is easily found in supermarkets and has a much cleaner taste than dried sage, which has a more musty flavor. Sage likes to pair up with other Mediterranean herbs such as rosemary, marjoram, oregano, and thyme. Sage also makes a lovely garden plant, sporting bright blue flowers in summer. This mint relative contains vitamins A and C and some calcium.

pineapple sage

Salvia elegans

*P*INEAPPLE SAGE IS ANOTHER ONE OF THOSE HERBS that North American cooks tend to ignore. This sage variety serves up a delightful contrast to common sage's musty, robust flavor. The hairy leaves of pineapple sage hold a surprising, subtle pineapple flavor and scent with just a hint of mint.

In fall, the pineapple sage plant will delight you with beautiful, scarlet, tube-like flowers you can also use to add a splash of color and flavor to many dishes. Pineapple sage is native to Mexico, but don't confuse it with Mexican sage, which is an ornamental sage with purple flowers.

You can use pineapple sage in place of common sage in just about any recipe to achieve a sweeter touch than would regular sage. Pineapple sage makes a great tea and complements chicken, pork, cheese, baked ham, fruit salads, and cantaloupe. Use pineapple sage as a flavoring for breads, sorbets, jellies, and honey. Judy Miles, owner of the Miles Estate Herb & Berry Farm, uses it in place of regular sage for her Thanksgiving stuffing. "The scent while it's cooking is just heavenly," says Miles, adding, "I just love the stuff." She also includes pineapple sage in a citrus marinade for roasted chicken.

Pineapple sage is a compatible partner for lemon verbena and citrus-scented geraniums such as lime geranium and lemon geranium. Pineapple sage contains vitamins A and C.

alice waters

chef/owner
❧❧

**Chez Panisse Restaurant
& Café**
Berkeley, California

❧❧

Café Fanny
Berkeley, California

*I*T'S ONLY NATURAL THAT THIS LONG-TIME ADVOCATE of fresh, organic produce would consider herbs one of her favorite things. Herbs, she says, can change the whole character of a dish.

"Fresh herbs bring a brightness and aroma to foods. When you have one ingredient you're working with for a whole season, you look for ways to change its character and make it different. That's what herbs do. They help you see other sides of these ingredients."

That makes herbs essential to Waters, who is adamant about using fresh, organic, in-season ingredients in her cooking. She says, for instance, "when you put basil on a tomato it becomes one thing; put tarragon on a tomato and it becomes another."

One of the things Waters likes to do is "surprise people with food." She likes to add something unexpected, an anise hyssop blossom in the salad perhaps.

She's attracted to lovage, inspired by anise hyssop's dramatic flowers, and loves to garnish with whole sprigs of bush basil. Yet, she considers sage an essential. She cautions to take a light hand with it, though, because it can easily overpower other ingredients.

She likes sage with winter squashes, considers it classic with chicken or veal saltimbocca, and likes to garnish with fried sage leaves. "The leaves turn very crisp," she says, "and their flavor is tamed, becoming mild and light."

After opening Chez Panisse in 1971, her insistence on cooking with local organic produce earned her the titles "food revolutionary," "green goddess," and "pioneer of California cuisine." She has cultivated, with the help of her full-time forager, about 75 local farmers who supply the restaurant with locally grown organic ingredients. Each week the forager compiles a list of available crops for the kitchen staff, and they create a menu based on those ingredients.

Waters has received numerous awards including Humanitarian of the Year in 1997 and Best Chef in America and Best Restaurant in America in 1992, all from the James Beard Foundation. She was awarded the National Education Diplomate Award, an honorary degree from Mills College in Oakland, California, and Le Tour du Monde en 80 Toques. Waters also received the Barbara Boxer Top Ten Woman Award, the Zonta Woman of the Year Award, the Academy of Friends Award, Wine and Food Achievement Award, and the Restaurant and Business Leadership Award from *Restaurants and Institutions* magazine. Chez Panisse was named to *Gourmet* magazine's 1998 Top Tables list.

Waters is author and co-author of several cookbooks: *Chez Panisse Vegetables* (Harper-Collins, 1996), *Fanny at Chez Panisse* (HarperCollins, 1992), *Chez Panisse Cooking* (Random House, 1988), *Chez Panisse Pasta, Pizza, and Calzone* (Random House, 1984), and *The Chez Panisse Menu Cookbook* (Random House, 1982).

Sugar Snap Peas with Brown Butter and Sage

2 tablespoons unsalted butter
16 sage leaves

½ pound sugar snap peas, strings removed
Salt and pepper

✦ Melt the butter over low heat in a sauté pan. Add the sage leaves and raise the heat. When the butter begins to brown, toss in the snap peas, and add salt and pepper to taste. Sauté the peas over high heat for about 3 minutes, stirring and turning them all the while.

Yield: 4 servings

Note: Do not overcook the peas. Sauté them just until they surrender their fresh, watery crispness and are still crunchy.

Recipe reprinted, with permission, from *Chez Panisse Cooking* by Alice Waters (Random House, 1988).

✦ This very simple recipe takes minutes to prepare. Very fresh sugar snap peas are firm and refreshingly sweet. The whole pod is edible and need not be shucked for the peas alone.

✦ Serve with roast chicken, veal, or grilled fish.

jean-louis dumonet

executive chef/co-owner

❧ ❧

Trois Jean Bistro
New York, New York

𝒟UMONET FIRST DISCOVERED SAGE in the south of France. He likes its "form and texture." He also likes its consistency. "When you touch it, it's very nice and it has a special taste."

"They have a proverb in Provence: 'qui a de sauge dans son jardin, a pas besoin de médecin,' which means, 'whoever has sage in his garden has no need of a doctor.' " In Spain, he says, they call sage *yerba buena,* which means "good herb."

In France, Dumonet frequently made a rabbit dish he seasoned with sage. He purchased rabbit and poultry from a nearby farmer who fed the chickens, guinea hens, squabs, and rabbits all-natural foods. Dumonet learned the animals' diet included carrots, salads, and sage, and that they seemed to like it.

"So, I said, if they like to eat sage, it would be a good idea to cook them with their favorite herb." Boneless loin of rabbit, its leg confit in a flavored sage juice became a regular menu item. "In the winter we served roasted chicken with sage, served with crushed potatoes mixed with olive oil (see opposite) and it's still on our menu at Trois Jean."

Born in Poitiers and raised in Paris, Dumonet grew up in a family of restaurateurs. He started cooking at age 14 and completed his formal training at l'École hôtelière Jean Drouant in Paris. He trained and cooked in various parts of the world before arriving in New York, including at Le Pré Catalan, Maxim's, and Joséphine in Paris; Hostellerie Georges in Merlimont; Les Dauphins in St-Raphaël in Provence; and the Gleneagles Hotel in Scotland. He also operated his own restaurant in Châteauroux, France, before opening the Parisian-style bistro Trois Jean in New York, with his two partners. Trois Jean's menu features "garden fresh, home-style food in the French tradition."

In the pâtisserie (pastry shop), an array of pastries, including tartlets and mousses, cream puffs, and chocolate ganache, are made fresh daily. Tea and pastries are served every afternoon.

In 1994, Dumonet was the youngest of 48 chefs in the United States to be awarded the Maître Cuisinier de France (Master Chef of France). He is a member of the James Beard Foundation and has cooked at the James Beard House. He was a professional guest at the Oldways Food Preservation & Exchange Trust educational seminar in Morocco in 1994, and he creates the Bordeaux wine menus for the annual bistro dinners for the Commanderie de Bordeaux, an international society of Bordeaux wine connoisseurs.

Trois Jean has been featured in *Town & Country* magazine, *Elle* magazine, *The New York Observer, The New York Times,* the *New York Post,* and a multitude of other publications.

Roasted Chicken with Sage, Served with Crushed Potatoes Mixed with Olive Oil

2 (3 to 4-pound) free-range chickens
Salt and pepper
1 large bunch sage leaves
¼ pound butter (½ cup)
½ cup chicken stock (page 219)

2 pounds Idaho potatoes (3 to 4 large), skins on
1 cup extra virgin olive oil
Tempura batter (page 222)
Oil

✦ Preheat the oven to 400°F. Wash the chickens, and season inside and out with salt and pepper. Insert 2 sage leaves between the skin and the meat of each leg and 3 sage leaves between the skin and the meat of each breast. Baste the chickens with butter and place them in a roasting pan. Roast the chickens for 20 minutes, turning them every 10 minutes and basting them often with the butter. Add ¼ cup of the chicken stock to the pan, and roast the chickens, turning and basting them occasionally, for another 10 to 15 minutes or until the juices run clear.

✦ Meanwhile, boil the potatoes. When they are cooked, peel them and crush them with a potato masher or fork. Mix in the olive oil, and season with salt and pepper to taste.

✦ Prepare the tempura batter. Heat some oil in a deep skillet. Dry off the remaining sage leaves well. Dip the sage leaves into the tempura batter, and deep-fry them in the oil until crisp. Drain the sage leaves on paper towels, and reserve.

✦ When the chicken is done, remove it from the pan. Heat the pan juices with the remaining chicken stock on top of the stove.

✦ To serve, cut the chickens in half. Place half a chicken on each plate with some crushed potatoes. Place the fried sage leaves on top of the crushed potatoes. Drizzle with some of the pan juices. Pour the remaining juices into a gravy boat for individual serving.

Yield: 4 servings

Timesaver Tip: Tempura batter mix is available in some supermarkets or in Asian shops.

✦ In France, we make roast rabbit with sage. Four or five years ago, Americans were not too fond of rabbit, so we created this version using chicken.
✦ Serve this dish in spring with baby vegetables such as carrots, turnips, beets, or asparagus. The vegetables can be cooked in chicken broth with a leaf or two of sage.

mario diventura

chef/co-owner

Filomena Cucina Italiana
Clementon, New Jersey

$\mathcal{M}$ARIO DIVENTURA IS NO STRANGER to restaurant kitchens. In fact, he was practically raised in them. At 13, he began learning from his grandfather, who opened Mama Ventura's in Voorhees, New Jersey, more than 40 years ago. In all, the DiVentura family, including brothers, sisters, and cousins, owns nearly a dozen restaurants in southern New Jersey and one in California.

It was mandatory for family members to work at Mama Ventura's when DiVentura was growing up. As a young boy, he learned, albeit reluctantly, all phases of the restaurant business. When he was well into his 20s, he realized he had begun to like the business. Now, he says, "it's my life."

In 1988, DiVentura and his brother Giuseppe opened Filomena Cucina Italiana, named in honor of their mother, Filomena. She still makes her famous gnocchi and other homemade pastas for three of the family-owned restaurants, Filomena, Mama Ventura's, and Filomena's Cucina Rustica.

In DiVentura's kitchen, sage is the rage. He likes sage's "nice robust flavor." Sage can often be substituted in recipes calling for rosemary; the two herbs are compatible with many of the same foods, he says. But mostly, he uses sage to make traditional central Abruzzi dishes such as veal saltimbocca (page 162) and osso buco. He likes sage in poultry stuffings and in chicken sausage, and brown butter sage sauce (see opposite) is a favorite that's a simple-to-make, tasty-to-eat sauce for most any pasta. He grows sage along with rosemary and basil in his home garden. DiVentura likes to experiment in the kitchen, creating new dishes and updating old classics.

Filomena Cucina Italiana is an intimate, 90-seat dining room with subdued lighting and is decorated in peach with rich wood accents. Tapestry table runners adorn the tables, and lush greenery helps give the restaurant a Mediterranean feel.

Both Filomena Cucina Italiana and its sister restaurant, Filomena Cucina Rustica, which opened in 1997 and features a wood-burning pizza oven, have received rave reviews from local critics, including those from *The Philadelphia Inquirer* and the *Courier Post*. DiVentura has been featured in a number of articles in the *Courier Post*.

Roasted Veal Ravioli with Brown Butter Sage Sauce

Veal:

1 pound veal, cubed

3 cloves garlic

1 tablespoon chopped sage

¼ cup diced carrot

¼ cup diced celery

¼ cup diced onion

Salt and pepper

1 egg

½ cup bread crumbs

¼ cup white wine

Pasta Dough:

5 eggs

3 cups all-purpose flour

Brown Butter Sage Sauce:

½ pound butter (1 cup), sliced

1 teaspoon minced sage

Freshly ground pepper

Grated Parmigiano-Reggiano cheese

Sage leaves

✤ To prepare the veal for the ravioli, preheat the oven to 375°F. Place the veal, garlic, sage, carrot, celery, onion, and a little salt and pepper in an ovenproof pan, and roast for about 30 minutes until tender. Place the veal mixture in a food processor, and process until smooth. Add the egg, bread crumbs, and wine, and pulse to combine. Set the veal mixture aside.

✤ To prepare the ravioli, place the eggs and flour in a food processor, and process until the dough clumps into a ball. Let the dough stand for at least 20 minutes. Divide the dough in half. With a rolling pin, roll out the dough as thinly as possible into 2 rectangles. Using a pastry wheel or ravioli cutter, cut the dough into 24 ravioli shapes (rounds or squares).

✤ To assemble the ravioli, place a spoonful of the reserved veal mixture in the center of half the ravioli shapes. Brush water around the edges, place another ravioli shape on top, and press the dough around the edges to seal the ravioli.

✤ To prepare the sauce, melt the butter in a hot skillet. Continue cooking over low heat until the butter begins to brown, lifting the skillet from the heat if necessary. Remove the skillet from the heat when the butter is almost burnt. Stir in the sage. Season with pepper.

✤ To serve, place the ravioli on a plate or in a serving bowl. Pour some sauce over the top. Garnish with sage leaves and some grated Parmigiano-Reggiano.

Yield: 4 servings (24 ravioli)

Timesaver Tips: You can purchase readymade pasta sheets from gourmet or pasta shops. Ravioli forms, available in kitchenware stores, make assembling ravioli easier.

✦ This is a traditional dish often served in northern Italy. The butter sauce is good with any stuffed pasta. Try it with tortellini.

✦ A traditional Italian mixed green salad with balsamic vinaigrette would complement this ravioli. You could also serve the ravioli as an appetizer, allowing two or three per person.

Veal Saltimbocca

8 (2 to 3-ounce) thinly sliced veal cutlets
All-purpose flour for dredging plus 1 tablespoon
1 tablespoon oil or clarified butter (page 220)
8 sage leaves, cut into chiffonade, plus extra
   sage leaves, left whole
4 cloves garlic, crushed or thinly sliced

2 cups sliced or chopped mushrooms, any variety
   or a mixture
½ cup dry sherry or Marsala
2 cups chicken broth
8 slices prosciutto
8 slices mozzarella, fontina, or provolone cheese

➤ Pat the veal cutlets dry, and dredge them in flour. Heat the oil in a sauté pan, and sear each side of the veal for about 30 seconds. Remove the veal, and keep it warm. Add the sage, garlic, and mushrooms to the pan. Toss lightly to blend, and sauté 1 to 2 minutes until the garlic is golden brown. Deglaze the pan with the sherry. Sprinkle 1 tablespoon flour into the pan, stirring constantly as the liquid and the flour form a roux. Add the chicken broth, and bring to a simmer. Continue simmering until the sauce thickens. Return the reserved veal to the pan. Place a slice of prosciutto over each veal cutlet. Place a cheese slice over the prosciutto. Cover, and cook another 1 to 2 minutes until the cheese melts.

➤ To serve, garnish each veal cutlet with sage leaves.

Yield: 4 servings

Note: You could also place the assembled veal, prosciutto, and cheese on a baking sheet, melt the cheese in the oven, and pour the sauce over the veal cutlets when you serve them. This method is especially helpful if you do not have a pan large enough to hold all the veal cutlets in one layer, or if you are making large quantities of this dish.

Shopping Tips: Look for well-trimmed veal with the gristle removed, or remove it yourself with a sharp knife. You may want to tenderize the veal by pounding it with a meat mallet.

➤ *Saltimbocca* means "jump in your mouth," which probably refers to the burst of flavors in this dish. Saltimbocca is a really rich, flavorful dish.

➤ Serve the veal and sauce over quick-steamed or sautéed spinach, over couscous, or over any pasta.

marc merdinger

Victor Cafe
Philadelphia, Pennsylvania

$\mathcal{A}$T Victor Cafe, you're served a slice of history with a dash of music on the side. In the dining room you, the diner, are for whom the bell tolls. And when that bell chimes, the singing wait staff come together for a performance that whets your appetite for both music and food. In the kitchen, executive chef Marc Merdinger composes a symphony of flavors to satisfy your culinary cravings. Chances are it's pineapple sage that flavors that symphony.

Merdinger first began using pineapple sage when he was a sous-chef at the Ebbitt Room of the Virginia Hotel in Cape May, New Jersey. What first attracted him to it, he says, was "how beautiful it was with those long stems and bright red flowers. I love its citrusy flavor," says Merdinger, who was already quite fond of both pineapple and sage when he discovered pineapple sage. "Sage is one of my favorite herbs. And pineapple, when ripe, is so delicious."

He likes harmonizing with pineapple sage. He makes an Italian flan, a panna cotta, and a broth he serves over tuna, all with pineapple sage. He uses it with fish, meats, game, and poultry, as well as with venison, and often prepares veal with pineapple sage.

It's a surprise to customers, though, who see pineapple sage on the menu and expect to find pineapple chunks and sage leaves on their plate, recounts Merdinger.

His culinary career began in Queens, New York, when, at 15, he worked in a pizzeria. "I was the only Jewish kid working in a pizzeria; they were afraid of me," says Merdinger, who once made a chicken liver and onion pizza and a smoked salmon pizza with cream cheese. "Okay, so I was a bizarre kid," he admits as he has the last laugh while composing a gastronomic ensemble behind the stove at the Victor Cafe. After all, he says, "I love cooking; I can't imagine doing anything else. And, if it wasn't for cooking, I wouldn't have met my wife, Valerie, who's one of the singers here."

The building originally housed a gramophone shop opened in the early 1900s by John DiStefano, a fan of classical music and opera. His broad knowledge of music was welcomed by musicians and directors at the nearby RCA Victor Company. The shop became a meeting place where music lovers gathered to share an espresso or a spumoni and listen to newly recorded arias, symphonies, and popular music of the day.

Upon the repeal of Prohibition in 1933, DiStefano transformed DiStefano's Gramophone Shop into the Victor Cafe, a music-lover's rendezvous. Record cabinets lining one room of the restaurant include thousands of the DiStefano family's extensive collection of 78 rpm records, relics of a bygone era. Many of the recordings are rare, out-of-print editions. Adorning the walls are signed photographs and operatic memorabilia that document DiStefano's musical legacy. And, standing guard near the front door is a life-sized statue of Nipper, mascot of the RCA Victor Company.

Grilled Beef Paillards over Pineapple Sage Panzanella and Roast Shallot Jus

Grilled Beef Paillards:

12 whole black peppercorns

6 cloves garlic, crushed

3 sprigs pineapple sage

3 sprigs rosemary

½ medium red onion, cut into julienne

1 cup olive oil

½ cup red wine vinegar

Juice of 2 lemons

Salt and pepper

4 (6-ounce) slices beef top round, sliced long and thin

Pineapple Sage Panzanella (bread salad):

12 cloves roasted garlic (page 222)

2 smoked plum tomatoes,* peeled, seeded, and diced

2 cups baby arugula

2 tablespoons chopped pineapple sage

¼ red onion, cut into julienne

1 cup (½-inch) cubes focaccia

3 tablespoons balsamic vinegar, reduced by one-half

3 tablespoons olive oil

Salt and pepper

If you don't have a stove-top smoker, use unsmoked plum tomatoes that are very fresh.

Roast Shallot Jus:

3 large shallots, roasted and chopped

¼ teaspoon chopped garlic

¼ teaspoon chopped pineapple sage

¼ cup Barolo

2 tablespoons balsamic vinegar

1 cup veal demi-glace (page 224)

2 tablespoons unsalted butter

Salt and pepper

➤ This dish is on our summer menu. The pineapple sage provides a nice light flavor that contrasts with the panzanella, an Italian bread salad, which packs a flavor wallop.

➤ This hearty dish can stand alone as a light summer dinner. I like thin-cut crispy French fries with this dish, but you could also cut potatoes thin and grill them. Add grilled summer vegetables for a complete meal.

➤ To prepare the beef, combine the peppercorns, garlic, pineapple sage, rosemary, onion, oil, vinegar, and lemon juice. Add a little salt and pepper, and mix well. Place the beef in a glass dish, and pour the marinade over the beef. Marinate, refrigerated, for 2 hours, turning the meat occasionally.

➤ To prepare the bread salad, squeeze the roasted garlic from its skin, and mash the garlic in a medium-sized bowl. Add the smoked tomato, arugula, pineapple sage, and onion. Set the smoked tomato mixture aside until just before serving time.

➤ To prepare the jus, sauté the shallots, garlic, and pineapple sage in a nonstick pan until the garlic is soft. If you do not have a nonstick pan, add a few drops of olive oil or spray the pan with cooking spray. Deglaze the pan with the wine, and reduce the liquid to about half. Add the balsamic vinegar, and again reduce the liquid to about half. Add the demi-glace, and reduce by about one-third. Set the jus aside, keeping it warm until serving time.

❧ To finish the dish, grill the beef to medium rare. Combine the reserved smoked tomato mixture gently with the bread, balsamic vinegar, olive oil, and a little salt and pepper. Combine the butter with the reserved jus, and season it with salt and pepper.

❧ To serve, mound the salad in the center of the serving plates. Cross some beef slices over the salad, and drizzle the jus over the beef.

Yield: 2 servings

Note: Because the beef is cut very thin, be careful not to overcook it when grilling.

Timesaver Tips: Roast the garlic and the shallots the day before. Prepare the veal demi-glace in advance, or use a commercial demi-glace product. Sources for demi-glace are included in the Mail Order Resources (page 228).

Pan Roasted Veal Medallions over Black Trumpet Mushroom Risotto with Pineapple Sage–Infused Veal Stock

Black Trumpet Mushroom Risotto:
1 small onion, diced
2 teaspoons chopped garlic
2 tablespoons olive oil
1 cup sliced black trumpet mushrooms
½ teaspoon chopped pineapple sage

½ teaspoon chopped rosemary
½ cup Arborio rice
5 cups simmering chicken stock (page 219)
¼ cup grated Parmigiano-Reggiano cheese
Salt and pepper

Veal Medallions:
12 (2-ounce) veal medallions cut from the tenderloin
Salt and freshly ground pepper
1½ tablespoons olive oil
2 tablespoons chopped pineapple sage
1 teaspoon chopped garlic

¼ cup Barolo
1 cup veal stock (page 218)
4 tablespoons unsalted butter
2 tablespoons peeled, seeded, and diced tomato

Fresh herbs, including pineapple sage blossoms

> ❧ I like to use pineapple sage with veal. The pineapple sage isn't overpowering; it just brings out the flavor of the veal. This dish is similar to saltimbocca, which traditionally is made with regular sage.

❧ To prepare the risotto, in a medium saucepan, cook the onion and garlic in the oil until they are translucent. Add the mushrooms, pineapple sage, and rosemary, and cook until the mushrooms are soft. Add the rice, and sauté for 2 to 3 minutes. Stirring continuously, slowly add the stock a little at a time, until the rice absorbs the liquid. This process should take

(continued on next page)

around 25 minutes. (Prepare the veal medallions toward the end of this period.) The rice should be al dente in the middle and creamy on the outside. Remove the risotto from the heat, and stir in the cheese. Season with salt and pepper.

✦ To prepare the veal medallions, season them with salt and pepper. Heat the oil in a large sauté pan over high heat. Once the oil has started to smoke, place the veal medallions in the pan. Brown them on both sides, and remove them from the pan. Keep the veal medallions warm. Add the pineapple sage and garlic to the pan, and sauté until the garlic is lightly browned. Reduce the heat to medium, and deglaze the pan with the wine until it has almost evaporated. Add the veal stock, and reduce until the sauce thickens. Stir in the butter and tomato, and adjust the salt and pepper.

✦ To serve, spoon some risotto into a large pasta bowl. Place 3 veal medallions tightly around the risotto. Drizzle some of the veal sauce over the veal. Garnish with fresh herbs.

Yield: 4 servings

Shopping Tips: Black trumpet mushrooms are exotic and can be hard to find. They are most plentiful from September to November. If necessary, you could substitute portobello mushrooms, but remove the dark gills to keep them from discoloring the dish.

✦ **The veal and risotto can stand alone, or add your favorite colorful vegetable and garlic bread or bruschetta.**

savory

Satureja hortensis (summer savory)
Satureja montana (winter savory)

AVORY BOASTS A 2,000-YEAR HISTORY and is most known for its affinity with beans. In fact, it's often called the bean herb and is used with lentils and all kinds of beans, including fava beans, green beans, and lima beans.

Still another Mediterranean native, savory was used by early Romans to flavor sauces. It was among the first herbs brought to the New World by early colonists; New Englanders were growing winter savory in their gardens by the late 1600s. Thomas Jefferson was so smitten with winter savory, he requested cuttings from his neighbor to include in his garden at Monticello. Shakespeare, too, thought savory worthy of frequent mention in his writings.

Savory's warm spiciness makes it a great salt substitute. Some say that a mixture of basil and winter savory can replace salt in many dishes. Savory pairs well with chervil and tarragon and often serves as catalyst to blend flavors together harmoniously.

There are two varieties of savory, winter and summer. While basically you can use these varieties interchangeably, each has its own characteristics. Winter savory is a perennial with a distinct peppery flavor. Summer savory is an annual, appearing for a short time during the summer. Winter savory's flavor is more intense, and summer savory is delicate with a touch of sweetness.

Use either variety in salads, in soups, and with vegetables such as eggplant, onions, brussels sprouts, squash, and peas. Savory adds spice to gravies, sauces, and stuffings and works well with meat, poultry, and eggs. It makes a tasty vinegar and a pleasant herb butter, and is one of the few herbs that retain their flavor fairly well when dried. Savory's peppery tones spice up bean soup, as well as chicken or beef stews and soups. Winter savory's sharper tones complement game.

summer savory

winter savory

167

elizabeth fox

chef
❧—❧
**Water Club Restaurant
and Courtyard**
Victoria, British Columbia

ELIZABETH FOX LIKES TO BRING HERBS and edible flowers from her garden into her kitchen both at home and on the job at the Water Club. She prefers summer to winter savory. "I love its scent; it's not as strong and overpowering as winter savory; it's much more gentle. One reason I enjoy it so much is because its growing season is so short compared to many other herbs, so the summer savory is a treat for me." The weather on southern Vancouver Island is mild, and quite a few herbs grow all year round while others grow from early spring to October, explains Fox.

Another reason she's such a fan of savory is that "it's a versatile herb with a wonderful fragrance. It's fantastic in marinades for my summer barbecues, and I always add some that I've dried from the summer garden to slowly simmered winter stews and roasts." She also thinks summer savory's "pretty trailing branches and small flowers look lovely in the garden."

Just after finishing her studies in computer science, Fox was sitting with some friends talking about what they would do differently if they were to do it over again. She said she'd become a chef. Her friends encouraged her. "They told me I was better at cooking than computer science. I realized that cooking was something that came naturally to me and that's what I wanted to do."

"If I were to have a culinary philosophy, it would be that if you can get fresh [ingredients], use them. I live where there are so many fresh foods available, and we're in an environment where more products are available all the time. I'm excited by finding different foods."

Fox has been the lunch chef at the Water Club since it opened in April 1997. She apprenticed under Mark Finnigan, executive chef at both the Herald Street Caffe and its sister restaurant, the Water Club. She has also worked in the Carden Street Cafe in Brentwood, just outside of Victoria, was executive chef at the Marina Restaurant in Victoria, and was a partner in the catering company Every Last Crumb. She has taught cooking classes for the past 10 years, and her recipes have been published in numerous British Columbia publications. Food writer Jurgen Gothe selected one of her recipes to include in his book, *Some Acquired Tastes: A Recipe Album.* Her culinary training was at Dubrulle Culinary Institute in Vancouver.

Described as casually elegant, the Water Club features a frequently changing menu based on in-season, local produce as well as locally produced chèvre and fresh herbs, some from a small garden on the premises. A pizza oven and a rotisserie provide the tools for such dishes as thin crust Roma style pizza with double smoked bacon, caramelized apple, grilled red onion, and fresh sage. Breads, too, are baked in-house and served with rosemary-flavored olive oil.

Apricot–Summer Savory Bread Pudding

1 loaf day-old French bread	4 tablespoons butter, softened
6 extra large eggs, lightly whisked	½ medium white onion, diced
Whole milk	1½ tablespoons finely chopped parsley
⅛ teaspoon salt	1½ tablespoons finely chopped summer savory
⅛ teaspoon freshly ground black pepper	1 tablespoon orange zest
Nutmeg	¼ cup diced dried apricots

⋆ Remove the crust from the bread. Cut the bread into pieces to fit your baking dish. (For a 9 by 5 by 2½-inch baking dish, cut the bread into rectangular pieces about 1 inch square and 5 inches long.) Place the bread in a medium bowl.

⋆ To the eggs, add enough milk to equal 6 cups. Whisk the egg mixture in another bowl with the salt, pepper, and a pinch of nutmeg.

⋆ In a small pan over medium heat, melt 2 tablespoons of the butter and sauté the onion until it is soft and golden. Remove the pan from the heat, and stir in the parsley, summer savory, orange zest, and apricot. Let the apricot mixture cool, and stir it into the egg mixture. Pour the egg mixture over the bread, combine gently, and let the bread mixture stand, refrigerated, for 60 minutes.

⋆ Butter the baking dish with the remaining 2 tablespoons of butter. Layer the bread in the dish, making sure that the apricot and onion get tucked between the layers of bread. Refrigerate overnight or at least 12 hours to let the bread absorb the custard.

⋆ Preheat the oven to 325°F. Cover the baking dish with foil. Place the baking dish in a larger one, and add enough boiling water to reach halfway up the smaller baking dish. Bake the pudding for 45 minutes. Remove the foil, and bake another 15 minutes to crisp the top of the pudding a bit. When the pudding is done, it will pull away from the sides of the baking dish and puff up in the middle.

Yield: 6 servings

⋆ Summer savory goes great with apricots, but I've also made this dish with sautéed apples and rosemary instead of apricots and summer savory. This pudding should be refrigerated at least overnight before it is baked.

⋆ This savory bread pudding is a great side dish with all meats and poultry.

Honey Mustard Baked Pork Chops Filled with Summer Savory and Chèvre

> ✤ This recipe was inspired by a similar dish, honey mustard baked chicken. In that recipe, I stuff chicken breasts with the cheese mixture and some prosciutto. I like to take one idea and come up with variations.

Summer Savory and Chèvre Filling:

8 ounces chèvre (or a combination of chèvre and cream cheese)
2 teaspoons chopped parsley
1 teaspoon chopped basil
1 tablespoon snipped chives
1 teaspoon chopped mint

1 teaspoon chopped summer savory
1 teaspoon chopped thyme
Cayenne
Freshly ground black pepper
Zest of 1 large orange

Pork Chops:

1 clove garlic, crushed
1½ cups bread crumbs
½ tablespoon chopped rosemary
½ tablespoon chopped summer savory
½ cup grainy Dijon mustard

3 tablespoons butter or olive oil
2 tablespoons honey
6 (1 to 1½-inch) pork chops, preferably center cut
Salt and freshly ground black pepper

Sauce:

6 cups chicken stock (page 219)
1 bay leaf
1 carrot, cut into ½-inch lengths
1 clove garlic, crushed
1 onion, cut into ½-inch pieces
1 stalk celery, cut into ½-inch lengths

1 sprig rosemary
1 sprig summer savory
1 sprig thyme
½ bunch parsley
6 ounces cold butter, cut into 1-inch cubes
Salt and pepper

✤ To prepare the filling, combine the chèvre, parsley, basil, chives, mint, summer savory, thyme, a pinch of cayenne and black pepper, and the orange zest. Store the chèvre filling in the refrigerator until the pork chops are ready to be stuffed.

✤ To prepare the pork chops, preheat the oven to 350°F. In a bowl, combine the garlic, bread crumbs, rosemary, savory, and mustard, and set aside. In a small saucepan, melt the butter with the honey, and set aside. Using a boning knife, make a lengthwise slit in the pork chops from the broad end to the narrow end, without piercing the sides. Stop about ½ inch from the end. Stuff the pork chops with the reserved chèvre filling. Roll them in the reserved bread crumb mixture, and place them in a baking dish. Sprinkle any remaining bread crumbs on top, and pour the reserved butter mixture over the pork chops. Sprinkle them with some salt and pepper. Bake the pork chops, uncovered, about 35 minutes, or until the juices run clear. If using a meat thermometer, the pork chops are done at 165°F.

✦ Meanwhile, prepare the sauce. In a large saucepan, combine the stock, bay leaf, carrot, garlic, onion, celery, rosemary, summer savory, thyme, and parsley. Simmer the stock mixture until there is just a bit more than 1½ cups of liquid left. Strain, and return the stock to the saucepan. Continue simmering the stock until only 1 cup remains. Whisk in the butter, one piece at a time, to thicken the sauce. Adjust the seasonings with salt and pepper.

✦ To serve, pour the sauce over the pork chops.

Yield: 6 servings

Note: You can substitute some of your favorite herbs for the ones in the filling if you wish or if some of these are not available to you.

Variation: Add about ¼ cup dried cranberries or about a third of a cup of dried cherries (available in gourmet shops) to the sauce. They will rehydrate nicely.

Timesaver Tips: You can often find pork chops already slit for stuffing in your grocery store, or you can ask your butcher to do it for you. You can also make the filling a day ahead of time.

✦ **Roasted garlic mashed potatoes are a great accompaniment for the pork chops. A little orange zest and chives can be added to them.**

debbie gold

co-executive chef

The American Restaurant
Kansas City, Missouri

*t*HE FLAVOR OF SAVORY IS WHAT MAKES it a staple in Debbie Gold's kitchen. "It's a cross between thyme and oregano. It adds accents to soups and sauces, stuffings, and even salads," says Gold. "It's just so versatile."

She likes both winter and summer savory and uses it pretty much in the same way as thyme. "I often use it as a garnish; it's great with rabbit, in grain salads, or in couscous." She includes it in a foie gras dish, and in a fresh spring salad of peas, artichokes, and mushrooms. "When you throw a few fresh herbs into mixed greens, they cause this little explosion of flavor. If people aren't used to it, it's a pleasant surprise. In fact, it's amazing how fresh herbs can make a salad more exciting." She also makes a short rib and noodle dish and a morel mushroom soup that's flavored with savory.

Gold first used savory while studying in France, then forgot about it. "A while back we had Patrick Clark as a guest chef at the restaurant, and he used it to make a fricassee of rabbit. Since then, savory has been a part of our pantry."

Gold and her husband and co-chef, Michael Smith, began a small herb garden the first year they were in their current home and are adding to it each year. They started with the basics, including savory, of course, along with thyme, oregano, and basil.

Gold's culinary training began in France at L'École Hôtelière de Tain L'Hermitage. She apprenticed at several Michelin-starred restaurants and with Michael Chabran, Albert LeCompt, and Jean-Marc Reynaud.

Upon her return to the United States in 1988, she worked in some of Chicago's finest restaurants, including Charlie Trotters, Everest, and Mirador.

In 1994, Gold and Smith were named co-executive chefs of The American Restaurant in Kansas City. For its contemporary American cuisine, extensive wine list, and exceptional service, the restaurant has received *Mobil Travel Guide*'s four-star rating, *Wine Spectator*'s Award of Excellence, the Distinguished Restaurants of North America Award, the AAA Four Diamond Award, and the Chaîne des Rôtisseurs Dining and Service Award and Hall of Fame Award.

In 1995, *Nation's Restaurant News* inducted The American Restaurant into the Fine Dining Hall of Fame. Gold and Smith have been featured in *Wine Spectator* magazine, and *Esquire* magazine named them Chefs to Watch in 1997. Both Gold and Smith were nominated for the 1997 and 1998 James Beard Foundation American Express Best American Chef: Midwest. The pair participate in culinary events worldwide to benefit organizations such as Meals on Wheels, the Bethesda Hospice of Cincinnati, March of Dimes, James Beard Foundation, and Taste of the Nation, as well as local farmers' markets and hunger relief programs.

Quinoa Barley Salad

Bulgur:
½ cup water, stock, or vegetable juice   ¼ cup bulgur

Barley:
1⅓ cups water, stock, or vegetable juice   ⅓ cup barley

Quinoa:
⅓ cup quinoa   ⅔ cup water, stock, or vegetable juice

Dressing:
1 small red onion, diced   ½ cup dried cherries
1 tablespoon finely snipped chives   ½ cup sherry vinegar
1 tablespoon thyme leaves   ¼ cup savory leaves
1 cup olive oil   Salt and pepper

➤ To prepare the bulgur, bring the water to a boil, and add the bulgur. Let stand until all the water is absorbed, about 20 to 30 minutes.

➤ To prepare the barley, bring the water to a boil, and add the barley. Cook the barley until tender, about 15 minutes.

➤ To prepare the quinoa, rinse it under cold, running water, and drain. Combine the quinoa and water in a medium saucepan, and bring to a boil. Reduce the heat to medium-low. Cook until the liquid is absorbed and the quinoa is transparent, about 8 minutes.

➤ To prepare the dressing, combine the onion, chives, thyme, oil, cherries, vinegar, savory, and a little salt and pepper.

➤ Combine the bulgur, barley, and quinoa, and toss with the dressing.

Yield: 4 servings

➤ This is a great salad that can be served hot or cold. The savory adds spiciness and contrasts with the dried cherries, which bring a sweet touch to the grains.

➤ Serve this hearty salad alone or with beef, chicken, pork, salmon, or shrimp, or top it with some fresh chèvre.

scented geranium

Pelargonium

*W*HEN VISITORS ACCIDENTALLY BRUSH AGAINST a scented geranium plant in her herb garden, they do a double take, says Lorraine Kiefer, co-owner of Triple Oaks Nursery & Herb Garden in Franklinville, New Jersey. She enjoys watching as they look all around for the source of the lemon, rose, or strawberry aroma wafting through the air. Most often, she says, they overlook the lowly scented geranium at their feet.

It's not a particularly showy plant, and it's the leaves, not the flowers, that produce the strong, copycat scents. There are hundreds of varieties of scented geranium that mimic flavors ranging from citrus to rose to spices to chocolate and even combinations such as mint-rose.

These fragrant plants have been enchanting us for centuries. Sailors first brought the plants to Europe on their return from the Cape of Good Hope in the early 1600s. They were brought to North America during colonial times, and during the very proper Victorian age, scented geranium leaves perfumed the finger bowls placed on dining tables. Scented geranium leaves were used in bouquets and potpourris, and they found their way into the kitchen as well. Teas, cakes, cookies, jams, and jellies were flavored with scented geraniums. Still today, many people make scented geranium sugar for use in baking. Add several leaves to a cup of sugar in a glass jar, alternating layers of leaves and sugar. In a week or so, the flavor and scent will have infused the sugar. Bruising the leaves slightly before adding them will release the oils that hold the scent. You can use this sugar, with the leaves removed, in your coffee, tea, or lemonade or on cereal or fruit, or substitute it for plain sugar in your favorite cake or cookie recipe. Some people place a layer of leaves in the bottom of a cake pan, then pour the batter over the leaves to make a scented geranium cake. Ice creams, sorbets, and puddings, too, can be flavored by infusing the scented geranium leaves into liquid ingredients. Whip up some scented geranium butter to wake up bland pancakes, waffles, or breakfast muffins. The flowers are also edible and can be tossed into fruit or green salads or floated in a punch bowl.

jerry traunfeld

JERRY TRAUNFELD WAS GARDENING before he was cooking, but just barely. He was sowing carrots in his garden plot at age 6 and experimenting with puff pastry at age 11. He's been doing both ever since, making him a perfect fit for his current job of chef at The Herbfarm Restaurant.

The restaurant sits amid five acres of herbs and other plants, providing Traunfeld with raw ingredients for his cuisine. Among his favorite herbs is the scented geranium. "It's an herb that provides all-around pleasure, even if you don't cook with it. I always have rose and lemon geraniums in the garden, then bring them inside in the winter. I just can never resist enjoying their scent. They have such a sweet perfume."

Although scented geraniums are not as versatile as other herbs, he says, "they are quite delightful in desserts and beverages." His favorite geranium flavors are attar of roses, and lemon, especially the Mabel Grey variety, which is the strongest of the lemon-flavored geraniums. The flowers have the same flavor as the leaves, he says, with an extra sweetness to them. He often uses the petals as a garnish.

He first started cooking with scented geraniums while working at Stars in San Francisco in the 1980s. He often infused the scented leaves in crème anglaise as a base for his berry tarts. He says the rose-flavored varieties go particularly well with berry and apple flavors. In fact, a traditional English jelly is made by adding a leaf of rose geranium to apple jelly.

Traunfeld worked in several California restaurants after graduating from the California Culinary Academy. He returned to the Northwest in 1986 and was named executive chef at the Alexis Hotel in Seattle. For the past eight years, he has created a new Herbfarm Restaurant menu each week, using the best of the Northwest's ingredients in season, as well as the herbs grown on site.

During Traunfeld's reign in the kitchen, The Herbfarm Restaurant has received four stars from the *Seattle P.I.,* four stars in *Northwest Best Places*, a four-star rating by *Mobil Travel Guide,* and was given a food rating of 29 out of 30 in the *Zagat Survey.* The restaurant has been featured in *The New York Times, The Chicago Tribune, Gourmet, Food & Wine, Victoria, Bon Appétit, Sunset,* and *Travel & Leisure*. The Herbfarm Restaurant was also featured on the television program *Burt Wolf's Table.* Traunfeld was selected *Simply Seafood* magazine's Chef of the Year, and he was a two-time nominee for the James Beard Foundation's Best American Chef: Northwest Award.

The Herbfarm Restaurant, destroyed by an electrical fire in 1997, is being rebuilt with the addition of six luxury suites. Meanwhile, Traunfeld is writing a definitive cookbook about using fresh herbs, tentatively titled *The Herbfarm Cookbook.*

chef

The Herbfarm Restaurant
Fall City, Washington

Rose Geranium and Saffron Panna Cotta with Honeyed Apricots

1¾ cups whole milk
½ cup heavy cream
8 rose geranium leaves
8 threads saffron
2 quarter-sized slices ginger

1 package unflavored gelatin
¼ cup sugar
Vegetable oil or nut oil
4 ripe apricots, pitted and quartered
3 tablespoons honey

❋ Bring 1½ cups of the milk and the cream to a boil in a small saucepan. As soon as the milk mixture comes to a full boil, add the rose geranium leaves, saffron, and ginger. Cover, and remove from the heat. Let the milk mixture steep for at least 30 minutes. Meanwhile, sprinkle the gelatin on the remaining milk to soften.

❋ Strain the milk mixture, squeezing out any liquid retained by the leaves. Reheat the infused milk in the saucepan with the softened gelatin and the sugar until the milk mixture is almost at a simmer and the gelatin and sugar are dissolved.

❋ Very lightly oil 4 (5-ounce) ramekins or cups (you can even use paper or plastic cups), and pour the milk mixture into them. Chill until set, about 2 to 3 hours.

❋ To serve, warm the apricots in the honey in a small pan. Unmold the panna cotta onto individual plates, and spoon the apricots and honey around each panna cotta.

Yield: 4 servings

Note: If apricots are not in season, you can substitute dried apricots. Just warm the dried apricots in the honey syrup with a piece of vanilla bean.

❋ This simple to prepare, eggless custard is a great vehicle for sweet herbal flavors. I especially like the exotic combination of rose and saffron.
❋ Although this dessert stands well on its own, you could serve it with shortbread.

Lemon Geranium Sorbet

16 Mabel Grey lemon geranium leaves*
1 cup superfine sugar

3 cups cold water
¼ cup freshly squeezed lemon juice (1 large lemon)

You may substitute an equivalent number of leaves of another scented geranium.

❋ Grind the lemon geranium leaves and sugar together in a food processor until the mixture is a fine green powder. Add the water and lemon juice. Strain the geranium mixture through a fine sieve. Freeze in an ice-cream maker following the manufacturer's instructions.

Yield: 1 quart or 8 servings

❋ This ultra-refreshing and very easy sorbet is the most delightful way I know to enjoy the lemon-times-ten flavor of Mabel Grey lemon geraniums.
❋ Serve with a shortbread cookie or a light, crisp tuile and/or fresh berries.

Chocolate–Rose Geranium Soufflé

1¼ cups whole milk
10 rose geranium leaves
¼ vanilla bean, split
Soft unsalted butter and sugar for preparing the soufflé dish
2 tablespoons unsalted butter

3 tablespoons all-purpose flour
4 ounces semisweet baking chocolate
1 ounce unsweetened chocolate
3 large egg yolks
4 large egg whites
½ cup sugar

✦ Bring the milk to a boil in a small saucepan. As soon as it comes to a full boil, add the rose geranium leaves and the vanilla. Cover, remove from the heat, and let the milk mixture steep for at least 30 minutes.

✦ Preheat the oven to 375°F. Heavily butter and sugar a 6-cup soufflé dish. Strain the infused milk, squeezing out any liquid retained by the leaves. Reserve the infused milk.

✦ Melt the butter in a medium-sized saucepan over medium heat. Whisk in the flour and cook for 1 minute. Pour in the infused milk, and continue to whisk vigorously until the milk mixture comes to a boil and thickens. Transfer it to a large mixing bowl, whisk in the chocolates, and then the egg yolks.

✦ Beat the egg whites until they form soft peaks. Gradually beat in the sugar until the meringue is stiff and glossy. Fold one-third of the meringue into the chocolate mixture to loosen it, then gently fold in the remaining meringue. Scoop the batter into the soufflé dish. Bake for 40 to 45 minutes until well risen. Serve immediately.

Yield: 8 servings

Timesaver Tip: If you wish, you can make the chocolate mixture ahead and store it, covered, in the refrigerator for 2 or 3 days. Bring the chocolate mixture to room temperature before continuing.

✦ Rose geranium is one of the few herbs that works well in chocolate desserts. In this dish, its perfume wafts alongside the seductive hot chocolate aroma. Rose geranium leaves vary not only in size, but also in strength according to the season in which they're harvested, so you may want to use fewer or more leaves. People's tolerance for their floral intensity varies, so keep that in mind as well.

✦ Serve this soufflé with lightly whipped cream, softened ice cream, or raspberry sauce.

sorrel

Rumex

a NATIVE OF EUROPE, SORREL HAS dark green, arrow-shaped leaves that contain calcium, potassium, iron, vitamin A, and so much vitamin C sorrel was once used to treat scurvy. Sorrel is also known as sourgrass, dock, or sour dock. There is also a variety called garden sorrel, but it's the French variety that's most prized for cooking. Early Romans ate sorrel because they believed it could counter the effects of overindulging in rich foods. In Tudor times, no herb garden was considered complete without it. Today, sorrel is often overlooked; in general, people either love it or hate it. Ironically, sorrel symbolizes affection. You'll find sorrel most often in French and Polish cuisine.

Sorrel's lemony tart flavor makes the young leaves an excellent addition to salads. Use this rhubarb relative to make sorrel soup, cook it with other greens such as spinach, and use it to garnish any dish that needs a little green. Sorrel is often used in cream sauces and stuffings. Simmered in butter and cream, sorrel adds zip to salmon and trout.

To store sorrel, wash and dry the leaves, wrap them in a paper towel, enclose them in a plastic bag, and store it in the refrigerator. You can also purée the leaves with water and freeze the purée in ice cube trays. Toss a cube or two into soup or vegetable dishes during the winter.

On a low salt diet? You need less salt when foods are flavored with sorrel. If you are using sorrel in a salad, because of sorrel's acidity you'll probably want to decrease the amount of lemon juice or vinegar in the dressing.

olivier de saint martin

executive chef/partner
⋙ ⋘

Dock Street Brasserie
Philadelphia, Pennsylvania

*t*RAINED BY THE BEST FRENCH CHEFS — Gaston Lenôtre, Claude Verger, Paul Bocuse, and Michel Guérard — De Saint Martin combines his classic French training with influences from his mother's kitchen.

He draws on the dishes she made during his childhood in northern France to create robust and hearty dishes such as lamb shank with tomato and sorrel sauce (page 181) for Dock Street Brasserie's menu.

He likes sorrel's acidity. "It puts a zing in the mouth," says De Saint Martin. "It's like putting lemon juice in sauce. In Normandy, we used to purée sorrel and serve it as a sauce with country-style veal." He uses a chiffonade of sorrel as a topping for veal chops, and tosses some in green salads. It provides a perfect balance to the sweetness of salmon, he says, and also goes well with chicken. Sorrel also perks up cream and butter sauces.

Despite its sometimes large leaves, sorrel is a fragile herb. De Saint Martin says that while it's strong in flavor, it's very delicate. He suggests washing the leaves in room-temperature water and "shredding the leaves to get the flavor out. Shredding right before serving brings its lemon astringency out." Add sorrel to hot dishes at the last minute, he says, or it turns gray.

De Saint Martin made his American debut as executive sous-chef at Le Bernardin in New York, came to Philadelphia in 1989 as executive chef at the Bellevue Hotel, and later opened La Coupole in the Bourse. He was executive chef at La Campagne in Cherry Hill, New Jersey, before coming to Dock Street in 1996.

He wants Dock Street Brasserie to be "a place to rendezvous, to discuss life, to eat fresh and wholesome food, to drink great beer." And, he says, "finally, my kitchen smells like my mother's."

At Dock Street Brasserie, patrons can watch brewery operations through a glass wall while dining on French brasserie food. A brasserie is a place to "enjoy good food and good beer," says De Saint Martin. To that end, his menu features reasonably priced French bistro food.

Each year, 65 different beers are brewed on the premises, and 10 different kinds are on tap each day. Too many choices? Not to worry, the wait staff is trained to help diners pair beer with their food.

The diners at the Dock Street Brasserie are as likely to be part of the black-tie, after-theater crowd as they are to be part of a college crowd celebrating the end of finals. Linen tablecloths grace the tables, and rich cherry wood, polished copper brew kettles, and terra cotta tiles adorn the main dining room and the bar area. Dock Street Brasserie also hosts monthly beer tastings and offers brewery tours.

Sorrel Soup

¼ pound butter (½ cup)
2 leeks, chopped
1 onion, chopped
2 pounds sorrel, sliced very fine, without stalks

2 quarts chicken stock (page 219), fat removed
Salt and pepper
½ cup crème fraîche
3 eggs

❧ In a 3-quart saucepan, heat the butter until it is bubbling but not brown. Add the leek and onion, and cook until tender. Reserve 6 teaspoons of the sorrel for the garnish. Add the remaining sorrel to the onion mixture, and cook until the sorrel becomes soft. Add the chicken stock and a little salt and pepper, and simmer for 45 minutes. Add the cream, and cook another 15 minutes. Place the soup in a blender or food processor, and process until the soup is smooth.

❧ Just before serving time, beat the eggs until fluffy in the top of a double boiler. Whisk the eggs into the soup. Garnish the soup with the reserved sorrel.

Yield: 6 servings

Pan Seared Cod with Caramelized Onions and Sorrel Butter Sauce

Caramelized Onions:
4 onions, sliced
2 cups red wine
2 cups red wine vinegar

Salt and pepper
⅓ cup honey
¼ cup butter

Sorrel Butter Sauce:
2 shallots, chopped
¾ cup dry vermouth
¾ cup white wine
1 cup heavy cream

½ pound butter (1 cup)
Salt and pepper
¼ cup sliced sorrel

Pan Seared Cod:
4 (8-ounce) cod steaks, skin on

Olive oil

❧ To prepare the onions, in a large saucepan combine the onion, red wine, vinegar, and a little salt and pepper. Cook the onion mixture over medium heat until all the liquid has evaporated. Add the honey, and continue cooking over medium heat until the onion has caramelized. Remove the saucepan from the heat, add the butter, and combine. Keep the onion mixture warm until serving time.

❧ Sorrel soup is popular in Sweden, as well as in France. We would pair this slightly bitter and velvety soup with a medium-bodied beer such as a Dock Street amber.

❧ A rustic bread would go well with this soup.

❧ With its tart lemon flavor, sorrel is a traditional accompaniment to fish. Here, the flavor is softened with sweet onions and a rich butter sauce. We would pair this dish with a medium-bodied beer such as a Dunkel.

❧ Roasted potatoes and a green vegetable salad would round out this meal.

✦ To prepare the sauce, in a skillet combine the shallot, vermouth, and white wine, and cook over high heat until the liquid has been reduced by about half. Add the cream, and boil the shallot mixture for 2 minutes. Add the butter, and whisk until combined. Season the shallot mixture with a little salt and pepper. Set the sorrel aside until just before the sauce is served.

✦ To prepare the fish, preheat the oven to 400°F. In an ovenproof skillet, pan sear the cod steaks skin side down in olive oil until they are golden brown. Turn the cod steaks, and finish cooking them in the oven for 5 to 8 minutes.

✦ To finish the sauce, add the reserved sorrel, and stir.

✦ To serve, spoon some of the onions onto the plate, place a cod steak on the onions, and top with some sorrel sauce.

Yield: 4 servings

Lamb Shank with Tomato and Sorrel Sauce

4 (¾-pound) lamb shanks	1 onion, quartered
Salt and pepper	1 bay leaf
4 tablespoons cooking oil	1 quart light beer
3 tomatoes, quartered	1 tablespoon tomato paste
1 carrot, quartered	4 tablespoons butter
1 head garlic, peeled	¼ cup sliced sorrel

✦ Season the lamb shanks with salt and pepper. In a large saucepan over high heat, sear the lamb shanks in the oil. Add the tomato, carrot, garlic, and onion, and combine. Cook the tomato mixture over medium heat for 5 minutes. Stir in the bay leaf, beer, and tomato paste, and simmer gently for 4 to 5 hours until the lamb shanks are tender and cooked through. Remove the lamb shanks from the saucepan, and place them on a plate.

✦ To finish the sauce, over high heat reduce the cooking liquid to 2 cups. Remove the bay leaf. Blend the cooking liquid and vegetables in a blender or food processor, and strain. Return to the saucepan. Just before the sauce is to be served, whisk in the butter and sorrel.

✦ To serve, place a lamb shank on the plate, and top with some sauce.

Yield: 4 servings

✦ Use very ripe tomatoes for this dish for their fuller flavor. The lemon flavor of the sorrel counters the fattiness of the lamb shank. We pair this hearty dish with a full-bodied beer such as a Dock Street double bock.

✦ Serve this dish very hot. Roasted vegetables such as carrots and potatoes go nicely with this country-style dish. You can also serve it over pasta.

stinging nettle

Urtica dioica

*h*ERE'S A REALLY DISTINCTIVE HERB that finds its way into many chef's kitchens across North America. There's a reason it's called stinging nettle, the same reason you should wear protective gloves when handling uncooked nettles. The leaves have stinging hairs that release formic acid when you brush against them. The acid causes a stinging sensation and sometimes welts on the skin. Stinging nettle's botanical name, *Urtica*, is from the Latin word *uro,* meaning "I burn." The acid is removed during cooking, leaving behind green leaves with culinary, medicinal, and cosmetic uses. Before adding stinging nettle to any recipe, boil it for 30 seconds and then plunge it into ice water.

You might wonder why folks would bother with an herb that harbors such aggression. Once used, believe it or not, to make fabric, this herb is rich in nutrients, especially vitamin C, and is still used by many as a spring tonic. Stinging nettle has a high calcium content and contains other nutrients such as magnesium, iron, and vitamins A and B. The plant is also a source of vitamin K, believed to be beneficial to the blood. Practitioners of homeopathic medicine prescribe stinging nettle for a number of ailments. It has also been used in cosmetics, to make dye, and as cattle fodder. Organic gardeners make an infusion of stinging nettle that they use as a spray to fight aphids. Early folklore decrees that when carried, stinging nettle gives the person carrying it courage and drives away fear.

Stinging nettle grows wild in moist, shady areas. In the kitchen, young, early spring shoots, which have no stinging hairs, are sometimes included in spring salads. The shoots can be steamed like spinach and other greens and add flavor, as well as nutrition, to stocks. Stinging nettle is also used to make soup, oils, and sauces, as well as tea.

sinclair philip

*P*HILIP AND HIS STAFF OF FIVE CHEFS include stinging nettle in a number of their dishes. Like sorrel and chervil, stinging nettle is used more often by European chefs than by North American ones. Philip says stinging nettle is widely available, in fact, "abundant in our area," and appears in many cookbooks.

Its stinging nature, he says, keeps it from being planted in many herb gardens. If you want to grow it, he advises placing it off in a corner away from areas with lots of traffic.

"It's very nutritious. You'll find many health food stores carry stinging nettle tea."

Stinging nettle can be prepared similar to sorrel and spinach and is often puréed and used as a sauce for meat or fish.

Philip says stinging nettle is best harvested in spring when the shoots are young and tender, but it can also be cut back to the ground during summer and early fall for a late harvest of new shoots.

"We don't use anything other than seasonal, regional, and organic produce, so they fit quite well into our cooking program. Our menu focuses on local fish and shellfish, as well as many organic herbs, vegetables, salad greens, and edible flowers grown in on-site, year-round, organic, outdoor gardens. The menu changes daily to take advantage of the local ingredients while they're at their peak of flavor."

Philip earned a doctorate in political economics from the University of Grenoble in France. During an 11-year sojourn in Europe, he became acquainted with the vegetable dishes and seafood cuisine of several regions of France, particularly that of the Mediterranean and the Alpine regions. As a scuba diver, beachcomber, and gardener, he learned a great deal about common and uncommon vegetables, herbs, and seafood varieties, including their handling and culinary applications in southern Europe.

He brought that education back to Sooke Harbour House, located at the southern tip of Vancouver Island, to create a seaside restaurant that has been rated one of the top 10 restaurants in Canada for 13 consecutive years by *Where to Eat in Canada.*

Sooke Harbour House, known as a "romantic little white inn by the sea," offers 15 rooms for overnight guests.

Sooke Harbour House has earned four stars from the *Mobil Travel Guide,* was among the top three on a list of romantic getaways in *Seattle* magazine and was deemed a favorite restaurant, and was rated among the top Victoria and Vancouver Island restaurants for food, service. and décor in the *Zagat Survey.*

The inn and restaurant have been featured in the *Los Angeles Times* and *The New York Times.* Canada's largest national newspaper, *The Globe and Mail,* named Sooke Harbour House the best restaurant in Canada for 1997.

*executive
chef/innkeeper*
❖❖

Sooke Harbour House
Sooke, British Columbia

Sooke Harbour House Egg Roulade of Smoked Salmon, Morel Duxelles, and Stinging Nettle Leaves with Stinging Nettle and Tulip Petal Sauces

❧ This recipe, which makes an elegant brunch entrée, was developed by co-chef Frank Von Zuben of Sooke Harbour House. "We have all these wonderful ingredients available; it's fun to incorporate them into our menu. Taking the time to pick [stinging nettles] or convincing someone else to, is the trick," says Von Zuben.

Egg Roulade:
4 cups whole milk
⅜ pound unsalted butter (¾ cup)
1½ cups all-purpose flour
6 large free-range eggs, separated
2 tablespoons dry white wine such as Canadian Gewürztraminer

2 tablespoons sour cream
1 teaspoon sea salt
¼ cup chopped herbs such as parsley, tarragon, and oregano

Stinging Nettles:
8 cups stinging nettle leaves

Morel Duxelles:
1½ pounds morel, cremini, or other strongly flavored mushrooms, or a combination
6 tablespoons unsalted butter

½ cup sunflower oil
1 cup finely diced onion
¼ cup dry white wine such as Canadian Gewürztraminer

Cream Sauce Base (for the two sauces):
3 cups light whipping cream

1 cup dry white wine such as Canadian Gewürztraminer

Roulade of Smoked Salmon (assembly):
Reserved egg roulade
½ pound smoked sockeye salmon,* sliced
You could substitute coho or Chinook.

Reserved morel duxelles
Reserved stinging nettles

Tulip Petal Sauce:
8 tulip petals, sliced into ¹⁄₁₆-inch julienne

1 cup reserved cream sauce

Stinging Nettle Sauce:
1 cup reserved cream sauce

¼ cup reserved stinging nettle juice

1 tablespoon reserved stinging nettle juice
Tulip petals (optional)

Whole chive leaves (optional)

❧ To prepare the egg roulade, preheat the oven to 350°F. Line a 17 by 11-inch jellyroll pan with parchment paper.

✦ In a medium-sized saucepan, heat the milk until it is steaming. Set the milk aside.

✦ In another medium-sized saucepan, melt the butter over medium heat. When the butter has melted and the bubbles have subsided, stir in the flour. Cook, stirring with a wooden spoon, for 3 to 4 minutes until the flour mixture starts to turn a golden color. Remove the flour mixture from the heat, and allow to cool for 2 minutes.

✦ Whisk the egg yolks into the flour mixture, one at a time, and combine thoroughly. Add the wine, sour cream, salt, milk, and herbs, and stir well to incorporate.

✦ In a stainless steel or glass bowl, beat the egg white with a wire whisk until stiff peaks form. Stir one-third of the beaten egg white into the herb mixture. Fold the remaining egg white into the herb mixture until it is evenly mixed and no egg white remains visible. Spread the egg mixture evenly into the jellyroll pan. Bake until the egg mixture becomes an even, golden color and has set firmly, about 20 minutes. Remove the egg roulade from the oven, turn it out immediately onto a tea towel, and set the egg roulade aside to cool.

✦ To prepare the stinging nettles, blanch the stinging nettle leaves in boiling water for 1 minute. Immediately plunge the blanched nettles into ice water. Remove the nettles from the ice water after 2 minutes. Squeeze the nettles well to remove any excess moisture. Set aside two-thirds of the nettles for the salmon roulade assembly.

✦ Juice the remaining nettles in a juicer with a fine-mesh screen, following manufacturer's directions. Cover the juice, and refrigerate it for the stinging nettle sauce, which is made just before the dish is served.

✦ To prepare the morel duxelles, clean the mushrooms by brushing them off. Avoid using any water to clean the mushrooms unless it is absolutely necessary. Chop the mushrooms finely by hand, or if using a food processor, chop them 1 cup at a time, pulsing until the mushrooms are finely chopped.

✦ Combine the butter and oil in a medium-sized sauté pan over medium heat. When the butter has melted and the bubbles have subsided, add the onion, and cook for about 3 minutes. Do not allow the onion to brown. Add the wine, and cook until it has evaporated and the onion is transparent, about 3 minutes. Add the mushrooms, and cook, stirring, until all the released mushroom liquid has evaporated, about 5 minutes. Set aside the morel duxelles for the salmon roulade assembly.

✦ To prepare the cream sauce base, bring the cream and wine to a boil in a large saucepan over medium heat. Whisk the cream mixture as it boils to prevent it from bubbling over. Reduce by one-half to make a smooth, thick cream sauce. Divide the cream sauce into 2 equal portions of 1 cup each. Set each aside, covered with plastic wrap, until the tulip and stinging nettle sauces are prepared. Meanwhile, assemble the salmon roulade.

(continued on next page)

> ✦ **The egg roulade, morel duxelles, and stinging nettle leaves are assembled with the salmon and served with the sauces.**

✦ To assemble the roulade, place the cooled egg roulade, still on the tea towel, in front of you on a flat surface with the longest side nearest you. Carefully remove the parchment paper. Lay slices of salmon on the egg roulade, starting at the edge closest to you and covering all but a 3-inch strip at the top (that is, the side farthest from you).

✦ Spread the reserved morel duxelles over the salmon slices. Chop the reserved stinging nettles, and spread evenly over the morel duxelles. Using the tea towel, gently roll the filled roulade away from you to form an evenly shaped log. Be patient; the roulade is fragile. Carefully transfer the roulade onto a 2-foot length of heavy-duty aluminum foil. Tightly wrap the foil around the roulade, pinching in the ends to seal the foil.

✦ Place the roulade on a baking sheet, and let it stand for at least 30 minutes to become firm. (The roulade may be stored in the refrigerator as long as overnight.)

✦ Preheat the oven to 350°F. Heat the aluminum wrapped roulade log for about 8 to 10 minutes. If the roulade has been refrigerated, heat it for 10 to 15 minutes or until warmed through. Warm the serving plates at the same time.

✦ To prepare the tulip and stinging nettle sauces, carefully heat each of the reserved cups of cream sauce in a separate small saucepan over medium-low heat for about 5 minutes. To finish the tulip petal sauce, combine the tulip petals with 1 cup of the cream sauce, and remove from the heat. To finish the stinging nettle sauce, combine ¼ cup of the reserved stinging nettle juice with the other cup of the cream sauce, and remove from the heat. Set aside the remaining stinging nettle juice for garnishing the serving plates.

✦ To serve the salmon roulade, carefully remove the aluminum foil and place the roulade on a cutting board. Slice the roulade into 8 (2-inch) slices, and place two of them on each of the heated plates. Spoon about 3 tablespoons of each cream sauce around the slices of roulade, and dot the sauces with the reserved stinging nettle juice. Garnish with the optional tulip petals and whole chive leaves, and serve immediately. Additional cream sauces can be served on the side.

Yield: 4 servings

Note: Be sure the tulips are from a source that grows them organically. Flowers from the florist are often sprayed with pesticides. You should also note that the tulip petals are edible, but the bulbs are toxic. Use only the solidly colored portion of the tulip petals and not the area from the base of the petal where it changes color. This portion is more bitter than the rest of the petal.

Timesaver Tips: The egg roulade, cream reduction, and stinging nettle juice can be prepared the day before and stored, covered, in the refrigerator. The tulip sauce and stinging nettle sauces can be finished just before the dish is served.

Sooke Harbour House Wild Sorrel and Stinging Nettle Oil

4 cups canola oil
2 cloves garlic
1 cup lightly packed wild sorrel*

Cultivated French sorrel can be substituted.

1 cup tightly packed stinging nettle leaves and tops, stems removed

❧ Place the oil, garlic, sorrel, and stinging nettle in a blender, and purée on high speed. Pour the oil mixture into a clean, sterile jar, and store it in the refrigerator for 24 hours to allow the sediment to settle. Ladle off the clear oil at the top, or strain the oil and sediment through a chinois or a few layers of cheesecloth.

❧ Store the infused oil in an opaque container in the refrigerator. If a film appears on the oil, skim the film off. The oil will keep for up to 1 month refrigerated.

Yield: 4 cups

❧ Infused oils are quite often used to replace cream and butter sauces in many North American restaurants. This oil is both nutritious and delicious and can be used to flavor a number of dishes or just drizzled on the plate as a garnish. This recipe was developed by Sooke Harbour House co-chef Edward Tuson.

❧ Use this oil as you would any oil — to sauté potatoes or other vegetables or meats, and for salad dressings and marinades.

tarragon

Artemesia dracunculus

*t*ARRAGON, ONCE CONSIDERED A CURE for snakebite, was introduced to Europe by crusaders who brought it back with them from the Near East. It's also been called the dragon herb because its roots resemble coiled up snakes. Its Latin name includes the word *dracunculus*, meaning "little dragon," and the English name (and the French *estragon*) also mean "little dragon." Tarragon is said to have been one of Charlemagne's favorite herbs and was grown in the royal gardens in Tudor times.

Both Russian and French varieties of tarragon exist, but the French one is the most prized for culinary uses. Its peppery licorice flavor is often paired with chicken and fish. Tarragon is the flavoring of the classic béarnaise sauce and of other cream sauces. This herb is often combined with mushrooms, leeks, tomatoes, and potatoes, goes well with steak and lamb, and is used in omelets, herb butters, and cream cheese. Vegetables such as cauliflower, cabbage, asparagus, artichokes, and beets are enlivened by a sprinkling of tarragon or a dollop of tarragon butter.

When combined with chives, chervil, and parsley, tarragon becomes the classic herb blend, fines herbes. Since tarragon has a strong flavor and aroma, this herb is rarely used with other robust herbs such as rosemary, sage, or thyme. Tarragon is also best used sparingly and should be added toward the end of the cooking time. The flavor of tarragon, unlike that of most herbs, intensifies during cooking. If cooked too long, tarragon will show its bitter side.

Tarragon contains potassium, small amounts of calcium, and magnesium.

bobby trigg

*b*OBBY TRIGG, A ONE-TIME WALL STREET BROKER, traded ticker tape for menus when he enrolled in The Restaurant School in Philadelphia. At the same time, he embarked on an old-world style apprenticeship with Jean Pierre Tardy, formerly of Le Bec-Fin in Philadelphia. From there, Trigg moved to a position at the prestigious Peacock Inn in Princeton, where he worked as a sous-chef.

In 1992, Trigg opened The Ferry House on the site of the original Coryell Ferry House, a popular colonial-era gathering place in Lambertville, New Jersey, across the river from New Hope, Pennsylvania. Now located in Princeton, The Ferry House boasts an innovative menu that displays creative use of fresh, locally farmed ingredients. "Keep it fresh, simple, and fun" is Trigg's motto.

Trigg likes to combine flavors to create surprising new tastes. Often, it's tarragon that helps him add a new twist to dishes on his menu, which changes every two weeks. He especially likes tarragon with mushrooms and fish.

"The late, great, Jerry Garcia of the Grateful Dead was once quoted as saying, 'Our fans are like licorice; they either love us or hate us.' I believe that's true [of tarragon]. Tarragon's licorice flavor is an incredible taste to some, while others refuse to eat it."

He says when a customer asks what herb is in one of his dishes, 99 times out of a hundred it's tarragon. "I use it a lot when I cook. I like its clean flavor; it lets you taste all the other ingredients in the dish as well. Then, when you least expect it, you taste it again. When used correctly, it has a subtle anise-like flavor that's comparable to the subtle sweetness of Jerry Garcia's guitar solos."

Trigg is most known for his lamb dishes, particularly a rack of lamb with a mustard-thyme crust that's nearly always on the menu. His signature dessert is crème brûlée. A popular lunch dish is grilled portobello burger — a portobello mushroom that is marinated and then slow roasted and grilled to order and topped with grilled vegetables and pesto.

Trigg has been featured in a number of area publications, including *New Jersey Monthly*.

chef/owner

The Ferry House
Princeton, New Jersey

Sautéed Scallops with Rhubarb Coulis and Tarragon Aïoli

Rhubarb Coulis:
2 tablespoons minced garlic
2 tablespoons chopped tarragon
1 cup Port
1 pound rhubarb, cleaned and cut into 2-inch chunks

1 tablespoon sugar
1¼ cups vegetable stock (page 218)
Salt and pepper

Tarragon Aïoli:
2 egg yolks
2 tablespoons apple cider vinegar
2 tablespoons minced garlic
1 tablespoon Dijon mustard

1¾ cups canola oil
¼ cup Pernod
3 tablespoons minced tarragon
Salt and pepper

Sautéed Scallops:
Oil

20 jumbo scallops

Baby greens tossed with fresh herb vinaigrette

❧ To prepare the coulis, preheat the oven to 350°F. Combine the garlic, tarragon, wine, rhubarb, and sugar in an ovenproof skillet. Bake until the rhubarb is soft, about 15 minutes. Place the rhubarb mixture in a food processor with the stock and some salt and pepper, and purée. Set the rhubarb coulis aside.

❧ Preheat the oven to 400°F for the scallops.

❧ To prepare the aïoli, place the egg yolks, vinegar, garlic, and mustard in a blender or food processor. Process the egg mixture, adding the oil in a fine stream until the egg mixture begins to look like mayonnaise. Add the Pernod, and process briefly. Add the tarragon and a little salt and pepper, and process briefly again. Set the aïoli aside.

❧ To prepare the scallops, heat a little oil in an ovenproof skillet. Add the scallops, and sear them over high heat until one side is golden brown, about 2 to 3 minutes. Turn the scallops, and place the skillet in the oven for 1 to 2 minutes to finish cooking the scallops.

❧ To serve, arrange the baby greens in the center of 4 plates. Pour the rhubarb coulis around the greens, and arrange 5 scallops on the coulis on each plate. Drizzle some aïoli over the top.

Yield: 4 servings

❧ The combination of the sweet scallop, the tart rhubarb, and the bitter and peppery baby greens with the licorice flavor of the tarragon makes this dish an interesting blend of flavors.

❧ Try garnishing this dish with some shredded carrot or some fried sweet potato matchsticks.

Red Snapper, Shrimp, Clams, and Oysters with Pernod Tarragon Butter Sauce

Pernod Tarragon Butter Sauce:
2 tablespoons minced garlic
2 tablespoons minced shallot
1 cup white wine
¼ cup fresh lemon juice

½ cup heavy cream
¼ cup Pernod
1 pound butter (2 cups)
Salt and pepper

Red Snapper, Shrimps, Clams, and Oysters:
4 (5 to 6-ounce) red snapper fillets
Oil
16 littleneck clams

2 tablespoons chopped tarragon

16 large shrimp, cleaned and deveined
16 oysters, shucked

❧ Preheat the oven to 400°F for the seafood.

❧ To prepare the sauce, combine the garlic, shallot, white wine, and lemon juice and reduce by two-thirds. Stir in the cream, and reduce again by one-half. Stir in the Pernod, and remove the cream mixture from the heat. Add the butter a small piece at a time until it's all incorporated. Season with a little salt and pepper. Set the sauce aside.

❧ To prepare the seafood, sauté the snapper in some oil, skin side up, in a large ovenproof skillet for 2 to 3 minutes. Turn the snapper, add the clams and shrimp, and finish in the oven until the clams begin to open, about 3 to 4 minutes.

❧ When the clams have opened and the snapper and shrimp are cooked, remove the seafood from the skillet and set the seafood aside. Add the oysters to the skillet, and cook them over high heat for 1 to 2 minutes.

❧ To serve, place a red snapper fillet on each plate. Top with shrimp, clams, and oysters. Ladle some sauce over the seafood, and sprinkle with some chopped tarragon.

Yield: 4 servings

❧ Here's another incredible combination involving seafood and the anise flavor of tarragon. The sweet shrimp, the succulent clams, the explosion of a fried oyster, the delicacy of the red snapper, the anise flavor in the butter sauce — all these result in a dish that is really appealing to seafood lovers.

❧ Serve this dish with light accompaniments such as spinach or kale and fresh asparagus.

Chanterelles with Apricot Brandy and Tarragon Cream

1 cup sliced chanterelles
2 tablespoons ginger oil*
2 tablespoons minced garlic
¼ cup apricot brandy

¼ cup heavy cream
2 tablespoons finely chopped tarragon
Salt and pepper

Ginger oil is available in Asian markets and specialty stores.

➤ Sauté the chanterelles in the ginger oil for 1 to 2 minutes. Add the garlic and apricot brandy, and flambé. Stir in the cream over low heat. Remove from the heat, add the tarragon, and season with a little salt and pepper.

Yield: 4 servings

Note: To make your own ginger oil, simply infuse 1 cup olive oil with several slices of ginger. Store the remaining infused oil in the refrigerator.

➤ My friend Tom, a wine salesman, suggested using apricot brandy with chanterelles. I gave it a try and found this combination very satisfying. Add tarragon and a touch of balsamic vinegar, and your taste buds will be most surprised.

➤ Serve these mushrooms on sautéed spinach with lots of garlic and a touch of balsamic vinegar.

raymond ost

*I*N 1993, RAYMOND OST WAS SELECTED from 275 chefs worldwide to receive the Master Chef of France award. His culinary background stretches back 25 years to when, at the age of 13, he served an apprenticeship in his native Alsace, France. At 19, he was named *chef de partie* at Restaurant Seeterrasse in Ingelheim, Germany, where he managed the entire kitchen, created a new menu, and supervised a staff of four that prepared 250 meals a day.

Ost confesses to a lifelong love of food, which was probably instilled in him by his mother. As a young boy, he often joined her in the kitchen and together they cooked. He's always liked tarragon because "it tastes and smells very good. I grew up with tarragon; everybody in our family had a garden." Ost still gardens, in fact, and grows tarragon along with another of his favorite herbs, thyme. He says tarragon's spiciness makes it a good herb to work with. He likes it for sauces, says it's great in salads, and good in meat marinades. But best of all, he likes it with fish.

His signature dish is *flammenküche*, a traditional Alsatian dish, which he makes in three savory varieties — a classic version with thinly sliced onion, hickory smoked bacon, and fromage blanc (a soft cheese); a smoked chicken version; and a portobello mushroom version. He also offers a dessert version, made with warm strawberries and pineapple.

Ost brings another bit of Alsace to Sandrine's with a *Stamtich*, known in France as *table d'hôte*. The Stamtich is a table that serves as a central meeting place for the owner, chef, and selected friends. It also serves as a place where solo diners can feel welcome.

Ost earned a bachelor's degree in hotel and restaurant management from L'École hôtelière in Strasbourg, France. At the same time, he worked full time at Restaurant de la Neinau, eventually becoming chef de partie. During that time he won three gold medals and two second place citations in various international culinary competitions.

He opened Sandrine's, named after his daughter, in 1996. The casual bistro features an Alsatian menu with New England influences. There are many similarities between Alsace and New England, says Ost. "They both have four distinct seasons and a bounty of regional ingredients. In both places, people enjoy food."

In 1977, he joined the Le Meridien Hotel Corporation, for which he worked at Le Meridien kitchens in Martinique, Kuwait, Abu Dhabi, and San Francisco. In 1988, he took over the reins at Le Meridien's Boston hotel, including those of Cafe Fleuri, the hotel's catering and pastry departments, and the dining room, Julien. During his tenure, Julien was ranked as Boston's number one lunch destination by *Zagat Survey*. The brunch, which was created by Ost, was named the best brunch in Boston for eight consecutive years by *Boston* magazine, and *Gourmet* magazine readers ranked Julien number one in ambiance and food in Boston.

chef/owner

Sandrine's
Cambridge, Massachusetts

Steamed Halibut with Zucchini and Carrot Scales in a Celeriac Sauce

1 pound Peruvian potatoes* (about 24)
2 pounds small zucchini, thinly sliced (about 5 cups)
1 pound carrots, thinly sliced (about 3 cups)
3 pounds halibut fillets
Salt and pepper
1 bunch tarragon
Oil

1 head celeriac, diced
8 large shallots, chopped (about 8 tablespoons)
2 tablespoons sherry vinegar
1 cup white wine
1 cup fish stock (page 217)
12 tablespoons butter

Peruvian potatoes are small purple potatoes available in specialty markets.

6 sprigs chervil

❧ Boil the potatoes until tender, about 8 to 10 minutes. Remove them from the heat, and immerse them in ice water to stop the cooking process. When the potatoes are cool, slice them thinly, and set them aside.

❧ Blanch the zucchini and carrot in boiling water. Drain, and set them aside to cool.

❧ Season the halibut with a little salt and pepper. Remove the tarragon leaves from their stems. Place about half the tarragon leaves on top of the halibut. Layer the zucchini and carrot slices in an alternating pattern on top of the tarragon leaves, overlapping the slices to resemble fish scales. Place the halibut on a rack in a large saucepan or steamer. Add boiling water, keeping the water level below the steaming rack. Cover the saucepan, and steam the halibut for 10 minutes.

❧ Place some oil in a medium sauté pan, and sauté the celeriac with the shallot and the remaining tarragon leaves until the celeriac is tender and golden. Deglaze the pan with the vinegar and wine. Add the fish stock, and simmer for 10 minutes. Pour the celeriac mixture into a blender or food processor, and purée until smooth. With the blender running, add the butter a tablespoon at a time, blending until the sauce is smooth.

❧ To serve, pour some sauce onto each plate. Arrange the potato slices on each plate, and lay a halibut fillet on top of the potatoes. Garnish each plate with a chervil sprig.

Yield: 6 servings

Note: While it's nice to use Peruvian potatoes for their color, you could substitute fingerling or new potatoes, or even use rice instead of potatoes. You could also substitute another mild, white fish for the halibut.

Shopping Tip: Choose zucchini with a small diameter for easier handling when forming the scales.

❧ Placing the tarragon leaves directly on the fish imparts its anise flavor to the fish. Covering the fish with the vegetables helps hold that flavor in similar to cooking en papillote.

❧ A good, crisp country bread would make this a complete meal.

thomas iatesta

*t*HOMAS IATESTA'S PASSION FOR TARRAGON is rooted in his childhood. "As a child, I grew up caring for my mother's herb garden. Next to basil, tarragon was the herb I most noticed because it is so aromatic and sweet." He says tarragon's strong flavor makes it a great seasoning when baking or grilling either poultry or mild fish. Iatesta urges home cooks to try using tarragon as an accent when baking breads or creating soups. Tarragon flavors a demiglace he uses for poultry and his smoked salmon mousse, and is often a central character in his meat crusts.

When he was growing up, hospitality was a priority in the Iatesta home. At The Gourmet's Table, a family-owned restaurant and catering service, he strives to "present exquisite cuisine, perfect ambiance, and professional service. We wanted to create a restaurant where people enjoy the taste and appearance of the food, and, at the same time, feel like guests in our home." Wood tables, white cotton napkins, candles, and jazz in the background help create the comfortable atmosphere.

Iatesta combines his Italian heritage with his classic French training and experience to create his "contemporary French and Italian cuisine." He is known for his light, healthy, colorful creations that are full of flavor due to the fresh herbs and seasonal produce he uses. He likes to emphasize the natural essence of foods. His technique is most evident in his signature soups, such as mussel bisque, lobster bisque, and vichyssoise. He uses seasonings and purées, rather than an excess of starch and cream, to give his soups body and flavor, not fat. A recent addition to the menu is a chilled tomato cucumber soup drizzled with basil purée. Iatesta's strength as a chef is in his ability to balance flavors and seasonings. When planning his menu, he asks himself, "Would I enjoy eating this and is it beautiful?"

After earning a culinary arts degree at the Academy of Culinary Arts in Atlantic County, New Jersey, Iatesta was chef de cuisine at Provence Restaurant in Philadelphia and was also sous-chef under Jean-François Taquet at Taquet Restaurant, also in Philadelphia, before opening The Gourmet's Table. Taquet, Iatesta's mentor, has described Iatesta as "a chef who creates cuisine with the utmost dedication to the highest standards of our profession."

The restaurant is frequently the site of special events. Iatesta orchestrated a special menu to coincide with a performance by local guitarist Russell Ferrara, for instance, and has also hosted wine tasting dinners in conjunction with the Chadds Ford Winery.

Shortly after opening in 1997, The Gourmet's Table, located in a Philadelphia suburb, was cited as a best bet of new restaurants by *Main Line Today* magazine. The restaurant has also been featured and reviewed in *The Philadelphia Inquirer* and the *Delaware County Daily Times* and was voted Best Restaurant by *Main Line Today* magazine.

executive chef/owner

The Gourmet's Table
East Goshen, Pennsylvania

Cream of Brie and Broccoli Soup with Fresh Tarragon

This soup is thickened naturally and simply with the Brie cheese, without the addition of arrowroot, cornstarch, or flour. Brie is named for the region in France where it originated.

This soup can serve well as a meal on its own accompanied by a nice, crusty bread and a glass of wine. It also makes a great first course for a hearty winter meal featuring poultry.

¼ cup chopped onion (about ½ medium-sized onion)
⅛ cup minced tarragon
2 teaspoons olive oil
½ cup white wine
1 large head broccoli, separated into florets
1 cup vegetable stock, homemade (page 218) or canned

2 tablespoons minced garlic (about 12 cloves)
1 quart heavy cream
1½ tablespoons salt
1 tablespoon pepper
1 cup chopped Brie cheese without the rind (about an 8-ounce wheel)

In a large saucepan, sauté the onion and tarragon in the oil over low to medium heat until the onion has caramelized, about 5 minutes. Deglaze the pan with the wine. Add the broccoli and stock, cover, and steam over low heat for about 2 to 3 minutes. When the broccoli is bright green, add the garlic, cream, salt, and pepper, and simmer over low to medium heat for about 5 to 10 minutes. Remove the broccoli mixture from the heat. Place the broccoli mixture in a blender, and blend at high speed until completely puréed. Pass the soup through a fine-mesh strainer.

Place the soup in a clean saucepan, and bring the soup to a slow simmer on low to medium heat. When the soup is hot, break up the cheese in your hands and add it to the soup. Vigorously whisk the cheese into the soup until the cheese is completely melted. Adjust the seasonings, if necessary.

Yield: 4 to 6 servings

Note: Do not steam the broccoli too long or it will turn brown. You want the broccoli to turn a bright green to make an attractive soup. Straining the soup is optional, depending on the texture you desire.

Pan Seared Tilapia Fillet with Fresh Tarragon Crust

1 medium-sized torpedo roll
¼ cup tarragon leaves
2 tablespoons grated Parmesan cheese
½ teaspoon minced garlic

¼ cup plus 1 tablespoon olive oil
Salt and pepper
1 (6-ounce) tilapia fillet

✢ Preheat the oven to 400°F. Slice the roll in half, and cut it into half moons. Toast the roll pieces in the oven for about 10 to 15 minutes or until they are completely toasted. Remove them from the oven, and leave the oven on for the fish.

✢ Place the toasted roll pieces in a food processor, grind them into coarse crumbs, and place the crumbs in a mixing bowl. Place the tarragon in the food processor, and process until the tarragon is coarsely minced. Add the tarragon to the bread crumbs, and mix well. Fold in the cheese, garlic, ¼ cup of the oil, and some salt and pepper. Mold some of the tarragon mixture in your hand to make sure it will hold together. If it stays molded, it is ready. If it does not, add a little more oil. Set the tarragon mixture aside.

✢ Rinse the tilapia and pat it dry with paper towels. Season it on both sides with some salt and pepper. Place the remaining oil in a frying pan, and heat until it begins to smoke slightly. Sear the fish for 2 minutes on each side, and remove it from the frying pan. Place the fish in an ovenproof dish. With your hands, pack the tarragon mixture tightly on top of the fish. Broil the fish in the oven for about 10 minutes or until the crust starts to brown.

Yield: 1 serving

✢ This is a light dish with the emphasis on natural juices and fresh herbs. There is so much flavor in the herb crust. The great combination of textures — light, flaky fish and crispy crust — delights the taste buds.

✢ This dish goes great with a dash of fresh lemon, roasted potatoes, and steamed vegetables, but you can simply add a green salad and a glass of white wine to keep it even lighter.

thyme

Thymus

*t*HYME IS ONE OF THOSE HERBS that goes with so many foods. It certainly helps that there are more than 400 different varieties of thyme, each with its own distinctive flavor and aroma. French and English thyme are the varieties most commonly used in the kitchen.

A member of the mint family, thyme is often paired with bay leaf and is used extensively in French cooking. It's also an essential ingredient in bouquet garni.

Use thyme for herb butters, salads, soups, and in butter sauces for fish. It goes swimmingly with fish and shellfish, in gumbo, and also with poultry. Try it with cottage cheese, eggs, artichokes, beets, beans, potatoes, mushrooms, onions, and carrots. Add some to the basting butter when roasting game birds, and sprinkle some over roast beef. Older, woody thyme sprigs can be used as skewers for vegetable kebabs. Thyme serves as a background herb, offering its own flavor but leaving room for other seasonings to come through. It pairs especially well with chives, chervil, parsley, basil, marjoram, lemon, garlic, or savory.

To strip the tiny leaves from their stem, hold a thyme sprig by its tender tip and run the thumb and forefinger of your other hand down the stem. Because the leaves are so small, they're usually just left whole, but they can be minced if you wish. Whole sprigs can be placed in soup and stockpots, then removed before serving.

Thyme is another Mediterranean native, and its name is believed to have derived from the Greek word *thymos* meaning "courage." Apparently, in the days of chivalry in early Greece, it was customary for ladies to embroider a bee hovering over a sprig of thyme on the scarves they presented to their knights. The bee symbolized its role as a messenger among the fairies and its part in the production of the famed thyme honey of Mount Hymettus, a stone's throw from Athens.

Fairies are said to live among the branches of thyme shrubs. Shakespeare speaks of this when, in *A Midsummer Night's Dream,* he refers to the fairy queen Titania taking shelter "in a bank where the wild thyme blows, where oxlips and the nodding violet grows." Just maybe, if you plant some thyme in your garden, you too will catch sight of the garden fairies.

lemon thyme

Thymus citrodorus

*t*HIS PLANT IS ONE OF THE MOST POPULAR thyme varieties. It's a bit larger and has greener leaves than garden thyme, although there is a variegated form that has green and yellow leaves.

Lemon thyme has an unmistakable citrus scent and flavor mingled with the rustic flavor of thyme, making it an excellent herb for chicken, fish, and vegetables. It makes a wonderful lemon butter that can be used to baste poultry, poach fish, or top steamed vegetables. Lemon thyme can be used to flavor ice cream, cakes, cookies, rice or grain dishes, and casseroles. Sprinkle the tiny leaves over green salads or into soups, and mix some into spreads. Consider using lemon thyme with fruits; it goes especially well with oranges and pears. Brew yourself a cup of lemon thyme tea. Use lemon thyme any time you want a delicate lemon flavor. It's best when added toward the end of cooking or when infused in a liquid.

Lemon thyme was once used as an antiseptic for the disinfecting properties of thymol, which is contained in the plant's oil, and for its fresh lemon scent.

emeril lagasse

chef/owner

❖

Emeril's
New Orleans, Louisiana

❖

Delmonico
New Orleans, Louisiana

❖

NOLA
New Orleans, Louisiana

❖

**Emeril's New Orleans
Fish House**
Las Vegas, Nevada

*L*OTS OF HERBS ARE NICE, but it's thyme that makes Emeril Lagasse "happy happy!" French thyme? English thyme? It really doesn't matter; for Lagasse, thyme rules. "There's nothing like it. Thyme is one of those robust herbs that has a dramatic impact on meats."

Thyme seasons his stocks and spices his gumbos. Thyme finds its way into some of his fish recipes and complements the beans and legumes in many side dishes. "There's something about thyme that also goes well with game birds and chicken."

The taste of thyme, he says, is unique. "I get a little acidic [taste]; I get a tiny bit of licorice; I get soil and ash — an earthiness, but all in a proper balance." Even dried thyme has its place in Lagasse's kitchen. He's developed a line of herb rubs made from dried herbs and spices. "For certain things I don't waste fresh herbs. I don't think fresh herbs should be in stock that cooks for hours. Long cooking allows dried herbs to reconstitute to almost their full flavor. For quicker cooking foods, however, you get more impact from fresh herbs."

At age seven, the Johnson & Wales University graduate helped his mom, Hilda, make vegetable soup in his home town of Fall River, Massachusetts. At age 26, he replaced Paul Prudhomme at Commander's Palace in 1981.

He opened Emeril's in the warehouse district in New Orleans in 1990, followed by NOLA in the French Quarter. He later opened Emeril's New Orleans Fish House in Las Vegas, and Delmonico, also in New Orleans. He's the host of two Food Network television shows, *The Essence of Emeril* and *Emeril Live!* and is the author of four cookbooks (all published by William Morrow and Company, Inc.), *Emeril's New Orleans Cooking* (1993), *Louisiana Real and Rustic* (1996), *Creole Christmas* (1997), and *Emeril's TV Dinners* (1998).

Despite Lagasse's on-camera antics, he's very serious about his food. "I think to have great cuisine, you have to have great ingredients. I keep to the philosophy that quality really produces quality." To get that quality, he contracts with several local farmers to grow ingredients to his specifications, and he makes his own andouille sausage, ham, bacon, cheese, Worcestershire sauce, and ice creams.

The AAA four-diamond Emeril's restaurant was granted the Ivy Award by *Restaurants and Institutions* magazine and was named to the American Express Fine Dining Hall of Fame by *Nation's Restaurant News*, and Lagasse was deemed the Best Southeast Regional Chef by the James Beard Foundation. Emeril's was nominated for the James Beard Outstanding Service Award in 1998.

Fall River Clam Chowder

½ pound unsalted butter (1 cup)
1 cup all-purpose flour
½ pound bacon, cut into medium dice
1 tablespoon chopped thyme
2 cups chopped leeks (about 1 pound leeks)
2 cups chopped yellow onions (about 2 medium onions)
6 cups heavy cream

2 cups clam juice
3 bay leaves
Salt and pepper
2 pounds littleneck clams, shucked and chopped
   (about 10 dozen)
2 tablespoons finely chopped parsley

✦ In a sauté pan over medium heat, melt the butter. Stir the flour into the melted butter until the mixture is smooth. Cook for 6 to 8 minutes to make a blond roux, stirring occasionally. Remove from the heat and set aside.

✦ In a stockpot over medium heat, cook the bacon until it is crispy, about 5 minutes. Add a pinch or two of the thyme to the bacon while it's cooking. Add the leek, onion, and another pinch of the thyme, and sauté until the vegetables are wilted, about 3 to 4 minutes. Stir in the cream and clam juice. Bring the cream mixture to a simmer. Add the bay leaves, the remaining thyme, and a little salt and pepper.

✦ Stir in the reserved roux, a ½ cup at a time, until it is all incorporated and the soup is smooth. Simmer for 20 minutes. Stir in the clams, and simmer for another 2 minutes. Stir in the parsley, adjust the seasonings if necessary, and remove the bay leaves.

Yield: 8 to 10 servings

Note: Littleneck clams are used in this recipe because they have better flavor than larger clam varieties.

✦ Traditional clam chowders in New England don't use thyme. I add a bit of thyme to the pot when rendering the bacon to get a tremendous flavor out of it. This is my version of a New England clam chowder with thyme, and it's named in honor of my home town.

✦ This chowder is wonderful with salt crackers, bread sticks — something with a little crunch to contrast with its creaminess.

Lemon Thyme Chicken with Rosemary New Potatoes

Lemon Thyme Chicken:
2 tablespoons olive oil
½ cup finely chopped lemon zest (zest of
    4 to 5 lemons)
½ cup finely chopped thyme

Juice of 1 lemon
1 whole chicken (about 3 pounds)
Salt and pepper
2 sprigs thyme (optional)

Rosemary New Potatoes:
10 small new potatoes, quartered and blanched
2 sprigs thyme
¼ cup chopped rosemary

2 tablespoons olive oil
Salt and pepper

4 sprigs rosemary

➤ To prepare the chicken, preheat the grill. In a small mixing bowl or sealable plastic bag, combine the oil, lemon zest, thyme, and lemon juice. Mix thoroughly. Season the chicken, inside and out, with salt and pepper. Rub the entire chicken, inside and out, with the thyme mixture. Insert a thyme sprig into the skin of each breast, if desired. Place the chicken on the grill over indirect heat. Grill for 10 to 15 minutes on each side, or until the juices run clear.

➤ To prepare the potatoes, preheat the oven to 400°F. In a mixing bowl, toss the potatoes with the thyme, rosemary, oil, and a little salt and pepper. Roast for 10 to 12 minutes or until the potatoes are golden.

➤ To serve, cut the chicken in half down the backbone. Place the potatoes on a platter. Arrange the chicken halves beside the potatoes, and garnish with the rosemary sprigs.

Yield: 2 servings

Note: Reserve stems from thyme and rosemary sprigs and store them in the refrigerator or freezer. Use these stems as skewers, or place them in the smoker box of your grill for an added flavor when grilling. You can also use them to flavor stocks.

Variation: You can also use this recipe for roasting, instead of grilling, chicken. Put everything in the same pan. Season vegetables such as carrots, turnips, beets, potatoes — whatever you like — with salt and pepper and a little olive oil. Use the vegetables as a base, or use a rack, and place the chicken on top. Roast the chicken at 400°F until the juices run clear, about 15 minutes per pound.

Timesaver Tips: To prepare a large quantity of lemon zest, peel the lemons with a potato peeler, cutting just deep enough to get the yellow part, not the white part, of the peel. Mince the zest in a mini food processor.

➤ This is one of my favorites. It's what I would cook for a Sunday dinner, and Sunday dinners are very special for me. The oil and the acidity of the lemon keeps the thyme in balance.
➤ If you want a change from white potatoes, you could substitute sweet potatoes for the new potatoes. Add your favorite vegetables.

ingrid croce

chef/owner

**Croce's Restaurant and
Jazz Bar**
San Diego, California

"*t*HYME IS A VIBRANT HERB, full of life and hope. My grandmother's kitchen always had the fragrance of thyme and, throughout my life, thyme has been an essence that centers me and makes me feel like I am welcome and that I belong," says Ingrid Croce.

She uses thyme to enhance the flavor of stocks, soups, seafood, poultry, light meats, vegetables, and sauces. "The vibrancy and perfume of fresh thyme gives a brightness to cuisine that dried thyme cannot give. The nice thing about thyme," says Croce, "is that you can't use it the wrong way; it's a very forgiving herb." Also, she adds, "thyme is readily available as opposed to time, which there never seems to be enough of."

If that seems like a familiar refrain to you, you're probably old enough to remember *Time in a Bottle,* a hit song by her late husband, singer-songwriter, Jim Croce. This tune was the inspiration for the title of her book, *Thyme in a Bottle: Memories and Recipes from Croce's Restaurant* (Croce's, 1998). The book chronicles Ingrid's life as a musician, artist, wife, mother, widow, and restaurateur and is seasoned with recipes she's developed along the way.

In 1985, she opened Croce's Restaurant, serving American regional cuisine, in tribute to her late husband Jim Croce and later added the Jazz Bar for A. J. Croce, the couple's son, who by then had developed a following for his own musical talents. Today, the Jazz Bar is home to many of southern California's finest jazz artists. In 1998, Croce expanded the original Croce's, and opened Croce's Top Hat Bar & Grille, which features national and local rhythm and blues music. Her most recent addition, Upstairs at Croce's, is a late-night, light dining and spirits bar.

Ingrid, a celebrity chef/author and spokesperson for QVC's The Book and The Cook event in Philadelphia for the last several years, has appeared on Food Network's *Chef du Jour* television program, on QVC and *The Today Show,* and numerous other national and local television and radio programs. Recently, Ingrid and her husband Jimmy Rock collaborated with VH-1 to produce a one-hour television special *Jim Croce: Behind the Music,* and assisted TNN with the television show *Jim Croce Life & Times*.

In 1993, the Roundtable for Women named Croce winner of the Pacesetter Award for small business in the food service industry. In 1994, she co-founded, with husband Rock and Connie Nelson, Croce-Rock-Nelson Presents, a company that produces a series of concerts to raise funds for community AIDS organizations. She also produced A Celebration of Women Chefs, a fund-raiser benefiting Rachel's Women's Center, and developed a food service, hospitality, and tourism curriculum for the San Diego Unified School District and Mesa College. Ingrid was honored as Restaurateur of the Year by the San Diego Restaurant Association, and was inducted into San Diego's Business Hall of Fame in 1998.

Salmon Coulibiac

Kasha:
1 large onion, finely chopped
3 tablespoons vegetable oil
½ cup minced carrot
½ cup minced celery

1 cup kasha (buckwheat groats), toasted
1 egg, beaten lightly
2 cups boiling chicken stock (page 219) or water
Salt and pepper

Mushroom Duxelles:
2 teaspoons clarified butter (page 220)
2 tablespoons chopped shallot
½ pound mushrooms, finely chopped

¼ cup white wine
Salt and white pepper

Salmon:
2 sheets puff pastry, cut into 12 (4 by 4-inch) squares
1 large bunch spinach
6 (2½-ounce) salmon portions

6 tablespoons butter, softened
Dash of lemon juice
1 egg, beaten

Lemon and Thyme Hollandaise Sauce:
6 egg yolks
6 tablespoons white wine
1 cup plus 5 tablespoons clarified butter (page 220)
1 teaspoon thyme leaves

¼ cup lemon juice
Cayenne
Salt and white pepper

➤ To prepare the kasha, in a small skillet cook the onion in the oil until the onion is translucent. Add the carrot and celery, and stir until the onion is golden. Set the onion mixture aside.

➤ In a bowl, mix together the kasha and the egg until the kasha is well coated. Cook the kasha mixture in a large, flat skillet over moderate heat, stirring, for 3 to 5 minutes until the grains are separated and toasted. Add the onion mixture, and stir in the boiling chicken stock. Simmer the kasha, covered, for 10 to 20 minutes or until it is tender and all the liquid has been absorbed. Season with a little salt and pepper. Set the kasha aside, covered, until you are ready to assemble the coulibiac.

➤ While the kasha is simmering, prepare the mushroom duxelles. Melt the butter in a large skillet. Add the shallot and mushrooms, and cook for 3 minutes. Deglaze the pan with the white wine. Bring the mushroom mixture to a boil, and reduce the heat to medium low. Let the mushrooms cook until all the liquid has evaporated. Season with salt and white pepper. Remove the mushroom duxelles from the heat, and allow it to cool.

❧ To prepare the salmon, place the pastry squares on a lightly floured surface. Place 6 spinach leaves in the center of each of 6 squares. Spoon 1 tablespoon each of the reserved kasha and mushroom duxelles onto the spinach. Place a salmon portion on top. Combine the butter and lemon juice, and spoon 1 tablespoon of the lemon butter on each portion of salmon.

❧ Preheat the oven to 350°F. Place the remaining 6 pieces of pastry on top of the filled pieces. Press down the edges to seal them securely, and crimp the edges with a fork or pastry crimper. Using a pastry brush, lightly cover the edges of the pastry with the egg. Bake the coulibiac for 15 to 20 minutes.

❧ To prepare the hollandaise sauce, bring some water to a boil, either in a large pot or the bottom of a large double boiler. In a stainless steel bowl or the top of the double boiler, whisk together the egg yolks and white wine for a few seconds until the egg mixture is light and frothy. Place the bowl or pot over, but not touching, the boiling water (do not put the bowl directly touching the water or you risk overcooking the egg). Whisk rapidly until the egg mixture becomes thick and has tripled in volume. Remove the egg mixture from the heat, and continue to whisk for 30 seconds to ensure the egg does not overcook. Slowly add the clarified butter while gently whisking until the sauce stiffens. Add the thyme and lemon juice and a little cayenne, salt, and white pepper, and combine.

❧ To serve, spoon some hollandaise sauce over each portion of coulibiac.

Yield: 6 servings

❧ Serve this dish with fresh vegetables, whatever is in season, and include slices of red pepper or another colorful vegetable. Any leftover kasha can be served as a side dish.

Thanksgiving Turkey with Thyme, Mushroom, and Onion Bread Stuffing

Turkey:

Thyme, mushroom, and onion bread stuffing
   (recipe follows)
6 tablespoons extra virgin olive oil
2 cloves garlic, finely minced
¼ teaspoon chopped rosemary
¼ teaspoon chopped sage
¼ teaspoon chopped thyme

¼ teaspoon paprika
¼ teaspoon salt
¼ teaspoon pepper
1 (20-pound) turkey, with giblets
4 cups water
½ lemon
1 to 2 cups chicken stock (page 219) or water

Gravy:

Reserved giblets
1⅓ cups pan drippings
4 cups chicken stock (page 219)

1⅓ cups reserved giblet stock
½ cup all-purpose flour
Salt and pepper

✤ Prepare the stuffing.

✤ To prepare the turkey, warm the olive oil in a small saucepan with the garlic, rosemary, sage, thyme, paprika, salt, and pepper. Set the oil mixture aside. Remove the heart, liver, neck, and gizzard from the turkey, and bring them to a boil in the water over moderate heat. Reduce the heat to a simmer, cover, and cook about 60 minutes until the giblets are tender. Reserve both the giblets and giblet stock for the gravy.

✤ Rinse the turkey inside and out under cold running water. Rub the inside and outside of the breast cavity with the lemon. Rub the inside and outside of the turkey with half the oil mixture. Reserve the remaining oil mixture for basting the turkey.

✤ Preheat the oven to 425°F. Stuff the turkey body and neck with the bread stuffing, and sew the openings together with a trussing needle and twine. Gently separate the skin from the body of the turkey with your fingers, and insert more stuffing underneath the skin on the breast or wherever else you can.

✤ Add 1 to 2 cups chicken stock to a large roasting pan, and set the turkey, breast side down, on a roasting rack in the pan. Bake for 45 minutes, basting the turkey with the remaining oil mixture every 20 minutes throughout the baking time. Reduce the oven temperature to 350°F, and turn the turkey breast side up. If necessary, add more chicken stock to the pan, to avoid burning. Bake the turkey for 15 to 20 minutes per pound (about 5 hours for a 20-pound turkey). At least 30 minutes prior to the end of this period, insert a meat thermometer in the thigh without touching the bone. Remove the turkey from the

✤ Each Thanksgiving, I try to prepare my fresh turkey so the meat will be tender and moist and the skin crispy and golden brown. Make sure your turkey has a healthy history, and, if you take the time to baste it every 20 minutes during roasting, you will get wonderful results.

✤ This makes a hearty meal with a nice green salad and hard crusted bread. You can use this recipe year round, not just for Thanksgiving.

oven when the temperature of the meat thermometer reaches 180°F. Allow the turkey to stand for 20 minutes before carving it. Reserve the pan drippings for the gravy.

❋ Meanwhile, prepare the gravy. Chop the reserved giblets finely. Pour the pan drippings into a 1-quart glass measuring cup, and remove any yellow fat that rises to the top. Combine the chicken stock and reserved giblet stock, and add to the defatted pan drippings. If you don't have 4 cups of liquid, add enough water or chicken stock to make 4 cups. Place this gravy mixture in the roasting pan used for the turkey. Place the roasting pan over two burners of the stove on medium heat. Sprinkle the flour onto the gravy mixture, and whisk, scraping up any brown bits from the bottom of the pan. Reduce the heat to a simmer, and add the reserved giblets. Continue whisking until the gravy thickens. Remove the gravy from the heat, and season with a little salt and pepper.

Yield: 20 to 24 servings

Note: For a smaller family, purchase a hen (8 to 16 pounds) and cook it for 20 to 25 minutes per pound. Halve the stuffing recipe.

Thyme, Mushroom, and Onion Bread Stuffing:

2 large yellow onions, sliced
2 medium carrots, diced
2 stalks celery, diced
1½ cups diced zucchini
5 tablespoons butter
1 cup chicken livers or parcooked, decased spicy
  sausage
10 cloves garlic, minced separately
1½ cups white or assorted mushrooms
Salt and pepper
3 tablespoons olive oil
10 cups bread cubes
Chicken stock (page 219), vegetable stock (page 218),
  or water

> ❋ Since my guests have enjoyed this stuffing immensely over the years, I prepare enough to fill every opening of a large turkey and a casserole as well.

❋ In a medium skillet, sauté the onion, carrot, celery, and zucchini in 3 tablespoons of butter for 7 minutes. In a separate large skillet, sauté the chicken livers in 1 tablespoon of the butter with 1 clove of the minced garlic until the chicken livers are brown. Chop the chicken livers into small pieces, and reserve them with the garlic with which they were cooked.

❋ Heat the remaining butter in the large skillet, and sauté 3 cloves of the minced garlic and the mushrooms with a little salt and pepper for 3 minutes. Add the onion mixture, combine it with the mushroom mixture, and set the mushroom mixture aside.

❋ In a large, flat-bottomed stockpot, combine 1 tablespoon of the oil with 2 cloves of the minced garlic. Place the stockpot over medium-low heat, add one-third of the bread cubes, and brown them for 2 minutes, stirring with a wooden spoon. Add one-third of the reserved mushroom mixture, and mix well. Set the bread cube mixture aside in a large bowl, and repeat the process twice more.

❋ In the large bowl, combine the bread cube mixture with the reserved chicken livers. Add stock, if needed, to moisten the bread cube mixture so that it can be used to stuff the turkey.

(continued on next page)

Season with salt and pepper. Set the bread stuffing aside to cool before using it to stuff the turkey.

Yield: sufficient for stuffing a 20-pound turkey and for a side dish of stuffing

Variations: If you have vegetarian guests, omit the chicken livers, use vegetable stock, and set aside one-third of the remaining ingredients to be baked and served in a separate casserole. If some diners don't like liver, substitute spicy sausage for the chicken livers. You can omit all meat and the stuffing is still hearty and engaging.

Timesaver Tips: Make chicken or vegetable stock for the stuffing well in advance and freeze it, or use purchased stock. You can make the stuffing the day before and store in a tightly closed container, refrigerated.

Baked Bread and Onion Soup

1 loaf crusty, country-style bread, preferably square
2 large onions, sliced
5 cloves garlic, slivered
¼ cup water or chicken stock (page 219)

1 teaspoon chopped thyme plus thyme sprigs
1 cup grated Parmigiano-Reggiano cheese, loosely packed
2 medium tomatoes, thinly sliced
6 cups chicken stock (page 219)

❧ Preheat the oven to 200°F. Slice the bread ¼-inch thick, and dry out in the oven until crunchy, about 15 minutes.

❧ Cook the onions and garlic in a stockpot with the ¼ cup water or chicken stock until completely soft.

❧ Preheat the oven to 350°F. Line a deep casserole dish with a layer of sliced bread. Place a layer of onions and garlic on the bread, and sprinkle with half the chopped thyme. Add a layer of cheese followed by a layer of tomatoes. Continue layering the ingredients, finishing with a layer of bread followed by a final layer of cheese.

❧ Fill the casserole dish to the top layer of bread and cheese with chicken stock, pouring it down the edges of the pan and being careful not to saturate the top layer of bread. Reserve the rest of the stock for serving. Let the soup stand for 15 minutes to soak up the stock, and fill the pan with stock again. Bake for 40 minutes or until golden brown.

❧ To serve, slice into squares and place in a bowl with additional stock. Garnish with a sprig of thyme.

Yield: 10 to 12 servings

Note: The chicken stock can be made the day before or even sooner if you freeze the stock.

Recipes adapted, with permission, from *Thyme in a Bottle: Memories and Recipes from Croce's Restaurant* **by Ingrid Croce (Croce's, 1998).**

❧ This soup is served at Croce's almost as a ritual. The bread is an inseparable accompaniment to the broth. It reminds me how basic nourishment helps us to restore health and happiness, too. And of how good soup can be!
❧ This is a robust soup that can be served alone as an appetizer or with a green salad.

barry squier

executive chef

Girafe
Basking Ridge, New Jersey

WHILE MOST PEOPLE CROSS THE PARKING LOT to get to their car, Barry Squier crosses it to get to his herb and vegetable garden.

Although he grows quite an array of herbs, there's always room for thyme, his favorite herb. "I love thyme; I use it in everything, well, almost everything. I like its sweetness and the aromatics of it."

He likes to tie thyme sprigs into little bundles and drop them into pots of soup or stock and into saucepans to infuse thyme's sweet, earthy flavor into the dish. Thyme is a base flavor, he explains, like black pepper and bay leaves. "These serve as the building blocks of soups, sauces, and stocks."

He likes to add thyme to risottos. Tiny thyme leaves swim in his caramelized onion broth made with chicken stock, balsamic vinegar, and onions. Herb-infused oils flavor his vinaigrettes, sizzle his sautés, and brighten his marinades. At the end of the growing season, he'll gather the remaining thyme, rosemary, and summer savory stems, dry them, and smoke with them throughout the winter. You'll get a great herbaceous aroma and flavor from tossing them right on barbecue coals or onto the grid of a gas grill, suggests Squier.

Squier especially likes English thyme. "It seems to grow real nice and the branches are woodier [than other varieties] so that a garnish of thyme sprigs holds up even under the heat of the dish." The leaves, he says, are "a little more compact," but the oils are stronger.

The garden at Girafe includes cilantro, savory, oregano, mint, marjoram, chives, garlic chives, cinnamon basil, lemon basil, sweet basil, and Thai basil. Anise, Johnny-jump-ups, nasturtiums, borage, and several sages, including purple sage, garden sage, and pineapple sage, grow among the lettuce, pepper, squash, and eggplant.

Girafe was named one of New Jersey's top tables by *Gourmet* magazine readers, and *New Jersey Monthly* rated it second in the top 10 New Jersey restaurants serving American cuisine. Girafe has also received *Wine Spectator*'s Award of Excellence for several years, and Squier frequently hosts wine-tasting dinners. Squier also teaches cooking classes at Kings Supermarket and was named one of North America's outstanding chefs by *Chefs in America*. His work has been featured in *New Jersey Monthly* magazine and *Country Roads* magazine. He studied at Le Cordon Bleu culinary school and worked at a number of restaurants before taking over the Girafe kitchen 17 years ago.

As to the restaurant's name, I wondered aloud if it's a touch of whimsy or if there is some practical explanation? "It's because the owner stuck his neck out when he opened it," quips Squier. Fact or fiction? "It's one of several stories floating around," he says. "Nobody seems to know for sure."

Pan Roasted Loin of Veal with Wild Mushrooms and Sherry-Scented Demi-Glace

For an elegant sit-down dinner when you're cooking to impress, this is a really wonderful, easy-to-make dish. Depending on the time of year, you could use morel, shiitake, black trumpet, or whatever mushrooms are available. The rich, earthy flavors of the mushrooms complement the nice whiteness of the veal.

Roasted potatoes and steamed asparagus or broccoli are great with this dish, or try it with fresh sautéed spinach.

1 teaspoon dried rosemary leaves
1 teaspoon dried thyme leaves
Kosher salt
½ teaspoon freshly ground black pepper
1 boneless loin of veal, silver skin removed
1 large shallot, minced
4 tablespoons unsalted butter

Rosemary sprigs

3 plum tomatoes, peeled, seeded, and chopped
2 pounds fresh wild mushrooms, sliced
½ cup dry sherry
2 cups demi-glace (page 224)
3 tablespoons vegetable oil
All-purpose flour

Thyme sprigs

Mix together the rosemary, thyme, some salt, and the pepper. Rub the herb mixture over the veal, and set it aside. (You could do this early in the day, and refrigerate the veal until about 30 minutes before cooking.)

In a heavy-bottomed saucepan, sauté the shallot in 2 tablespoons of the butter for 2 minutes. Add the tomatoes and mushrooms, and continue cooking for 2 minutes. Deglaze the pan with the sherry. Add the demi-glace, and bring the mushroom mixture to a boil. Reduce to an almost syrupy consistency. Keep the demi-glace mixture warm until just before serving.

Heat a large, heavy-bottomed sauté pan over medium-high heat. Add the vegetable oil, and when it is hot, add 1 tablespoon of the butter to the pan. Heat the butter until it reaches a light brown color. Dredge the seasoned veal in flour, and shake off the excess. Sear the veal in the browned butter on all sides. You may have to increase the heat to get the veal evenly browned, but be careful not to let the butter burn. Place the veal on a meat rack, and continue cooking it, covered, either on the stove or in the oven at 325°F, until the temperature of the veal reaches 125°F on a meat thermometer. Remove the veal from the heat, and let it stand on the rack for about 15 minutes.

To finish the demi-glace, whisk the remaining butter into it, and adjust the seasoning with salt and pepper to taste.

To serve, slice the veal and drizzle the mushrooms and demi-glace over the top. Garnish with fresh rosemary and thyme sprigs.

Yield: 4 to 6 servings

Note: Use dried herbs in the mixture rubbed on the outside of the meat before searing. Fresh herbs tend to lose their flavor and color when exposed to the high heat required for searing. You could also sear the veal on a grill instead of in a pan on the stove.

Roast Leg of Lamb with Fresh Rosemary and Thyme

8 large cloves garlic, minced
3 tablespoons finely chopped rosemary
3 tablespoons finely chopped thyme

Kosher salt and freshly ground black pepper
1 butterflied leg of lamb, about 4 to 5 pounds
Oil

⇻ Preheat the oven to 350°F. Combine the garlic, rosemary, thyme, and a little salt and pepper in a small bowl. Open the leg of lamb, and season it with the garlic mixture. Tie the leg of lamb closed with butcher's twine. Season the outside with salt and pepper.

⇻ In a heavy-bottomed saucepan, brown the leg of lamb in the oil over high heat. Transfer it to a roasting pan, and roast the leg of lamb until the interior temperature reaches 125°F on a meat thermometer. Let the leg of lamb stand for at least 15 minutes before carving it.

Yield: 4 to 6 servings

Note: The lamb could also be cooked on a grill or rotisserie.

⇻ When I think spring and Easter, I think spring lamb. It's always available and is one of the most economical meats. I like to serve a tomato and apple chutney with it. The sweet and sour flavors go really well with the lamb.

⇻ Lamb is a spring dish, so serve young spring vegetables such as nice little baby turnips, baby gold beets or glazed carrots, little pearl onions, and maybe little red bliss or fingerling potatoes.

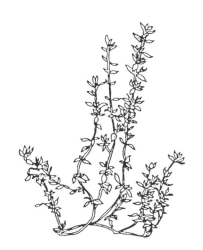

roland liccioni

chef/owner
❦
Le Français Restaurant
Wheeling, Illinois

*r*OLAND LICCIONI ESPECIALLY LIKES THE FRAGRANCE of lemon and the flavor of thyme, so it's only natural that lemon thyme would be on his list of favorite herbs. "It's a good combination of flavors. It's delicate with a not too strong taste." He likens lemon thyme to lemon grass. Some people, he says, can't tell the difference when one or the other of these herbs is used in cooking. "Both are delicate, but lemon grass is more spicy."

He's fond of lemon thyme as a flavoring for his sauces and au jus gravies, which he makes with a light hand. He uses reductions, rather than heavy sauces, to focus attention on the freshness of the foods and the intricacies of flavors. His lighter style of cuisine first appeared in the light, transparent, intensely flavored sauces he prepared while working as *chef de cuisine* at Carlos in Highland Park, a north Chicago suburb. He earned the restaurant its four-star rating and gained national attention, appearing in the PBS *Great Chefs* series.

Born into a Corsican–Vietnamese family, Liccioni began his formal training at age 13 in France at L'École hôtelière de Biarritz. After graduating with first prize, he traveled to Paris where he tested and developed his culinary skills at Bofinger on the Rue de la Bastille for five years. He was then offered the opportunity to work with the Roux brothers at their renowned London restaurants, La Gavroche and the Waterside Inn.

After two years of tutelage under his mentor, Michel Roux, Liccioni moved to the United States. Following his stint at Carlos, where he met and married pâtissière Mary Beth, the couple took over the reins of Le Français from the retiring Jean Banchet.

They've consistently maintained an AAA five-diamond rating as well as the *Mobil Travel Guide* five-star rating. *Wine Spectator* magazine has rated their wine list as "one of the greatest wine lists in the world for the past 10 years." Le Français was named one of the top 10 restaurants in the United States by *Condé Nast Traveler*, and the *Zagat Survey* awarded it the highest rating for food and service. The restaurant has also been honored by *Traditions & Qualité* and the exclusive Relais & Châteaux hotel and restaurant group. In 1997, Liccioni was named Best Chef of the Midwest by the James Beard Foundation. In 1998, *Gourmet* magazine readers rated Le Français the Top Table in Chicago, with top marks for food, service, presentation, and wine list.

Liccioni is a perfectionist, happiest at work in his kitchen. He once considered playing professional soccer but refused an invitation to join a pro club when it conflicted with his culinary career.

Liccioni also loves to garden and grows many of the herbs, vegetables, and fruits he uses in the kitchen at Le Français. "Use only the best quality ingredients that are fresh and pure" is his motto. Among the herbs he grows in his 500-square-foot garden are parsley, chives, chervil, several varieties of thyme and basil, rosemary, and lovage.

Sautéed Sea Scallops with Lemon Thyme

Marinade:
Leaves from 7 or 8 lemon thyme sprigs
¼ cup olive oil

16 jumbo or 24 medium sea scallops

Sauce:
2 tablespoons chopped shallots
1 cup dry white wine
1 cup vegetable stock (preferably made from leeks, fennel, celery, and mushrooms)

4 tablespoons butter
Fresh lemon juice
Salt and freshly ground white pepper

Frisée
Champagne vinegar

Olive oil

✦ To prepare the marinade, mix together the lemon thyme leaves and oil in a bowl. Add the scallops, and marinate them for about 60 minutes in the refrigerator, turning them once.

✦ To prepare the sauce, combine the shallot, wine, and vegetable stock in a medium saucepan. Over high heat, rapidly reduce the liquid by half. Whisk in the butter to create an emulsion. Season the sauce to taste with a squeeze of lemon juice and a little salt and pepper. Reserve the sauce, keeping it warm.

✦ To finish the scallops, preheat a nonstick sauté pan. Sauté the scallops on one side until they are nicely browned, turn, and brown the other side. Do not overcook the scallops; they cook very quickly and become tough when overcooked.

✦ To serve, divide the scallops among each of 4 warm plates. Toss the frisée with some champagne vinegar and olive oil. Spoon the sauce around the scallops, and garnish with the frisée.

Yield: 4 servings

✦ This scallop dish is very rich. The delicate lemon thyme adds a hint of citrus. I made this dish in France with English thyme, but English thyme is too strong for me. I find lemon thyme to be more delicate and well matched with the scallops.

✦ This dish can be served as an appetizer or an entrée. Add a root vegetable such as salsify when serving the scallops as an entrée. Salsify, also known as oyster plant, is sometimes available in Spanish, Italian, and Greek shops. It can be sautéed, braised, or roasted.

Chicken Breasts with Lemon Thyme and Grilled Vegetables

Chicken Breasts with Lemon Thyme:

4 chicken breasts with bones
1 teaspoon lemon thyme leaves
    plus 1 sprig lemon thyme
Olive oil
2 stalks celery, cut into 1-inch chunks
1 clove garlic
1 large carrot, cut into 1-inch chunks

½ onion, cut into 1-inch chunks
Small handful mushroom stems
1 cup dry white wine
½ cup brandy
5 to 6 peppercorns
1 whole clove
Salt and pepper

Grilled Vegetables:

Lengthwise slices of eggplant, zucchini, and red
    and yellow peppers

Olive oil

> ◈ I like this dish because in France my mother made a similar dish. She used lemon grass, but I discovered lemon thyme is just as good.

◈ Remove the chicken breasts from the bones, and reserve the bones. Rub the chicken breasts with the lemon thyme leaves and some olive oil. Marinate them in the refrigerator for at least 60 minutes.

◈ Chop the chicken bones. Place them in a 2-quart saucepan, and brown them in oil over medium heat. Add the celery, garlic, carrot, onion, and mushroom stems, and cook until the vegetables start to turn brown. Add the wine and brandy, and reduce until the liquid is nearly gone. Add enough water to cover the bones and the sprig of lemon thyme, peppercorns, and clove. Simmer for 60 minutes. Strain the liquid, and discard the vegetables and bones.

◈ Return the liquid to the saucepan, and reduce by half to form a sauce. Season the sauce with some salt and pepper.

◈ To prepare the grilled vegetables, preheat the grill, season the vegetable slices with a little olive oil, grill them briefly, and set them aside, keeping them warm.

◈ To finish the chicken breasts, grill them thoroughly.

◈ To serve, drizzle the sauce over the chicken breasts and grilled vegetables.

Yield: 4 servings

Lemon Thyme Ice Cream

5 or 6 sprigs lemon thyme
4 cups milk
1 cup heavy cream
1 cup sugar

1 vanilla bean
10 egg yolks
Ice bath

✦ Combine the lemon thyme, milk, cream, ½ cup of the sugar, and the vanilla in a medium saucepan, and bring to a boil. In a bowl, whisk together the egg yolks, and remaining sugar. Whisk some of the hot milk mixture into the egg yolks and whisk the egg yolk mixture into the remaining milk mixture. (Combining the egg yolks with the hot milk mixture all at once will cook the egg yolks.) Return the milk mixture to the heat, and cook gently, stirring constantly, until thickened.

✦ Pour the milk mixture into another container, and place it in an ice bath to cool. When cold, strain the milk mixture through a fine sieve. Process the milk mixture in an ice-cream maker following the manufacturer's instructions.

Yield: 1½ quarts

✦ Who doesn't like ice cream? Lemon thyme gives ice cream a spicy-citrus flavor that adds intrigue to a popular dessert.

✦ This ice cream is a wonderful accompaniment to warm chocolate desserts.

down to basics

*M*ANY OF THE BEST RECIPES are built upon the basics, things like stocks, roasted peppers, or roasted garlic. This chapter is dedicated to just such things.

stocks

*S*TOCKS ARE THE BASIS OF SOUPS but can also be used to make sauces and gravies or as the cooking liquid when cooking vegetables or meats. The recipes given here are basic stock recipes; other ingredients can be added or substituted. Stocks generally include the aromatics — onion, carrot, and celery — along with bay leaves and other herbs such as thyme. Before making stock, look through the refrigerator and in the garden to see what other fresh vegetables and herbs are available. Chefs often use stems and peelings to help flavor their stocks. Follow their example: place herb and vegetable stems in a plastic bag, store it in the freezer, and use them when you make stock. If, for example, you like to eat broccoli florets but not the tough stems, you can give flavor to stocks by adding those stems to the stockpot. Other commonly included vegetables are potatoes, turnips, leeks, spinach and other greens, mushrooms, and fennel. These are especially good additions if you're making vegetable stock.

Most stocks are best made ahead and refrigerated. Scrape off the congealed fat and discard it before using the stock. Stocks can also be frozen. Freeze them in 1-cup containers (the 8-ounce tubs that soft margarine comes in are excellent) because that's a common amount called for in recipes. If you don't want to make your own stock, check your supermarket, gourmet shop, or the Mail Order Resources (page 228) for bases, available in many flavors, that you simply combine with water or pan drippings.

fennel

Beef Stock

2 cloves garlic
2 large carrots, scrubbed
2 medium onions, quartered
2 stalks celery
Oil
1 cup red wine

5 cups water
2 bay leaves
2 pounds beef bones
Several sprigs of herbs such as parsley, thyme, rosemary, or a combination
Salt and pepper

➤ Sauté the garlic, carrot, onion, and celery in oil in a large stockpot until the carrot and celery are lightly browned. Deglaze the pan with the wine. Add the water, bay leaves, beef bones, and herb sprigs. Bring to a boil, reduce the heat, and simmer for 60 minutes. Season with salt and pepper to taste. Strain. Store the beef stock in the refrigerator or freezer.

Yield: about 4 cups

Fish Stock

2 carrots, cut into 4-inch pieces
2 cloves garlic
2 stalks celery, cut into 4-inch pieces
1 leek, cut into 4-inch pieces
1 medium onion, quartered
½ cup white wine
2 pounds fish bones and scraps,* rinsed

2 quarts water
10 peppercorns
3 to 4 sprigs thyme
2 bay leaves
1 bunch parsley
Salt and pepper

Many fishmongers will provide these free of charge.

bay

➤ Sauté the carrot, garlic, celery, leek, and onion in a large stockpot until the carrot and celery are lightly browned. Deglaze the pan with the wine. Add the fish bones and scraps, water, peppercorns, thyme, bay leaves, and parsley. Bring to a boil, reduce the heat, and simmer for 45 minutes. Season with salt and pepper to taste. Strain. Store the fish stock in the refrigerator or freezer.

Yield: about 4 cups

down to basics

Vegetable Stock

2 carrots, scrubbed, cut into 4-inch pieces
2 leeks, cut into 4-inch pieces
2 onions, quartered
2 stalks celery, cut into 4-inch pieces
1 fennel bulb, quartered
Olive oil

¼ cup white wine
3 tomatoes, quartered
2 bay leaves
Several sprigs of herbs or bouquet garni (page 15)
8 cups water
Salt and pepper

✦ In a large stockpot, sauté the carrot, leek, onion, celery, and fennel in a small amount of olive oil until the vegetables are lightly browned. Deglaze the pan with the wine. Add the tomatoes, bay leaves, and herbs, and continue cooking for 2 minutes. Add the water, bring to a boil, reduce the heat, and simmer for 60 minutes. Season with salt and pepper to taste. Strain. Store the vegetable stock in the refrigerator or freezer.

Yield: about 4 cups

Veal Stock

2 to 3 pounds veal bones
½ cup white wine
8 cups water
2 bay leaves
2 carrots, cut into 4-inch pieces

2 leeks, cut into 4-inch pieces
2 stalks celery, cut into 4-inch pieces
1 medium onion, quartered
Salt and pepper

✦ Preheat the oven to 375°F.

✦ Place the veal bones in a roasting pan, and roast them until they are brown. Deglaze the pan with the wine. Place the bones and juices from the pan in a large stockpot, and add the water, bay leaves, carrot, leek, celery, and onion. Bring to a boil, reduce the heat, and simmer for 60 minutes. Season with salt and pepper to taste. Strain. Store the veal stock in the refrigerator or freezer.

Yield: about 4 cups

Chicken Stock

1 (3 to 4-pound) chicken, washed, giblets removed
Kosher salt and freshly ground pepper
6 quarts cold water
Bouquet garni of parsley, bay leaf, and thyme

5 carrots, cut into 2-inch pieces
4 stalks celery with tops, cut into 3-inch pieces
2 yellow onions
1 parsnip, cut into 3-inch pieces

➤ Rub the chicken inside and out with salt and pepper. Place the chicken in a large stock-pot with the water. Place the bouquet garni in the pot, along with the carrots, celery, whole onions, and parsnip. Bring to a boil, lower the heat, and simmer for 2 hours. Skim the foam from the top of the stock periodically.

➤ Remove the chicken, and set aside for another use. Strain the stock through a fine strainer or cheesecloth. It may be necessary to strain it twice to get a good clear stock. Refrigerate the stock until the fat rises to the top and hardens. Skim off the fat and discard. The stock may be stored in the refrigerator for a couple of days or frozen.

Yield: about 20 cups

Note: Make bouquet garni by placing several springs of parsley and thyme along with 2 bay leaves in a square of cheesecloth. Bring the ends of cheesecloth together and tie with kitchen string, leaving the string long enough to tie to the handle of the pot. Place the bouquet garni in the stock, and tie the string to the handle of the pot. You can also purchase muslin herb bags or herb balls from gourmet shops to place the herbs in.

Recipe reprinted, with permission, from *Thyme in a Bottle: Memories and Recipes from Croce's Restaurant* **by Ingrid Croce (Croce's, 1998).**

parsley

down to basics

other basics

*i*N ADDITION TO STOCKS, many recipes call for other flavor enhancing ingredients that require some preparation. Roasting peppers, for instance, brings out their sweetness while roasting garlic makes it more mellow. Clarified butter is sometimes used for sautéing or roasting long-cooking items because with the milk solids removed it can withstand higher temperatures before beginning to burn.

Most of these items are available readymade from supermarkets and gourmet shops but since it can be rewarding to make your own, instructions for these "other basics" are provided below.

Clarified Butter

To clarify butter, melt unsalted butter over low heat. Let the butter stand for 2 or 3 minutes until the butter and milk solids separate. Skim any foam from the top, and pour the butter into a cup, leaving the milky solids in the pan. Discard the milky solids. The clarified butter will keep, refrigerated, for about a month.

Clarified butter is used in the veal saltimbocca recipe (page 162), in the salmon coulibiac recipe (page 204), as a seafood condiment, and in some emulsified sauces.

Roasted Peppers

Roasting peppers makes them tender and gives them a sweeter flavor. Cut the peppers in half lengthwise, and discard the seeds and membranes. Put the pepper halves on a baking sheet, and place them under the broiler until the skins are charred, about 10 to 15 minutes. (You can also do this on the barbecue grill.) Place the peppers in a tightly closed paper bag for about 10 minutes. The steam will loosen the skin, making the peppers easy to peel. Discard the skins. The roasted peppers will keep about a month when placed in a jar, covered with oil, and stored in the refrigerator. Use them in salads, on pizza, with pasta, or over grilled meat.

Simple Syrup

½ cup sugar   1 cup water

❧ Combine the sugar and water in a small saucepan. Place it over medium heat, and boil a minute or two until the sugar is dissolved and the liquid is clear.

Yield: about 1 cup

❧ Simple syrup is used as a thickener in some dessert and sauce recipes.

Fresh Pasta

3 to 3½ cups pasta flour   2 tablespoons olive oil
1 teaspoon salt   1 cup warm water

❧ Sift 3 cups of the flour onto a flat surface. Make a well in the center of the flour, and add the salt, the oil, and a small amount of the water.

❧ Mix the ingredients gradually with a fork, bringing more flour from around the edges and adding the remaining water a little at a time, until a smooth dough is formed. If the dough is sticky, add more flour slowly until the dough is no longer sticky. Knead until the dough is a soft, workable ball, about 10 minutes. Cover the dough with plastic wrap, and refrigerate for at least 1 hour or up to 2 days.

❧ Divide the dough into 3 pieces, and roll each into a one-eighth-inch thick sheet. Let the pasta sheets stand for 5 minutes. Cut the pasta into shapes, or press it through a manual pasta machine. Dry the pasta on a rack for at least 60 minutes before cooking it.

Yield: 1 pound

Note: Pasta flour should be stored in the refrigerator.

Timesaver Tips: Use your food processor, equipped with the steel blade, for kneading pasta dough. Begin by combining the salt, olive oil, and ½ cup of the water. With the machine running, slowly add the pasta flour and the remaining ½ cup of water. Process until the dough is soft enough to handle. If the dough is too dry, add additional water drop by drop.

Variations: Flavor your pasta with your favorite herb or other flavoring such as spinach or tomato paste. For herb-flavored pasta, add 3 tablespoons herb pesto or 2 tablespoons finely chopped herb leaves.

Recipe courtesy of Antoine's Pasta, Fair Lawn, New Jersey.

❧ Pasta flour is also called semolina. Semolina is of durum wheat, a hard wheat, that is ground more coarsely than normal wheat flour. Semolina is the basic ingredient in all good-quality commercial pasta, both imported and domestic.

down to basics

Tempura Batter

½ cup all-purpose flour
⅛ teaspoon baking soda
⅛ teaspoon salt

⅛ teaspoon pepper
1 egg yolk
½ cup ice water

❧ In a medium-sized bowl, sift together the flour, baking soda, salt, and pepper. In a small bowl, beat the egg yolk with the water until frothy. Continue beating, and gradually add the flour mixture until the batter is smooth. Dip meat or vegetables into the batter, and deep-fry them until golden brown.

Yield: about ¾ cup

Note: There are a number of variations to tempura batter, some calling for whole egg, others for just the yolk. The batter should be mixed and used immediately while the water is still ice cold. You can also buy tempura batter mixes in grocery or gourmet shops.

Roasted Garlic

1 head garlic
¼ teaspoon olive oil

Salt and pepper
½ teaspoon chopped herbs,* optional

*Thyme goes particularly well with garlic, but you could use any herb you like or that will complement your meal.

❧ Preheat the oven to 325°F.

❧ Remove the outer skin from the garlic. Slice off the top of the head so that each clove is open. Place the garlic in a garlic baker or ovenproof dish. Drizzle the olive oil over the garlic. Season it with a little salt and pepper, and sprinkle the optional herbs over the top.

❧ Cover the garlic, and bake for 20 minutes. Uncover, and bake it an additional 30 minutes or until the garlic is tender and golden brown, basting with additional olive oil, if necessary. You can also cook the garlic in a microwave oven, but the longer, slower oven roasting produces a richer flavor. For microwave baking, cook at full power for about 1 minute or until the garlic is soft. To enhance the garlic's color and flavor, drizzle some Worcestershire sauce or balsamic vinegar over the garlic before microwaving. To use, simply break the cloves apart and squeeze out the roasted garlic.

Yield: 1 head roasted garlic

glossary

Acidulated water: water to which a small amount of lemon juice or vinegar has been added. Certain foods are soaked in it to prevent them from browning.

Adobo sauce: a spicy sauce made of chiles, vinegar, and spices. It is available canned.

Aïoli: a kind of mayonnaise originating in Provence. Traditionally, aïoli was created with garlic as the flavoring, but today, a wide range of herbs, hot peppers, and other flavors are often used. Aïoli is used to dress fish, meats, vegetables, and salads.

Amontillado: a Spanish sherry with a nutty flavor.

Anaheim chile: a mild chile available in green and red. It is also known as New Mexican chile.

Apéritif: a light alcoholic drink customarily served to stimulate the appetite before dining.

Arborio rice: an Italian rice traditionally used for risottos because its high starch content creates the creamy texture characteristic of that dish.

Arugula: a salad green with a somewhat bitter, peppery flavor.

Banyuls: a French dessert wine.

Barley: a chewy grain often included in grain salads and in vegetable soup.

Blanch: to submerge food (usually herbs, fruits, and vegetables) first into boiling water briefly and then into ice water. Blanching is used to lightly precook vegetables before grilling them or combining them with other ingredients. When vegetables and herbs are to be frozen, or when herbs are to be preserved in vinegar, blanching them first retains their color and flavor.

Blanquette: a creamy stew, which frequently includes pearl onions and mushrooms, made with white meat such as veal, lamb, or poultry.

Blood orange: a slightly tart orange with red flesh that is often used to make sauces.

Bruschetta: a traditional Italian garlic bread served warm.

Bulgur: wheat kernels that have been steamed, dried, and crushed. They're often used in salads such as tabbouleh.

Caperberry: the fruit of the *Capparis spinosa* plant. The caperberries form after the bush blossoms. The blossom buds are known as capers.

Celeriac: a root vegetable that tastes like a cross between celery and parsley. Because celeriac discolors when cut, soak it in acidulated water after cutting. Celeriac is also known as celery root.

Chiffonade: very thin slivers of ingredients such as lettuce, sorrel, chicory, or other herb leaves. The leaves are usually stacked and then rolled and cut crosswise. Chiffonade is often used as a garnish.

Chinois: a cone-shaped fine strainer used to strain particles from soups, stocks, jellies, and such. Chinois usually come with a pestle for pushing the food through the mesh, which may be extremely fine.

Chipotle chile: a smoked chile, usually a jalapeño. Chipotle chiles are sometimes sold in cans with adobo sauce.

Confit: potted meat. French cooks from the Gascony region preserve duck, goose, and sometimes pork by cooking and storing these meats in their own fat, which seals and preserves them. Confit will keep, refrigerated, for up to six months.

Consommé: a fish, chicken, or meat broth that has been clarified. Consommé is available in cans from supermarkets.

Coulis: a thick sauce of puréed fruits or vegetables that is often used as a garnish or as a bed for other foods.

glossary

Couscous: a traditional North African dish of semolina wheat. The preparation style of couscous varies from country to country.

Crostini: a small, thin slice of toasted bread often served with a topping as an appetizer.

Deglaze: to heat a small amount of liquid, often wine or sometimes stock, in a sauté pan while stirring to release from the bottom of the pan bits of food left after browning meat.

Demi-glace: a rich brown sauce made from espagnole sauce enriched with veal stock and wine and reduced to a thick consistency. Authentic demi-glace can take hours, even days, to make and involves a couple of different stocks, wine, and several reductions. The process is time-consuming and is rarely done in home kitchens. A more simple process is to make a veal stock (page 218), and reduce it by about half; add sherry or Madeira equal to half the amount of reduced stock, and reduce again. The result of the simplified process is not quite the same as that of the authentic demi-glace process. Today you can buy demi-glace concentrates by mail order or in gourmet shops. You can also buy a frozen demi-glace product at some supermarkets and gourmet shops. See the Mail Order Resources (page 228) to find a supplier.

Dredge: to coat food lightly with flour or cornmeal before frying.

Dulse: a seaweed from the coastal regions of New England and Atlantic Canada. It's available in other parts of North America dried and should be soaked in liquid to rehydrate it. Dulse is used in soups and salads and is rich in iron.

Duxelles: a preparation of mushrooms that are chopped and combined with aromatics such as onions and shallots and then sautéed in butter. Duxelles is often used as a garnish or stuffing or is included in sauces.

Emulsion: a mixture of two liquids, such as oil and vinegar, that normally do not combine thoroughly. An emulsifier is needed to make an emulsion. The most common emulsifier is egg yolk.

Fish sauce: a pungent, salty liquid that is used in a way similar to soy sauce. Fish sauce is also called *nuoc nam* (Vietnamese) or *nam pla* (Thai) and is available in Asian stores.

Flambé: to ignite brandy, rum, or whisky that has been poured over food. The alcohol burns off but a concentrated flavor is left behind.

Flan: a baked custard dish that can be sweet or savory. Baked caramel flan is a traditional Mexican dessert.

Fumet: a concentrated fish stock added to sauce or another stock to enhance the flavor. The term may also refer to mushroom stock.

Galangal: a rhizome, similar to ginger, that is available in Asian markets, sometimes in powdered or dried form. Galangal is also known as galanga root.

Granita: an Italian frozen sweet or savory dish similar to sorbet but with a grainy texture. It's often served as a palate cleanser between courses or as a light dessert.

Habanero chile: the hottest chile in the world.

Ice wine: wine made from grapes that are left to freeze on the vine before harvesting. When pressed, these grapes make a very sweet dessert wine often served chilled with fresh fruit and ripe creamy cheeses, or as an after-dinner wine.

Incorporate: to mix ingredients thoroughly.

Jícama: a root vegetable also known as the Mexican potato. It can be used both raw and cooked.

Julienne: foods, usually vegetables, cut into very thin matchstick-like pieces.

Juniper berry: fruit of the juniper shrub. Juniper berries have the flavor of gin and are used to flavor sauces and marinades for game, duck, rabbit, pork, ham, beef, and lamb. Crushing the berries before adding them releases more of their flavor into the dish.

Kaffir lime leaf: an aromatic leaf with a bright citrus aroma. It comes from Southeast Asia and is used extensively in Thai and Indonesian cooking. It's available in specialty markets and Asian groceries. Substitute lemon grass or lime peel if necessary. Kaffir lime leaf can be used in a way similar to bay leaf but will add citrus overtones.

Kefalograviera: according to cheese guru Steven Jenkins, author of *Cheese Primer*, "a sort of sheep's milk Gruyère cheese offering a rich, robustly nutty flavor." Kefalograviera is available in cheese shops and Greek or specialty markets.

Kosher salt: a coarse salt. It's sometimes sold as coarse salt and is available in most supermarkets.

Leek: a vegetable belonging to the onion family. Leeks are milder and sweeter than onions. Generally, only the white part of the leek is eaten; the green part is used for flavoring soups and stocks.

Lillet: a French apéritif.

Mandoline: a hand-operated utensil with different blades, used for cutting vegetables. It's the forerunner of our modern food processors. Many chefs prefer mandolines to food processors for their more uniform cuts.

Mascarpone cheese: a rich cream cheese from the Lombardy region of Italy, often used in desserts and frequently paired with fruit.

Mesclun: mixed greens, usually young, baby greens. The ingredients may vary depending on the time of year but often include arugula, dandelion, radicchio, and sorrel.

Mirepoix: a combination of vegetables, usually carrots, onions, and celery, and herbs sautéed in butter and used to season sauces, soups, and stews. Mirepoix is sometimes used as a bed upon which meats are placed during braising.

Mirin: a low-alcohol rice wine available in the ethnic or gourmet section of some supermarkets or in Asian stores.

Miso: a bean paste, which is made from soybeans, used extensively in Japanese cooking. Store miso in an airtight container in the refrigerator.

Mojo: a spicy condiment similar to salsa, although usually it is slightly more liquid than salsa. Mojo, often used as an alternative to rich sauces, is usually served with cooked foods rather than cold ones.

Nonreactive utensil: a utensil that will not be affected by acids or other substances. Utensils made of glass, stainless steel, or ceramic materials, and those coated with enamel, are nonreactive.

Nopales: the fleshy, oval leaves of the prickly pear cactus. They taste like a combination of green pepper, green beans, and asparagus with a hint of lemon. Peel off the eyes with a vegetable peeler. Nopales are available year round in Mexican markets and some supermarkets, and will keep in the refrigerator for two weeks.

Orzo: a tiny pasta that resembles rice and is often used in soups and as a substitute for rice.

Parchment paper: a moisture-resistant paper used to line baking pans and to make parchment bags for piping icing, mashed potatoes, and other stiff foods into designs. It's available in some supermarkets and in gourmet shops.

Pâtissier: the French word for "pastry chef."

Pear eau de vie: a clear, pear-flavored brandy.

Pernod: a European anise-flavored liqueur.

Pico de gallo: a Spanish relish made of finely chopped ingredients. There are a number of versions of pico de gallo; it may include jalapeño chiles, cucumbers, onions, and bell peppers.

glossary

Pizzelle iron: is similar to a waffle iron. In fact, many models have reversible grates, one side for waffles and one side for pizzelles. Pizzelle irons are available in kitchenware and department stores.

Poblano chile: a common Mexican chile. When dried, it's known as an ancho chile. Ancho chiles should be rehydrated in a little boiling water before use.

Prosciutto: a dry-cured ham available in Italian markets.

Purslane: a salad herb with tear-shaped leaves. It's sometimes included in mesclun and is usually available from late spring through summer. Purslane is sometimes cooked like spinach or added to sauces and omelets.

Quinoa: a high-protein grain native to South America, often used as a side dish or in salads and soups.

Reduce: to boil a liquid until it reduces to a lesser volume. This reduction results in concentrated flavor.

Roux: a mixture of equal amounts of flour and butter or oil that is used to thicken many sauces and gravies. A white or blond roux is used for cream sauces. Further cooking results in a brown roux for darker sauces.

Sea salt: a salt made from the evaporation of sea water rather than salt obtained from mines. Sea salt is more expensive than table salt and is available in some supermarkets and in gourmet shops.

Serrano chile: a small, very hot chile also known as a serranito pepper. It's often an ingredient in salsas.

Star anise: the dried, star-shaped fruit of an evergreen tree native to southern China and Vietnam. Its flavor is a combination of anise and fennel with sweet overtones. Star anise is the main ingredient in Chinese five-spice powder. Use star anise whole to infuse soups and broths, or grind it to a powder for other uses. It's available in grocery stores, gourmet shops, and Asian markets. Buy it in small quantities; its flavor diminishes with prolonged storage.

Tomatillo: a green fruit that looks like a small green tomato and is enclosed in a papery husk. Sometimes called Chinese lanterns, tomatillos and are often used in Mexican sauces and salsas. Remove the husks and rinse off the sticky residue. Tomatillos can be used cooked or raw. Store them, refrigerated, for up to a month.

Triple Sec: an orange-flavored liqueur. It is an ingredient in margaritas.

Udon: thick Asian noodles made from hard wheat flour and often used in soups. Udon are available in gourmet shops or Asian markets.

selected bibliography

Barash, Cathy Wilkinson. *Edible Flowers from Garden to Palate*. Golden, Colorado: Fulcrum, 1993.

Bremness, Lesley. *Herbs*. 1st American ed. London; New York: Dorling Kindersley, 1994.

DeWitt, Dave, Mary Jane Wilan, and Melissa T. Stock. *Hot and Spicy Mexican*. Rocklin, California: Prima, 1996.

Doole, Louise Evans. *Herbs: How to Grow and Use Them*. New York: Sterling, 1962.

Herbst, Sharon Tyler. *The New Food Lover's Companion*. Hauppague, New York: Barron's Educational Series, 1995.

Hersey, Jean. *Cooking with Herbs*. New York: Scribner, 1972.

Hom, Ken. *Ken Hom's Asian Ingredients*. Berkeley, California: Ten Speed Press, 1996.

Jamison, Cheryl Alters, and Bill Jamison. *The Border Cookbook*. Boston: Harvard Common Press, 1995.

Jenkins, Steven. *Cheese Primer*. New York: Workman, 1996.

Lang, Jenifer Harvey, ed. *Larousse Gastronomique*. New York: Crown, 1984.

Leek, Sybil. *Sybil Leek's Book of Herbs*. 1st ed. Nashville: Thomas Nelson, 1973.

Lima, Patrick. *The Harrowsmith Illustrated Book of Herbs*. Camden East, Ontario: Camden House, 1994.

McVicar, Jekka. *Herbs for the Home: A Definitive Sourcebook to Growing and Using Herbs*. New York: Viking Studio Books, 1995.

Ortiz, Elisabeth Lambert. *The Encyclopedia of Herbs, Spices and Flavorings*. New York: Dorling Kindersley, 1992.

Owen, Millie. *Herbs, Greens and Aromatics*. New York: Lyons & Burford, 1979.

Phillips, Roger. *The Random House Book of Herbs*. New York: Random House, 1990.

Riggs, Carol. *Herbs: Leaves of Magic*. Boulder, Colorado: Sycamore Island Books, 1979.

Rinzler, Carol Ann. *The Complete Book of Herbs, Spices, and Condiments: From Garden to Medicine Chest*. New York: Facts on File, 1990.

Rodale's Illustrated Encyclopedia of Herbs. Emmaus, Pennsylvania: Rodale Press, 1987.

Rohde, Eleanour Sinclair. *A Garden of Herbs*. New York: Dover Publications, 1969.

Sanecki, Kathleen Naylor. *The Complete Book of Herbs*. New York: Macmillan, 1974.

Saville, Carole. *Exotic Herbs*. New York: Henry Holt, 1997.

Simmons, Adelma Grenier. *Herb Gardens of Delight, with Plants for Every Mood and Purpose*. New York: Sterling, 1962.

Stobart, Tom. *Herbs, Spices and Flavorings*. New York: McGraw-Hill, 1970.

mail order resources

A Cook's Wares
211 37th Street
Beaver Falls, PA 15010-2103
(800) 915-9788
e-mail: cookware@ccia.com
www.cookswares.com
➤ ingredients and cooking supplies

Adriana's Caravan
409 Vanderbilt Street
Brooklyn, NY 11218
(800) 316-0820
e-mail: adricara@aol.com
➤ herbs, spices, and international ingredients

ALLSERVE, Inc.
PO Box 21743
Cleveland, OH 44121-0743
(800) TASTE-2-U
www.allserv.com
➤ food bases, sauce preparations, gravies, and concentrates

Caviar Assouline
314 Brown Street
Philadelphia, PA 19123
(800) 521-4491
e-mail: joel@caviarassouline.com
www.caviarassouline.com
➤ caviar and gourmet foods and ingredients

CMC Company
PO Box 322
Avalon, NJ 08202
(800) CMC-2780
➤ hard to find ingredients

Dean & Deluca
560 Broadway
New York, NY 10012
(800) 221-7714
www.dean-deluca.com
➤ gourmet foods and ingredients

Indian Harvest Specialtifoods, Inc.
PO Box 428
Bemidji, MN 56619-0428
(800) 294-2433
www.indianharvest.com
➤ rice, grains, and beans

Indian Rock Produce
530 California Road
PO Box 317
Quakertown, PA 18951-0317
(800) 882-0512
➤ fresh herbs and produce

Kalustyan's
123 Lexington Avenue
New York, NY 10016
(212) 685-3451
➤ spices, nuts, dried fruits, grains, beans, and Middle Eastern specialties

Melissa's World Variety Produce, Inc.
PO Box 21127
Los Angeles, CA 90021
(800) 588-0151
www.melissas.com
➤ specialty foods and ingredients

Miles Estate Herb & Berry Farm
4308 Marthaler Road NE
Woodburn, OR 97071
(888) 810-0196
www.herbs-spices-flowers.com
➤ herb plants, spices, and specialty items

More Than Gourmet
115 West Bartges Street
Akron, OH 44311
(800) 860-9385
e-mail: demi-glace@worldnet.att.net
➤ demi-glace

Nueske's Hillcrest Farm
RR 2, PO Box D
Wittenberg, WI 54499-0904
(800) 392-2266
www.nueske.com
➤ apple wood smoked products

Penzeys Ltd.
PO Box 933
Muskego, WI 53150
(414) 679-7207
➤ herbs, spices, and blends

Redi-Base
PO Box 846
Whitehall, PA 18052-0846
(800) 820-5121
www.redibase.com
➤ sauce bases

Richters Herbs
357 Highway 47
Goodwood, ON L0C 1A0
(905) 640-6677
e-mail: inquiry@richters.com
www.richters.com
➤ herb plants and seeds

San Francisco Herb Co.
250 14th Street
San Francisco, CA 94103
(800) 227-4530 / East Coast: (800) 316-7965
e-mail: spice@sfherb.com
www.sfherb.com
➤ dried herbs, spices, teas, and other ingredients

The Baker's Catalogue
King Arthur Flour
PO Box 876
Norwich, VT 05055-0876
(800) 827-6836
www.kingarthurflour.com
➤ variety of flours and other baking ingredients and supplies

The Herbfarm
32804 Issaquah-Fall City Road
Fall City, WA 98024
(800) 866-4372
www.theherbfarm.com
➤ herb seeds, plants, herbal crafts and gifts, and books

The Oriental Pantry
423 Great Road
Acton, MA 01720
(800) 828-0368
www.orientalpantry.com
➤ hard to find Asian foods, spices, and sauces

Vann's Spices
6105 Oakleaf Avenue
Baltimore, MD 21215
(800) 583-1693
e-mail: vanns@balt.mindspring.com
➤ dried herbs, spices, and blends

Walnut Acres Organic Farms
Walnut Acres Road
Penns Creek, PA 17862-0800
(800) 433-3998
www.walnutacres.com
➤ grains, nuts, flours, condiments, dried herbs, and spices

Williams-Sonoma
PO Box 7456
San Francisco, CA 94120-7456
(800) 541-2233
➤ cookware, including a kitchen blowtorch, and gourmet ingredients

chef/restaurant listing

Jody Adams
Rialto
One Bennett Street
Cambridge, MA 02138
(617) 661-5050

Anthony Ambrose
Ambrosia on Huntington
116 Huntington Avenue
Boston, MA 02116
(617) 247-2400

Bruce Auden
Restaurant BIGA
206 East Locust Street
San Antonio, TX 78212
(210) 225-0722

Marty Blitz
Mise en Place
442 West Kennedy Boulevard
Tampa, FL 33629
(813) 254-5373

Colin Cameron
Esplanade Restaurant
1510 Southwest Harbor Way
Portland, OR 97201-5105
(503) 228-3233

Jonathan M. Cartwright
White Barn Inn
37 Beach Street
Kennebunkport, ME 04046
(207) 967-2321

Richard Chamberlain
Chamberlain's Prime Chop House
5330 Belt Line Road
Addison, TX 75240
(972) 934-2467

Alfonso Contrisciani
Opus 251
251 South 18th Street
Philadelphia, PA 19103-8168
(215) 735-6787

Ann Cooper
The Putney Inn
Depot Road
Putney, VT 05346
(802) 387-5517

Ingrid Croce
Croce's Restaurant and Jazz Bar
802 Fifth Avenue
San Diego, CA 92101
(619) 232-0077

Olivier De Saint Martin
Dock Street Brasserie
Two Logan Square
Philadelphia, PA 19103
(215) 972-8158

Anne Desjardins
L'Eau à La Bouche
3003 Boulevard Sainte-Adèle
Sainte-Adèle, QC JOR 1L0
(450) 229-2991

Mario DiVentura
Filomena Cucina Italiana
1245 Blackwood-Clementon Road
Clementon, NJ 08021
(609) 784-6166

Ed Doherty
Olive
482 Evesham Road
Cherry Hill, NJ 08003
(609) 428-4999

Jean-Louis Dumonet
Trois Jean Bistro
154 East 79th Street
New York, NY 10021
(212) 988-4858

Diane Forley
Verbena
54 Irving Place
New York, NY 10003
(212) 260-5454

Elizabeth Fox
Water Club Restaurant and Courtyard
703 Douglas Street
Victoria, BC V8W 2B4
(250) 388-4200

Clark Frasier
Arrows
Berwick Road, PO Box 803
Ogunquit, ME 03907
(207) 361-1100

Mark Gaier
Arrows
Berwick Road, PO Box 803
Ogunquit, ME 03907
(207) 361-1100

David Garrido
Jeffrey's
1202 West Lynn
Austin, TX 78703
(512) 477-5584

Debbie Gold
The American Restaurant
200 East 25th Street
Kansas City, MO 64108
(816) 426-1133

Thomas Iatesta
The Gourmet's Table
2 Waterview Road
East Goshen, PA 19380
(610) 696-2211

Erasmo "Razz" Kamnitzer
Razz's Restaurant and Bar
10321 North Scottsdale Road
Scottsdale, AZ 85253
(602) 905-1308

Zov Karamardian
Zov's Bistro
17440 East 17th Street
Tusten, CA 92680
(714) 838-8855

Emeril Lagasse
Emeril's
800 Tchoupitoulas
New Orleans, LA 70130
(504) 528-9393

Delmonico
1300 St. Charles Avenue
New Orleans, LA 70130
(504) 525-4937

NOLA
534 St. Louis Street
New Orleans, LA 70130
(504) 522-6652

Emeril's New Orleans Fish House
3799 Las Vegas Boulevard
Las Vegas, NV 89109
(702) 891-7374

Roland Liccioni
Le Français Restaurant
269 South Milwaukee Avenue
Wheeling, IL 60090
(847) 541-7470 or (800) 499-7794

Scott Mason
Ketchum Grill
250 East Avenue
Ketchum, ID 83340
(208) 726-4660

Frank McClelland
L'Espalier
30 Gloucester Street
Boston, MA 02115
(617) 262-3023

Marc Merdinger
Victor Cafe
1303-05 Dickinson Street
Philadelphia, PA 19147
(215) 468- 3040

chef/restaurant listing

Kim Miller
Belleview Biltmore Resort & Spa
25 Belleview Boulevard
Clearwater, FL 33756
(813) 442-6171

Jay Moore
Hudson's on the Bend
3509 Ranch Road 620 North
Austin, TX 78734
(512) 266-1369

Trish Morrissey
Philadelphia Fish & Company
207 Chestnut Street
Philadelphia, PA 19106
(215) 625-8605

Daryle Ryo Nagata
Herons Restaurant & Lounge
900 Canada Place Way
Vancouver, BC V6C 3L5
(604) 691-1991 or (800) 441-1414

Michael Olson
On The Twenty
3836 Main Street
Jordan, ON LOR 1S0
(905) 562-7313

Raymond Ost
Sandrine's
8 Holyoke Street
Cambridge, MA 02116
(617) 536-5352

Mai Pham
Lemon Grass Restaurant & Cafes
601 Munroe Street
Sacramento, CA 95825
(916) 486-4891

Sinclair Philip
Sooke Harbour House
1528 Whiffen Spit Road
Sooke, BC V0S 1N0
(250) 642-3421 or (800) 889-9688

Nora Pouillon
Nora
2132 Florida Avenue NW
Washington, D.C. 20008
(202) 462-5143

Asia Nora
2213 M Street NW
Washington, D.C. 20037
(202) 797-4860

Tracy Pikhart Ritter
Whistling Moon Cafe
402 North Guadalupe
Sante Fe, NM 87501
(505) 983-3093

Jamie Shannon
Commander's Palace
1403 Washington Avenue
New Orleans, LA 70130
(504) 899-8231

Joe Simone
Tosca
14 North Street
Hingham, MA 02043
(617) 740-0080

Michael Smith
The Inn at Bay Fortune
Highway 310
Bay Fortune, PEI C0A 2B0
(902) 687-3745 (summer) / (860) 296-1348 (winter)

Costas Spiliadis
Milos
5357 avenue du Parc
Montreal, QC H2V 4G9
(514) 272-3522

Milos
125 West 55th Street
New York, NY 10019
(212) 245-7400

Barry Squier
Girafe
Route 202
Basking Ridge, NJ 07920
(908) 221-0017

Lili Sullivan
The Rebel House
1068 Yonge Street
Toronto, ON M4W 2L4
(416) 927-0704

Michael Thomson
Michaels Restaurant and Ancho Chile Bar
3413 West 7th
Fort Worth, TX 76107
(818) 877-3413

Jerry Traunfeld
The Herbfarm Restaurant
32804 Issaquah-Fall City Road
Fall City, WA 98024
(800) 866-4372

Bobby Trigg
The Ferry House
32 Witherspoon Street
Princeton, NJ 08540
(609) 924-2488

Alice Waters
Chez Panisse Restaurant & Café
1517 Shattuck Avenue
Berkeley, CA 94709
(510) 548-4795

Café Fanny
1619 5th Street
Berkeley, CA 94710-1714
(510) 526-7664

Janos Wilder
Janos
150 North Main Avenue
Tucson, AZ 85701
(520) 884-9426

John Zenger
Esplanade Restaurant
1510 Southwest Harbor Way
Portland, OR 97201-5105
(503) 228-3233

recipe index

recipe index

credits

Front cover photos (from top right counter-clockwise): Sorrel, Laurel Keser. Chef Emeril Lagasse, courtesy of the chef. Chef Ann Cooper's charbroiled salmon on a bed of bouillabaisse with lemon basil pesto (page 27), courtesy of the chef. Chef Daryle Ryo Nagata, courtesy of the chef. Chef Mai Pham's Thai hot and sour prawn soup (page 86), courtesy of the chef. Scented geranium, courtesy of The Herbfarm. Chef Nora Pouillon, Mahdavian.

Back cover photos (from left to right): Chives, Laurel Keser. Chef Sinclair Philip, Simon Desrochers. Chef Alfonso Contrisciani's sun-dried tomato crusted snapper with fennel, artichokes, and lemon balm (page 81), courtesy of the chef. Chef Jean-Louis Dumonet, Michel Verdure.

Interior photos: Page 22, Fayfoto. Page 25, Jeff Baird. Page 43, Angela Cousins. Page 72, Bob Carey. Page 85, Kent Lacin. Page 101, Jack Leclair. Page 106, Dan Root. Page 122, Thia Konig. Page 141, Mahdavian. Page 148, Andy Hanson. Page 156, Franklin Avery. Page 158, Michel Verdure. Page 175, Angie Norwood Browne. Page 183, Simon Desrochers. Page 212, Stuart Rodgers Ltd. Pages 17, 28, 31, 36, 40, 47, 50, 55, 58, 62, 66, 76, 80, 88, 93, 96, 113, 115, 120, 125, 130, 134, 137, 144, 151, 160, 163, 168, 172, 179, 189, 193, 195, 200, 203, 209, courtesy of the chef.

Illustrations: QuickArt® Herbs and Spice art collection (© 1985 – 1988 Wheeler Arts).

metric equivalents

General Formula for Metric Conversion

➤ **Ounces to grams:** multiply ounce figure by 28.35

➤ **Pounds to grams:** multiply pound figure by 453.59

➤ **Pounds to kilograms:** multiply pound figure by 0.45

➤ **Ounces to milliliters:** multiply ounce figure by 30

➤ **Cups to liters:** multiply cup figure by 0.24

➤ **Fahrenheit to Celsius:** subtract 32 from the Fahrenheit figure, multiply by 5, then divide by 9

➤ **Inches to centimeters:** multiply inch figure by 2.54

Volume

1 teaspoon = 5 milliliters
1 tablespoon = 15 milliliters
¼ cup = 60 milliliters
⅓ cup = 80 milliliters
½ cup = 120 milliliters
⅔ cup = 160 milliliters
1 cup = 230 milliliters

Weight

1 ounce = 28 grams
1 pound = 454 grams

Oven Temperatures

300°F = 150°C
325°F = 165°C
350°F = 175°C
375°F = 190°C
400°F = 200°C
425°F = 220°C
450°F = 230°C
475°F = 245°C